THE IMPROVEMENT OF TEACHER
EDUCATION

COMMISSION ON TEACHER EDUCATION

Appointed by the American Council on Education

E. S. EVENDEN, Teachers College, Columbia University, *Chairman*

RALPH W. TYLER, University of Chicago, *Vice Chairman*

HAROLD BENJAMIN, University of Maryland

MILDRED ENGLISH, Georgia State College for Women

HARRY M. GAGE, Lindenwood College

HELEN HAY HEYL, New York State Education Department

CHARLES W. HUNT, Oneonta State Teachers College (New York)

HAROLD E. JONES, University of California

FRED J. KELLY, United States Office of Education

LEWIS MUMFORD, Amenia, New York

SHELTON PHELPS, Winthrop College*

W. CARSON RYAN, University of North Carolina

PAYSON SMITH, University of Maine†

ALEXANDER J. STODDARD, Philadelphia Public Schools

FRANK W. THOMAS, Fresno State College (California)

GEORGE F. ZOOK, American Council on Education, *ex officio*

KARL W. BIGELOW, *Director*

* Retired in 1943.
† Chairman from 1938 to 1942.

THE IMPROVEMENT OF TEACHER EDUCATION

A Final Report
by the
COMMISSION ON TEACHER EDUCATION

AMERICAN COUNCIL ON EDUCATION
Washington, D. C.
1946

Manufactured by
Universal Lithographers, Inc.
Baltimore 2, Md.
U. S. A.

10-22-53

Foreword

THE COMMISSION on Teacher Education, created in February 1938 and formally dissolved in September 1944, devoted most of its time, energy, and means to the conduct of an extensive field program. Included was a national cooperative study in which a large number of representative school systems, colleges, and universities participated, and a series of statewide cooperative studies involving the teacher education interests of ten states. Service to these enterprises was provided by a central staff located in Washington and a collaboration center on child growth and development housed at the University of Chicago. Eight published reports have resulted from the Commission's field experience and from its own deliberations. Six of these were prepared by members of the staff and dealt in detail with different large phases of the program. The other two have been reports from the Commission itself. *Teachers for Our Times* was an orienting statement of the Commission's own point of view respecting present-day problems in the education of teachers. *The Improvement of Teacher Education* concludes the series. In it, the Commission summarizes what it did, lists the more significant findings, and sets forth its own recommendations.

The present work naturally reflects the various staff volumes which were themselves drawn largely from the records and reports submitted to the Commission by representatives of the more than sixty institutions and cooperating groups that took part in the field study program. This volume accordingly owes much to the work and thinking of many persons. It is particularly indebted to the ability of Karl W. Bigelow to analyze and digest voluminous reports and to find and express elements of agreement among divergent points of view. As director of the Commission, Dr. Bigelow was assigned the task of the actual composition of the final report. To him, as well as to all others, the Commission acknowledges its indebtedness.

v

These acknowledgments, however, imply no lack of responsibility on the part of the Commission for the points of view and the recommendations in this report. Original drafts of the several chapters were discussed at a series of meetings, revised in the light of those discussions, and resubmitted for further criticism by the members. The report thus constitutes an official Commission statement and represents the result of a pooling of thought by a group of men and women deeply and professionally concerned with the improvement of teacher education, men and women who brought to the Commission a wide variety of experiences and points of view.

The Commission, in now bringing its work to a close, wishes to express its appreciation of the opportunities it has had to study intensively the important problems of teacher education during the critical years just past. It is grateful to the American Council on Education for having sponsored its program, and also to the General Education Board for having provided so generously for the support of its work. It desires especially to recognize the encouragement and help provided by two officers of that board, Robert J. Havighurst and Flora M. Rhind.

E. S. EVENDEN
Chairman

Introduction

THERE ARE several temptations to which men and women who have devoted long and earnest attention to any given subject are prone to succumb. One is to believe that their subject is of the widest and most critical importance. Another is to feel that the circumstances of their times call for particular attention to that subject. A third is to be convinced that what they themselves have concluded and have to say is worth especial consideration.

The Commission on Teacher Education has felt all of these temptations. Moreover, it has yielded to them. But it has not done so uncritically. It does not believe itself self-deluded. It is of the sober opinion that the improvement of teacher education is of the greatest national importance in our times. And it cannot but believe that its own unique experience provides a basis for suggestions and recommendations that are of genuine significance.

Our nation is today facing unprecedented challenges. Many of these reflect problems that had already made themselves dramatically felt in the period between the two world wars. These problems—political, economic, social, and moral—were not solved; indeed they were often further complicated, by the experiences attendant upon the waging of the last war. The end of that war has brought them back to us clamoring for solution. They are domestic and international in character, intermixed.

Our task of dealing with these persistent problems is enormously increased by the necessity of now reconverting our lives from a wartime to a peacetime basis and by the novel impact of developments speeded up under the stimulus of war. How to deal constructively with the new atomic power with which we have been presented is only the most striking of many new issues that we now must face. There has been no time in American history when greater dangers threatened or greater opportunities were offered.

If, as a people, we are to meet these challenges successfully we must have knowledge, we must have understanding, we must have skill. We must also have sound purposes, devotion to the common welfare, and ability to live and work together cooperatively. All of these characteristics are the goals of democratic education. Upon the quality of education in our country, therefore, must clearly depend our ability to make the age now opening up a great one.

From this it follows that the improvement of teacher education is a critical national necessity, for teachers are the key element in most educational processes. Upon their quality more than on any other factor depends the quality of instruction offered in the schools, the colleges, the universities, and the educational institutions provided for adults. And that quality is largely determined by the excellence of the arrangements provided for the education of teachers. Such arrangements are not at present satisfactory.

It was, of course, because of a widespread recognition that teacher education required improvement that the Commission was created by the American Council on Education in February 1938. Prior to that time the Council had carefully explored the need for such a body, working through its Committee on Problems and Plans and enjoying the assistance of many leaders in American education. It received encouragement on every hand. Students of every aspect of education testified that their researches invariably revealed that the improvement of teacher education was a key necessity if their own immediate problems were to be dealt with successfully.

The demand, moreover, was for the encouragement of experimental action at the points where teachers were actually being prepared and employed. It was felt that further systematic inquiry into existing practices was not called for. It was believed that added specialized research would be a less useful activity for a national commission than stimulation of a testing in practice of hypotheses already developed through processes of careful study. It was considered that deliberative pronouncements would be less valuable than a series of reports based on experience in the field.

Accordingly when the Commission was established, following a generous grant of funds by the General Education Board, it was understood that its task was to be basically one of implementation. It consequently set about developing a field program. A national cooperative study was first organized in which fifty cooperating units undertook to participate. About half of these were institutions of various types in which teachers were being prepared, and about half were school systems concerned with the growth of teachers on the job. Later a second study was set up, the units of which were cooperating groups representing the teacher education interests of ten particular states.

Since the character of these studies is fully described in the body of this report little need be said about them at this point. It should, however, be remarked that each continued from three to three and a half years and that together they constituted the major activity of the Commission. The staff of the Commission worked closely with each cooperating unit and a wide variety of services was rendered in response to expressed needs. The emphasis was on local deliberation and local action and while the various units were kept in touch with one another there was no effort to press for uniformity.

The natural consequence was a program of diversified activities relating to nearly every aspect of in-service and pre-service teacher education. Careful records of experience were maintained, evaluation of outcomes was emphasized, and periodical reports were prepared by each unit for presentation to the Commission. Meanwhile Commission staff members kept in close touch with developments in the field and formulated their individual judgments as to the effectiveness of the various experimental efforts.

With the cumulation of experience it became evident that the processes employed for arrival at decisions and for carrying out of action were of critical importance. Considerable attention was accordingly given to the various ways of working together that were utilized and to an estimation of their effectiveness. Testimony respecting these matters was gathered from the field and the judgments of staff members were systematically pooled. It was concluded that some important discoveries had been made.

When the period of field activity on the part of the Commission was concluded staff members were asked to prepare a series of reports based on the rich experience that had been enjoyed. Drawing on the cumulated materials and their own insights these authors produced six volumes, already published. These dealt respectively with the preparation of teachers, their in-service education, evaluation in teacher education, child growth and development, statewide programs for the improvement of teacher education, and problems of graduate instruction leading to the Ph.D.[1] In the meantime the Commission itself had published a preliminary report, *Teachers for Our Times*, in which it set forth its basic point of view respecting the problems with which it had been asked to deal.

The present volume constitutes the Commission's final report. The book is a summary of its main experience, and of the experience of the various units that cooperated with it, as well as a formulation of its own conclusions and recommendations. For the record, but also—and mainly—because everything the Commission has to say is deeply rooted in its experience, Chapter I is mainly devoted to a running account of what the Commission did. This should serve a useful orienting purpose. However, it is recognized that some readers may feel that they are already adequately acquainted with this story, parts of which have been told elsewhere. These may wish to turn at once to the succeeding chapters.

Chapter II deals with the subject of the preparation of teachers, and Chapter III with in-service education. In each of these the focus is upon action available to colleges, universities, and school systems acting more or less independently. Chapter IV, contrariwise, has to do with cooperative activities, that is, with those that involve the working together of various institutions or of the representatives of such institutions. In the final chapter the Commission has summed up. Here it has provided a concluding statement of its views respecting the importance of teacher

[1] A complete list of Commission publications will be found in the appendix to this report.

education and of the basic ideas that it considers must control if teacher education is to be adequately improved. It has added a summary discussion of leading problems and promising trends. Some readers may wish to examine this chapter before tackling the more detailed presentations that precede it.

The chairman of the Commission, in his foreword to this report, has expressed certain acknowledgments for the Commission. The director would like, at this last opportunity, to exercise a similar privilege. He is grateful for the guidance and support of the Commission and of the American Council on Education, for the loyal and effective cooperation provided by his staff colleagues, and for the numberless contributions to the success of the Commission's program made by the thousands of men and women who participated in the field aspects of that program. For him there can be no doubt that what is reported in this volume constitutes a heartening demonstration of the possibilities inherent in the cooperation of persons dedicated to a worthy cause.

KARL W. BIGELOW
Director

Contents

I

The Commission and Its Work

THE CREATION, activities, and conclusions of the Commission on Teacher Education need to be viewed in perspective. The decision of the American Council on Education to call this body into being in 1938 was a response to significant circumstances in the educational world. The planning that preceded and accompanied its program was influenced not only by those circumstances but also by broader social developments. The Commission's interpretation of its own experiences reflects its attitude toward the fundamental issues with which Americans—as individuals and as members of a great society—are today so compellingly faced.[1]

BACKGROUND: CIRCUMSTANCES AND IDEAS

When the decision to establish the Commission was reached the first century of public teacher education in the United States was drawing rapidly to a close. The last decades of that century, moreover, had been marked by many changes, much expansion, and a good deal of criticism both from within the teacher education world and from without. The first world war had very adversely affected education in this country. Financial support had been reduced. Experienced teachers had been drawn away from their posts in large numbers and enrollments in institutions where teachers were being prepared had declined sharply. Teaching vacancies had frequently had to be filled by persons not qualified even according to the modest standards of

---

[1] This attitude has been somewhat fully expressed in the Commission's first report, *Teachers for Our Times* (Washington: American Council on Education, 1944), especially Chapter II. Chapter I of that book offers a more extended analysis of the situation in teacher education when the Commission began its work than can be presented in this report.

that time. The end of the war found many of these inferior teachers immovably fixed in their new positions.[2]

Teacher education after 1918

The years following 1918, on the other hand, were marked by extraordinary educational expansions and advances. While elementary school enrollments began, eventually, to decline in reflection of falling birthrates, the numbers of students swarming into the secondary schools more than compensated for such losses. The growth in attendance at this latter class of institution was accompanied by an almost equally spectacular enlargement of enrollments in the nation's colleges and universities. All these developments, of course, led to an increase in the demand for qualified teachers, and this demand was made effective by an upward trend in salaries and by improving provisions for tenure and retirement. Moreover, as shortages were repaired, and particularly after the onset of the depression in 1929 caused a teaching career to appeal to more and more young people, it became possible to raise notably both the requirements for certification to teach and the standards for programs of preparation.[3]

A steady increase in the amount of college education possessed by beginning teachers on the average was one of the more striking characteristics of this period. This development particularly applied to elementary school teachers. It was between the wars that the chief institutions in which these teachers were prepared changed rapidly and all but universally from one- or two-year normal schools to four-year, degree-granting teachers colleges. While by 1940 only a third of the states had undertaken to require that all elementary school teachers should be college graduates, the movement in this direction was clearly pronounced. The four-year standard was, indeed, being widely met in many states where it was not yet mandatory. There were similar developments bearing on secondary school teachers, who have traditionally been expected to undergo a longer preparation

[2] The story of the period has been told in some detail in *Teacher Education in a Democracy at War*, prepared for the Commission by Edward S. Evenden (Washington: American Council on Education, 1942), especially in Chapter II.

[3] *Ibid.*, Chapter III.

than their colleagues in the lower grades. In their case, by 1940 all but four states had adopted a minimum requirement of four years of college education, while a half dozen—to say nothing of a good many cities—had begun to insist on a fifth year of pre-service preparation.

These trends toward lengthening the period of preparation for teaching were accompanied by developments bearing upon teachers in service. An atmosphere grew up in which such persons found themselves strongly stimulated to complete the four-year college program and to move on to the attainment of a master's or even of a doctor's degree. Pressure in these directions was often exerted by linking promotions and salary advances with degree attainment, but this reflected as much as it created a general feeling of prestige attaching to advanced study for teachers. The colleges and universities, naturally, did not fail to encourage this movement, and the times were marked by a rapid growth in the provision of summer sessions and extension offerings.

All these increases in periods of institutional study by prospective and experienced teachers were inevitably accompanied by curricular changes. It became possible, for example, for the teachers colleges to make better provision for the general education of their undergraduates. Advancing educational research resulted in the enrichment and expansion of professional courses. Better opportunities for student teaching were provided, and more and more institutions acquired campus schools where their own students could conveniently observe and share in model educational work. As student bodies grew in size staff enlargement became necessary; and the expansion of graduate schools—both of education and of arts and sciences—that was simultaneously occurring made possible the filling of vacancies with instructors of superior training.[4]

It is not, of course, to be supposed that developments so numerous and so rapid were unaccompanied by difficulties or

[4] An account of graduate school development in the United States and an analysis of current graduate school problems will be found in *Toward Improving Ph.D. Programs*, prepared for the Commission by Ernest V. Hollis (Washington: American Council on Education, 1945).

that the opportunities provided were made use of with unalloyed wisdom. While the period was marked by a good deal of intelligent and imaginative experimentation bearing on the education of teachers, patterns of more antiquity than demonstrable worth were often retained and elaborated. As elsewhere in the educational—and not only the educational—world, specialization was enjoying great prestige. This inclined staff members in all departments—those of the various arts and sciences as well as of education—to offer more and more courses of limited focus and consequently, despite the increasing amount of student time at their disposal, to compete more and more vigorously for their respective shares of student attention. No little acrimony and a good many lopsided programs resulted. Feeling was apt to run particularly high between the educationists on the one hand and the subject-matter specialists, as a group, on the other.

The situation became particularly confused and unsatisfactory at the level of graduate instruction, both for those preparing to teach and those already employed in the schools. There developed here a still unresolved conflict between the guardians of the established patterns of departmental specialization for the master's and doctor's degrees and those primarily concerned that the candidates should spend their time in activities clearly calculated to advance their professional competence. Since members of the latter party were by no means in agreement among·themselves the resultant controversy was —and remains—many-sided. A special complication came from the fact that teachers in service were rarely able to devote a full academic year to their advanced studies: practical necessity usually forced them to rely on repeated attendance at summer sessions or extension centers. This militated against the achievement of any integration of the graduate programs, encouraging rather the piecemeal accumulation of "credits" through successive courses each of which might be a relatively independent experience.

If the twenties and thirties, then, constituted a period of unprecedented growth in American teacher education, that

same period brought many problems and issues into the fore-
front of professional consciousness. Naturally there were numerous attempts to deal boldly and intelligently with these matters.
Three trends were particularly notable. The first was in the
direction of attaining a greater degree of integration and
continuity in programs both for prospective teachers and for
those in service—a swing away from some of the evils that have
been suggested in the preceding paragraphs. Then there was a
tendency to strive more vigorously to make certain that educational experience was functionally related to the real needs of
teachers, as private persons and citizens no less than as professional workers; in its last mentioned aspect this movement
was distinctly related to mounting criticism from the field,
shortly to be examined. Finally, teacher education showed an
increasing concern with the implications of general social
developments and of the related conflicts of basic social ideas:
there was growing preoccupation with the nature and requirements of democracy.

Promptings from the educational world

The conclusion has been reached that while teacher education
in the late thirties had for several decades been enjoying remarkable growth and had benefited from many improvements, it
was, nevertheless, marked by various unresolved conflicts and
a healthy spirit of self-criticism. In all these respects it was
typical of the whole educational scene, of which it was a significant part. Indeed, its own problems and uncertainties in no
small measure reflected those of the schools that it was designed
to serve. These institutions were not only changing in many
ways; they were also pressing more insistently than ever before
for modifications that would bring teacher education into
closer consonance with their own purposes and needs.

Several facts combined to account for these important developments. In the first place enlargement of enrollments had brought
many schools face to face with new and difficult problems.
This was particularly true of the secondary schools, the democ-
ratization of which had forced the introduction of curricula

and practices suited to a new clientele. For the conduct of this work traditionally educated teachers were not well prepared. Also influential was the tendency of teachers to remain in active service for steadily lengthening periods: this had the effect of placing a rising premium on in-service education closely related to the realities of the working situation. A third and connected factor was the movement toward curricular revision.

Responding to the demands of "new" students, social changes, and emergent educational ideas, school leaders had become increasingly preoccupied with the possibilities of local program improvement. Sometimes they moved autocratically, sometimes democratically, but in either case they always found that the understanding, skill, responsiveness, and initiative of the teachers were critical factors for determining in what degree and with what speed reforms could be carried through. In a number of instances statewide programs for curricular revision were initiated, and these resulted in particularly vocal demands for changes in teacher education that would increase the supply of teachers able to put the new ideas into effect successfully. The implications for both teacher preparation and in-service assistance were equally emphasized. The view was increasingly expressed that teacher education, by and large, was failing to keep up with the needs of the schools as seen by the more sensitive of their leaders.

Also contributing to the spreading notion that teacher education in the United States would benefit from intensive study were the examples and implications of various national and regional inquiries that had recently been concluded or were being pursued at the time creation of the Commission was being considered. The several commissions of the Progressive Education Association, the Educational Policies Commission of the National Education Association and the American Association of School Administrators, the American Youth Commission of the American Council on Education, and certain surveys and studies sponsored by the United States Office of Education, the regional accrediting associations, and a number of subject-matter groups had served both to influence thinking with respect to school practice and to emphasize the responsibilities of teachers. Not dissimilar was the impact of much contemporary research respecting children, the community, the larger social order, and various aspects of the educative process. All pointed at last to the teacher and his education as of key importance if educational change was to keep pace with evolving personal and social needs.

It will be useful to list some of the educational ideas that were in the ascendant during the period under review and that had significant implications for the modification of teacher education in both its preparatory and in-service phases. First, there was mounting sensitivity to the importance of understanding the growth and development of children and of adjusting educational practice to the needs that reflect the years, experiences, prospects, and individual differences of children. There was also increasing realization that the school, its teachers, and its students are integral parts of the community and of the larger social order and that this relationship should be better understood and more effectively cultivated.

Again, the whole question of the content and organization of the curriculum was being more and more debated, with a distinct trend evident in the direction of experimentation designed to achieve a closer relationship to needs and a greater degree of integration and continuity. Another idea to which special attention was being paid had to do with the roles of the various actors in the educational drama: it held that teachers and students alike should participate more generally in planning and carrying out programs and projects, that education should be a process of shared creation rather than of mechanical performance of tasks externally assigned. Finally, the period was marked by rising concern on the part of educational leaders with democracy as idea and as reality. Such persons shared with other students of the national and international scene a sense of mounting crisis with respect to the status of many traditional values and institutions.

The challenge of democracy

The Commission was created in a time of great social stress. Its plans and actions were from its beginning affected by the war, which broke in Europe as the program was being launched and which engulfed the United States as that program reached mid-career. The implications of domestic and international events for education demanded attention throughout the period of activity, as did the effects of war-related developments on children and youth.[5] The Commission became increasingly impressed by the critical nature of our times and by the necessity of teaching and teacher education being better adjusted to basic social needs.

But the Commission saw the war as only the most instant and dramatic evidence of the great social crisis that marks our age. It looked backward at the turmoil of events that, through a generation or more, had led up to formal warfare. It also looked ahead in an effort to anticipate the situations with which men would be faced when the fighting had ceased. It concluded that many of the basic issues of our times would still require the most urgent attention for years to come and that it was essential that the resources of education be ever more fully mobilized to the end that wise popular decision and wise social action might ensue.

When the canvas of recent history is examined every aspect of human existence, every social institution is seen to be under strain. Agriculture, industry, and trade are changing rapidly in consequence of new discoveries, new inventions, new methods of operation. Religious and family attitudes and habits are in flux. Political customs and instrumentalities—local, national, and international—are being modified. Basic human convictions have been shaken and a conflict of ideas rages. Traditional concepts and patterns of behavior no longer command general allegiance. Change makes more change inevitable, and the great questions are whether its course can be purposively controlled and, if so, how this had best be done.

[5] When the United States entered the war the Commission sponsored the special volume, *Teacher Education in a Democracy at War*, already referred to.

It is the Commission's conviction that man can play a part in the control of his own future, that democratic planning is both possible and desirable.[6] It is aware, however, of serious obstacles to such a course. In so unfamiliar, so unstable a situation as the present, man is inevitably uncertain and afraid. He feels an impulse to return to the past, to recapture a life that seems simple and secure in retrospect. He also feels an impulse to withdraw, to fly from the arenas of conflict, to avoid human entanglements with their accompanying necessity of give as well as take. Yet neither of these escapes is possible. The course of history is irreversible; human interdependence—increasing steadily—makes isolation of any sort daily less feasible. The times call for understanding, imagination, and boldness; for mutual acceptance, mutual trust, and general participation. These are possible. The alternatives are chaos or tyranny.

The challenge to education is evident. This institution, too, is affected by the forces at work in our times. It has shared the strains of war and used its opportunities to contribute to the winning thereof. Upon it also impinge the deeper, longer running social forces. Education's responsibility is simultaneously and equally to the society that supports it and to the persons —children and young people—that it directly serves. It must be responsive to social needs with their mingled elements of permanence and change. It must equally respond to the similarly blended needs of boys and girls. Upon its effectiveness must depend the ability of our future citizens to deal constructively with the problems of our times.

That education can be employed as a powerful instrument of social policy has recently been demonstrated by its effectiveness in the hands of the totalitarian dictators. It must now be used—as it can be—as a means for the perfection of democracy. This requires that education not only develop understanding but also aid in the achievement of emotional maturity and of the capacity for free social action. For if our democracy is to be preserved and improved in our critical times we need, above

[6] For an elaboration of its views see *Teachers for Our Times*, Chapter II.

all, citizens who can work together cooperatively, with due respect for each other, while at the same time thinking, feeling, and acting under the guidance of their own independent powers of reason.

For reasons such as have just been suggested the Commission has felt obligated to concern itself constantly with basic issues of human nature and of human relationships. It has asked itself how human beings can best live and work together in the homes, in the classrooms, in the school systems, in the colleges, in the communities, in the nation, in the world. How can they meet their problems—the old and the new, the simple and the complex—intelligently, effectively, rightly? The Commission has found no better answer to these questions than the answer of democracy. And it has tried to carry out its tasks and formulate its views consistently with that answer.

The Commission recognizes, of course, that the nature of democracy is precisely one of those issues about which misunderstanding and disagreement currently cluster. What it understands by the term ought to be made clear. Because, however, the Commission has already expressed its views at some length elsewhere[7] and because an understanding of its meaning will come best from a study of the specific recommendations scattered throughout this volume, only a relatively brief statement is called for at this point.

The basic democratic values are respect for personality, acceptance of social responsibility, and reliance upon reason. The democratic individual thinks, feels, and acts for himself and encourages in others behavior of an equal integrity. But the freedom he thus exercises and fosters he recognizes as being subject to two conditions—conditions that both ought and also must be observed if, in the long run, freedom is to persist and prosper. The first condition is that behavior must be reasonable —thought, feeling, and action must be rationally adjusted to purpose and to the facts of the situation. The second condition is that decision must be taken with consideration for social consequences—affirmative, active respect for the rights, person-

[7] *Ibid.*, especially Chapter II.

alities, and welfare of others is as essential as respect for oneself.

In group situations democracy implies participation by all concerned, an earnest effort to respect and learn from each other, to make and welcome contributions designed to benefit the group. It implies resistance to the temptation to impose upon others limitations that group well-being does not actually require and the necessity for which is not clearly evident. It requires readiness to respond to the authority of expert knowledge and experienced wisdom, and willingness to bear a full share of responsibility for the consequence of decisions shared in. Above all it calls for ability to move with reasonable promptness through the stage of discussion and debate to that of policy agreement, to fix and delegate responsibility intelligently, and to give loyal support and all reasonable scope to those selected for the discharge of such responsibility. Ultimate powers of decision and control will always remain with the group but these will be exercised with discretion and restraint. Democracy does not require that every question to arise be submitted to the group; indeed its success as a way of life demands that the risks of individual and mass frustration through perpetual and indiscriminate debate be deliberately avoided.

The democratic ideal insists, of course, that decisions taken should be in accordance with basic democratic values—they should be rational and they should manifest regard for human personality and the common welfare. Just because of these requirements such decisions must also be responsive to the circumstances that define and the increasing knowledge that illuminates the problems to be met. In our time circumstances are in notable flux and the accumulation of knowledge proceeds at a rising tempo. Because of these facts old habits of thought and action require critical re-examination, and the experimental testing of new solutions needs to be encouraged.

The contemporary crisis gives a special urgency to the aims of education in a democracy. Democratic citizens must understand, esteem, and be guided by democratic values. They must have a general knowledge of men—including themselves—and of the nature and functioning of the social order. They must be able to derive and grasp generalizations from experience and know how to use them to guide behavior. They must possess integrity of thought, feeling, and action, and a sense of personal responsibility for participation in social action. They must be able to communicate effectively with their fellows, to teach them and learn from them, to work with them freely and in common cause. Education in a democracy should help to produce such men. It should concern itself with purpose and capacity rather than with the inculcation of readymade answers.

The Commission has wished to emphasize the implications for teacher education of such views as these. The nature of our times has made it all the more essential to operate from such a fundamental base. Not to have done so would have revealed a culpable insensitivity to the great dangers and opportunities with which we are all faced. But there is another reason for the emphasis: it focuses the attention of teachers and the teachers of teachers upon considerations of principle and upon their personal responsibility for working together, wherever they may be, to improve education in the situations over which they have control. These situations have been powerfully affected by war; they are being powerfully affected by the events that are following the war. Moreover, they vary, have varied, and will vary from place to place. In view of such facts a national commission on teacher education ought to stress basic principles and their general applications. The details must be worked out finally by those on the several firing lines.

Summary

This introductory statement may now be concluded by a brief summarization of the convictions which have controlled the Commission's thought and action and which its experience, during its existence, has served to strengthen.

1. The crisis of our times calls for a renewal of devotion to genuine democratic values, an extension of the use of proper democratic procedures, and a mobilization of intelligence, imagination, and good will in a positive attack upon emergent social problems.

2. These problems are—and promise to continue to be—so novel and complicated that it is of prime importance that education should promote general ability to understand them and to deal with them intelligently by the methods of democracy. The same can be said with respect to the personal problems that are created by the circumstances of our times.

3. The needed improvement of education implies the improvement of teaching and of the performance of all educational workers. It is, therefore, critically important that teachers in our times should be able persons, well prepared, enabled constantly to realize their full powers, and growing continuously in competence while on the job.

4. It follows that teacher education, which is responsibly concerned with all these matters, needs to be raised to the highest possible degree of excellence. This calls for a present rededication to their tasks by all whose behavior influences the development and performance of teachers, and a redoubling of their efforts to choose and carry out courses of action with a deep and intelligent sense of social responsibility.

5. If teacher education is to make the social contribution thus called for it must be guided by democratic values and must strive for self-improvement through the use of democratic procedures. The individuals, groups, and institutions involved must demonstrate—and must be encouraged to demonstrate—respect for personality, the use of group methods, and reliance upon critical thinking.

The Creation of the Commission

The general circumstances, social and educational, that characterized the time at which the Commission on Teacher Education was established having been described, and some basic related ideas of the Commission having been set forth, it will now be useful to consider precisely how that body came into being and just what responsibilities were assigned to it.

The proposal that eventuated in its creation was first made to the Committee on Problems and Plans of the American Council on Education in January 1936. Following extended discussion by that body, a series of conferences was arranged in which representatives of teachers colleges, colleges of liberal arts, publicly and privately controlled universities, state departments of education, school systems, and leading educational associations and deliberative bodies participated. In this way, as well as through correspondence with individuals and other inquiries directed by two specifically appointed members of the Council staff, views regarding the need for a national study of teacher education and the character it might wisely assume were gathered, and an analysis and general formulation was begun. Later a special committee was appointed to take responsibility for preparing a formal report regarding these matters.[8] Such a document was presented, reviewed, and accepted in February 1937. This report subsequently served as a basis for further discussion in which an additional number of representative educators took part. For example, its proposals were approved in mid-1937 by a specially called conference of representatives of certain educational associations directly concerned with questions of teacher education. From all the above it can be seen what care was taken to make certain that the proposals would reflect the thinking of a large and representative group of persons concerned with the problems of teacher education.

The committee's report, published under the title *Major Issues in Teacher Education,*[9] constituted a charter for the Commission later to be formed and as such needs to be briefly reviewed.

[8] Payson Smith, formerly state commissioner of education in Massachusetts, served as chairman of this committee. The other members included a second state commissioner, Sidney B. Hall of Virginia; three teachers college presidents: Charles W. Hunt of Oneonta (New York), O. R. Latham of Cedar Falls (Iowa), and Roscoe L. West of Trenton (New Jersey); two presidents of colleges of liberal arts: Meta Glass of Sweet Briar College and James L. McConaughey of Wesleyan University; three representatives of graduate schools of education: Dean Doak S. Campbell of George Peabody College, E. S. Evenden of Teachers College, Columbia University, and Dean W. E. Peik of the University of Minnesota; and a superintendent of schools, A. J. Stoddard of Denver. Positions and locations are given as of the date of service on the committee. Dr. Smith and Dr. Evenden were particularly active in carrying out preliminary inquiries and in developing a report. Jesse B. Sears of Stanford University also shared in this work.

[9] *Major Issues in Teacher Education,* American Council on Education Studies, Series I, Vol. II, No. 4 (Washington: American Council on Education, February 1938).

In this report the committee explicitly denied that it had attempted an exhaustive listing of needs in American teacher education, or an appraisal of the relative urgency of those that it chose to list. To do either of these things was not thought to be a requisite part of the task that it had been assigned. Nevertheless, an analysis of what it did mention is important as helping to explain the background against which the Commission was later to operate.

The committee began by pointing out a need for thorough revision and restatement of the objectives of teacher education. It expressed the view that better students should be recruited for the profession and selected by the institutions where they were to be prepared. Looking at preparatory programs, it called for more attention to the development of an understanding of child nature and its implications for teaching; command of subject matter (improvement was deemed especially needful in the case of secondary school teachers); understanding of community educational agencies with which the schools should cooperate; ability to share creatively in forming and putting into effect policies and plans respecting school administration, curriculum building, the school library, and equipment; and professional attitudes toward questions of professional ethics, tenure, and academic freedom. The frequent inadequacy of experience in student teaching was remarked. The problem of determining how teachers might best be prepared for specialized work—as in art, music, home economics, industrial subjects, and physical education, or with atypical children or adults—was also separately mentioned.

Viewing from another angle the institutions preparing teachers the committee called attention to the inadequacy of their financial support, the frequent lack of essential preparation and understanding of education on the part of their staff members, the fact that they were often without contact with the social and educational problems of the schools within their regions, and the existence of a degree of competition for student enrollment that constituted a menace to the integrity of professional education for teachers. Questions further declared to call for study had to do with the probable effect of the junior college movement on programs for the education of teachers and the place and proper organization of graduate work in the education both of teachers and of school administrators.

Some of the items already listed had evident implications for programs of in-service education; however, the need for a great extension and improvement of such programs was also given separate mention. The committee further stated that the existing system of teacher certification was unsatisfactory and should be changed.

In recommending creation of a commission to study such issues as those it had suggested, the committee did not undertake to predetermine just how the proposed body should operate. Certain ideas as to procedure were, however, set forth that were later to exercise considerable influence. Of these the most important had to do with the desirability of decentralized study with major responsibility to be borne by local working groups. It was suggested that each such group should determine its own particular points of attack and plan and carry out its own program of self-study and self-improvement. At the same time the values that might be obtained through cooperative relationships between groups—for purposes of mutual stimulation and assistance—and through the central provision of consultant and similar services were pointed out. The importance of bringing about the participation locally of as many staff members as a given problem had relevance for, and of striving in this and other ways for an increase in staff unity, was emphasized.

All of these ideas were later followed by the Commission and determined important aspects of its program. In other respects, however, it may be said that the Commission went beyond suggestions offered by the committee. The latter body, for example, thought only of colleges and universities as prospective participants in the contemplated study, and while sensitive to the need of greater program coordination, it visualized such institutions as committing themselves, not in general, but in terms of specific problems specially selected for attack. Thus one group would be formed for the re-examination of objectives, another for attention to the improvement of instruction respecting child growth and development, and so on. As will be reported more fully a little later on, the Commission after its establishment determined to include school systems and statewide cooperating groups as well as colleges and universities in its program. It also chose to bring all these in as general participants. Although they usually came, in time, to focus attention on a selection of problems they were not required to do so; they were free to shift emphasis in the light of changing circumstance and developing judgment, and they were always encouraged to consider the bearing of specific activities on their programs viewed as a whole.

The way in which later developments both followed and deviated from suggestions contained in *Major Issues in Teacher Education* has been touched on for a reason. It reveals, as other parts of this report are intended to reveal, how plans become modified as a result of expanding thought and experience. Because of the wisdom of the Council's special committee in refraining from undertaking to predetermine a program, the Commission when it came into existence was free to exercise its own best judgment as to what it should undertake to do. Inevitably it was influenced by the careful thinking that had preceded its creation. But being constituted in major part by different personalities and having the advantage of opportunity for still further deliberation, it quite as inevitably made contributions of its own. It is worthy of mention at this point that, as will later more fully appear, the Commission followed the committee's example in leaving its own staff and the institutions with which it became associated free to make modifications in their original plans as experience demonstrated the desirability of such action.

As was stated earlier the report of its special committee was received and approved by the American Council in February 1937. Following this, the Council sought a grant of funds from the General Education Board to make possible undertaking the recommended venture. This request met with favorable action and in January 1938 the Council was able to announce that basic support for a commission on teacher education had been provided to cover a period of five years. Subsequently additional grants were received and the life of the project was eventually extended to six and three-quarters years, coming to a close in September 1944.

The Commission was organized during the early months of 1938, meeting for the first time in June of that year. It was slightly enlarged the following year. Its members were selected so as to provide representation of various groups concerned with teacher education. Thus the sixteen members included four · college presidents—two from teachers colleges and two from colleges of liberal arts—three heads of university schools or departments of education, two university professors of education, a director of laboratory schools in a state college for women, a superintendent of schools, a representative of the United States Office of Education, a curriculum specialist for a state department of education, the director of a university institute of child welfare, a literary and social critic who later became head of a university school of humanities, and—ex officio—the president of the American Council on Education. Publicly and privately controlled colleges and universities were represented in about equal proportions. One of the professors of education had but recently retired from many years of service as a state superintendent of education. Four members of the Commission had served on the Council committee that had produced *Major Issues in Teacher Education*, two of them with special prominence, and several had been or still were conspicuously associated with the work of various educational associations, commissions, and special studies.[10]

The director of the Commission was also appointed early in 1938, and other members of the staff were gradually added. These persons, too, were selected because of the relevance and

[10] A list of Commission members appears on a preliminary page of this report. Payson Smith, its first chairman, found it necessary to resign that post in February 1942 and was succeeded by E. S. Evenden, the original vice chairman. Ralph W. Tyler was then elected to the vice chairmanship. Harold Benjamin was unable to participate in Commission deliberations after July 1942 when he was commissioned in the United States Marine Corps and assigned to active duty.

variety of their experience. In addition to numerous individuals who rendered special services, usually of a temporary and consultative nature, there were fifteen who gave all—or in a very few cases half—of their time to responsible staff work for from two to nearly seven years. Among these latter were represented administrative and teaching experience in universities, teachers colleges, colleges of liberal arts, and public and private elementary and secondary schools. Several staff members had at one time or another been attached to state departments of education. The special fields in which these individuals had earned their doctor's degrees, done published research, and offered advanced instruction, included elementary, secondary, and higher education, educational administration, evaluation, psychology, child growth and development, sociology, philosophy, and economics.[11]

PLANNING THE PROGRAM

The first task of the Commission was, of course, to formulate a policy and a program. Its members began by discussing their new responsibilities and by exchanging views and suggestions as to how these might best be discharged. The director participated fully in these deliberations as did, as soon as they were appointed, the other members of the Commission staff. The principle of participation in planning by those responsible for the administration of decisions was thus followed from the outset. The same principle was later employed by the staff in its relations with others.

Evolution of the study plans

By the close of a second Commission meeting, held in October 1938, certain controlling agreements had been reached. These were in full accord with the basic recommendations of *Major Issues in Teacher Education* although including new developments in certain directions. Fundamental was acceptance of the idea that emphasis was to be laid on experimentation and demonstration in the field, with procedure to be through the establishment of working relations with selected institutions where teacher

[11] A list of staff members is given in the appendix.

education was a major responsibility. Alternative possibilities were, of course, carefully considered. But the exhaustive survey of the education of teachers carried out by the United States Office of Education from 1930 to 1932 made further use of this technique unnecessary for some time to come, and it seemed wiser to press for the implementation of existing research rather than to promote further inquiries of this character. The situation appeared to be ripe for use of a relatively novel method. That this method could not be expected to yield some results that might have been anticipated had other techniques been employed was fully understood, but it was believed that the approach promised peculiar advantages of its own. It emphasized the responsibility of persons working at the points where action must take place and encouraged these to put to the acid test of experience the hypotheses of current educational thought.

The basic decision reached, the Commission had to consider how many field contacts it should seek to establish, of what character, and with what types of institution, where located. In recognition of the large number of institutions concerned with teacher education there was a strong inclination to seek extensive contacts, but deliberation led to the conclusion that a more intensive relationship with a relatively small number of centers would prove more profitable. The Commission's resources while substantial were not unlimited, and the danger of attempting more than could be competently carried out had to be recognized. The Commission was greatly concerned with its responsibility to be of wide service to those concerned with teacher education, but it concluded that in the long run such service could be better rendered if it did not attempt to cover too much ground in the field program phases of its work.

The decision to establish direct contacts with only a limited number of institutions became more clearly necessary as the character of the relationships to be worked toward was agreed upon. The Commission was deeply impressed by the importance of emphasizing and fostering institutional unity, institutional freedom, and institutional dynamics. It determined, therefore, to invite institutions to join its projected study as wholes, and then permit them to choose for themselves what special problems they should, in view of their own needs, resources, and developmental trends, undertake to attack with special vigor. This implied an extensive responsibility on the part of the Commission to each such associate, one that could not be adequately performed if relations were too numerous.

Another important implication should also be observed: each institution was to retain full responsibility and a maximum of freedom to determine its course of action in the contemplated study and to modify that course as experience directed. The program was to be decentralized. The Commission understood that this decision involved risks and would encourage variations in attack that would make comparisons difficult. But it believed it to be consistent with its own philosophy and to promise advantages not otherwise obtainable. As things turned out the decision proved particularly fortunate; when the impacts of war began to be felt the institutions associated with the Commission were able to adjust their courses to the new realities without any deviation from the commitments they had made.

When the Commission came to consider criteria for selecting the institutions to be associated in its program it at once reached a decision of great significance. It determined to make its main approach to the problems of the in-service education of teachers through the establishment of contacts with representative school systems. This was a reflection of the view that the continued personal and professional development of teachers is fundamentally a responsibility of these individuals themselves and that it must be planned and brought about in particular relation to their working situations. The Commission did not underestimate the contributions of colleges and universities to the in-service growth of teachers, but it believed that the school system setup must always be of basic influence in determining the extent to which an active teacher is enabled to realize his existing powers and is stimulated and assisted to increase them.

It should be noted that the Commission was particularly concerned about the whole matter of development in service, believing that far too often teachers cease to grow in competence

—and even retrogress—after they enter employment. It also believed that programs of in-service education should be keyed to the working teacher's needs and that these must powerfully reflect the circumstances of his employment. For these reasons, then, the Commission determined to invite as many school systems as colleges and universities to cooperate in its study. At first it contemplated dealing with the two groups separately, but upon further consideration it was thought wiser to bring them together in order that the advantages of interaction might be obtained.

Because the Commission represented a national organization it felt obligated to select its prospective associates so as to provide for geographical spread. Because it was sensitive to the variety of the teacher education scene it thought it essential to choose representatives of different types and sizes of college, university, and school system. While the Commission itself generally leaned in the "progressive" direction so far as educational philosophy was concerned, it did not propose to make sympathy with this inclination a criterion for choice. It did, however, think it essential to seek assurance that its associates would not prove self-satisfied but would, rather, be eager to devote unusual energy to self-study and self-improvement.

The above decisions made, the Commission asked itself what services it should plan to make available to the colleges and school systems that were to become partners in its study. At this point consideration was given to a rather elaborate plan contemplating the creation of six service divisions—in evaluation, curriculum, personnel, human growth and development, social understanding, and the aesthetic and communicative arts—each of which was to be staffed with expert consultants and authorized to arrange conferences, finance special collaborators in local situations, and otherwise facilitate developments in the field. The Commission soon concluded, however, that it would be unwise to set up so much machinery in advance of the establishment of relationships with the field units. This was primarily because it believed that the cooperating colleges, universities, and school systems should share from the outset in molding the course of the proposed study, and that pressures that might unnaturally distort the normal processes of institutional development should be avoided. It accordingly decided that with a single exception only general coordination should be provided for in advance. The exception, dictated by special considerations, was to be the immediate creation of a combined division of human growth and development and teacher personnel.

While the thinking that has been described was done in explicit relation to plans for a nationwide cooperative study of teacher education, it had many implications for other enterprises that the Commission was beginning to consider. This was particularly true of a plan to encourage statewide attacks on the improvement of teacher education which would be participated in by state departments of education, state universities and teachers colleges, privately controlled universities and colleges of liberal arts, and representatives of the schools. As will become evident later on, the Commission's statewide program came to share with the cooperative study emphasis upon the following: experimentation and demonstration; the unity, freedom, and dynamics of particular institutions; local control and the use of group methods; the closer working together of colleges and universities on the one hand and school systems on the other; and the use of consultants, conferences, and workshops. In contrast with the national study, however, the statewide studies were characterized—with rare exceptions—by the participation of all eligible colleges and universities. In some states, moreover, the attention given to in-service education was slight.[12]

Announcement of plans

The actual launching of the national cooperative study along the lines agreed upon by the Commission called for additional

[12] It should be noted that the statewide studies were quite as much entitled to be called "cooperative" as that established on a national basis. However, the latter, which was put into operation a year before the others, came to be referred to from the outset as "the cooperative study of teacher education." Because this usage has become familiar to many in the course of the Commission's existence it has seemed best to retain it in this report. It has, however, no implications of contrast with the statewide programs.

funds, and these were made available in the fall of 1938. With support thus assured the Commission moved ahead, the next important step being the publication, in February 1939, of a statement in which it set forth its principles, described its plans, and invited would-be participants in the projected study to make their interest known.[18]

It seems desirable, at the risk of some repetition, to rehearse the basic decisions reported in this document. There were nine of them, as follows:

1. The Commission should, so far as possible, work directly with and through already existing groups and agencies that are professionally concerned with the education of teachers.

2. The Commission should especially endeavor to facilitate the efforts of the various groups and agencies to put into use and test in practice the best available knowledge regarding the problems in the field.

3. The Commission should concern itself with all the experiences which have educational significance for the teacher at any particular time. (This was explained as meaning that too much distinction ought not to be drawn between such elements as "general" and "professional" education, and that programs of teacher education should be cooperatively planned in terms of the total needs of those who are involved.)

4. The Commission should concern itself with the education of teachers from the time they determine to enter the profession to the time they withdraw from it. (This justified the proposal to work with schools as well as colleges.)

5. The Commission should stimulate, in every feasible way, cooperation in the attack upon problems of teacher education. Such cooperation should be between those working at any given stage of teacher education and also between those working at succeeding stages.

6. The Commission should not seek to impose any plan or pattern on the individual groups with which it may be associated. Variations in circumstance and in conviction clearly justified

---

[18] *Cooperation in the Improvement of Teacher Education* (Washington: American Council on Education, 1939).

variations in practice. Particular groups must formulate their own objectives, study their own situations, set up and evaluate their own programs. This did not, of course, mean that one may not learn from the experience of others; what it did imply is that such lessons must be truly assimilated.

7. The Commission should encourage each group associated with it to continue or enter upon experimental activities related to that group's own recognized needs and to broaden emphases as new needs became evident and as circumstances permitted.

8. The Commission should, however, be particularly concerned with facilitating attacks on problems and issues in the field of teacher education that have the widest and deepest significance.

9. The Commission should encourage continuous evaluation of programs for teacher education wherever occurring.

Having set forth these principles of operation the Commission expressed its intention of inviting fifteen institutions where teachers were being prepared and fifteen school systems concerned with the continued growth of staff members to join in the cooperative study for a period of three years. It explained that the primary criterion for the selection of participants would be the presence of plans or programs for dealing intelligently and vigorously with recognized local problems of teacher education, but that considerations of type and size of institution, as well as of geography, would also be taken into account. The intention was to include institutions serving Negro as well as white constituencies.

The responsibilities to be undertaken by cooperating groups were then described: they were to be expected to commit themselves wholeheartedly and for the full three years to positive efforts to improve their work in teacher education, to free a portion of the time of staff members for local duties related to the cooperative activity and for participation in conferences and workshops, to keep careful records of plans and procedures and evaluate outcomes as fully as possible, and to share with others the results of their experimentation. The Commission declared that it would be particularly interested in evidence of a general eagerness on the part of staff members of would-be cooperating units for participation in the study: it avowed its belief that superior programs are most likely to result from cooperation on the part of all those responsible for the various opportunities for educational experience provided in any given pre-service or in-service situation.

The Commission concluded its statement by sketching the contributions it itself expected to make to the cooperative enterprise, stressing its desire, however, to adjust these to the needs of the institutions to be associated with it as such needs became manifest. The services of a central staff of general consultants and coordinators were promised, along with those of special part-time consultants as demanded. The plan was announced to establish a special division of child growth and development and teacher personnel, with a collaboration center to be set up where research materials in both fields would be brought together and studied for their educational implications. Provision of conference and workshop opportunities for representatives of cooperating institutions was forecast, as well as the collection and dissemination of information regarding experiments being carried forward. The hope was expressed that the contemplated program would be found to have values for many groups besides those most intimately involved and that eventually a process of cooperative attack upon the improvement of teacher education would be demonstrated which would prove widely adaptable, even in the absence of special subsidization.

Selection of the cooperating centers

Even before the public announcement of its plan for a nationwide cooperative study of teacher education the Commission had taken first steps toward the selection of a group of participants. Suggestions as to teachers colleges, colleges of liberal arts, universities, Negro colleges, and school systems that ought to be considered for inclusion were sought from a large number of educational leaders. As responses to the Commission's announcement were received all were carefully considered. Eventually staff members visited as many places as possible—approximately one hundred—in an effort to learn more about local interests, plans, and facilities at first hand. The problem of choice proved a difficult one: there were many more colleges, universities, and school systems with which the Commission would have liked to be associated than it was in a position to select. In the end it was unable to stick to its original intention of limiting the study to thirty centers. Not only did it issue invitations to thirty-four such units but of these six were clusters, so that fifty administratively distinct bodies were actually included. Even so, many omissions were made with very great regret.

The participants in the cooperative study were as follows:

Institutions of higher learning

Claremont Colleges, Claremont, California
College of St. Catherine, St. Paul, Minnesota
College of William and Mary, Williamsburg, Virginia
Colorado State College of Education, Greeley, Colorado
Columbia University, New York, New York: including Barnard, Columbia, and Teachers Colleges
Eastern Kentucky State Teachers College, Richmond, Kentucky
Middlebury College, Middlebury, Vermont
New Jersey State Teachers College, Newark, New Jersey
Oberlin College, Oberlin, Ohio
Ohio State University, Columbus, Ohio
Prairie View State College, Prairie View, Texas
Southern Illinois State Normal University, Carbondale, Illinois
Stanford University, Palo Alto, California
State Teachers College, Milwaukee, Wisconsin
State Teachers College, Troy, Alabama
Tuskegee Institute, Tuskegee, Alabama
University of Nebraska, Lincoln, Nebraska
University of North Carolina, Chapel Hill, North Carolina: including also the State College of Agriculture and Engineering, Raleigh, and the Woman's College, Greensboro
University of Texas, Austin, Texas
Western Michigan College of Education, Kalamazoo, Michigan

School systems

Bedford County, Virginia
Caledonia Central Supervisory Union, Danville, Vermont
Colquitt County, Georgia: including the county and Moultrie city systems

Denver, Colorado

Des Moines, Iowa

Detroit, Michigan

Greenville County, South Carolina: including the county, city, and
Parker District systems, and with the cooperation of the Green-
ville County Council for Community Development and Furman
University

Houston, Texas

Los Angeles County, California: including the county, city, Burbank,
Pasadena, and Santa Monica systems

Newton, Massachusetts

New Trier Township, Illinois: including the township high school,
the elementary systems of Glencoe, Kenilworth, Wilmette, and
Winnetka, and the North Shore Country Day School

Norris, Tennessee

Philadelphia, Pennsylvania

Spokane, Washington

Classified according to types this list includes: seven state
teachers colleges; seven colleges of liberal arts, all but one
privately controlled; one publicly supported technical college;
seven universities or graduate institutions, three of them privately controlled; two Negro colleges, one public, one private;[14]
three of the five largest city school systems in the country in
cities with a population exceeding 1,000,000; four systems in
cities with a population of from 100,000 to 1,000,000; twelve
smaller city systems; six county or other nonurban systems; and
one private school. Twenty-three states, in all parts of the
Union, were represented. It should be added that seven of these
states—Alabama, Colorado, Georgia, Kentucky, Michigan,
New York, and Ohio—as well as three additional ones—
Florida, Mississippi, and West Virginia—were later affected
by the Commission's statewide program. In each of these ten
states relations were eventually established with all or most of

---

[14] The Commission sought throughout its existence and in a variety of ways to
serve the needs of Negro as well as of white teacher education. It assumed that
those needs were basically similar. Some of the colleges and universities with
which the Commission worked were attended by representatives of only one race,
others by representatives of both; some of the school systems practiced segregation,
others did not. The Commission accepted these local differences as it did differences of many other kinds. Its own conferences and workshops were attended by
members of both races without discrimination.

their colleges and universities, and in most instances with a representative group of their school systems.[15]

LAUNCHING THE COOPERATIVE STUDY

The first act of the Commission, once the membership of the national cooperative study was determined, was to arrange a two-week planning conference to be held on the campus of Bennington College during the latter half of August 1939.[16] One hundred and twenty-four persons attended this gathering, all but a few being present throughout. Of these, 104 were representatives of the institutions that were to participate in the study, the delegations ranging in size from two to seven persons. Four Commission and six staff members were present and there were ten specially invited guests. The college representation, totaling 67, was made up of nine presidents, ten deans of education, five deans of liberal arts, one administrative and two personnel deans, four other educational administrative officers, twenty-one professors of education and twelve of various academic subjects, a registrar, a librarian, and a psychiatric social worker. The delegation from school systems included twenty superintendents and associate or assistant superintendents, eleven additional representatives of central offices (supervisors and the like), three principals, and a classroom teacher, besides a dean of education and a sociologist from related universities. The Commission members and guests who participated regularly included a university president and a Negro college president, two officials from the United States Office of Education, and three representatives of other nationwide educational enterprises.

The chief purpose of the Bennington conference was to settle basic plans for the cooperative study about to get under way. It was hoped that important objectives and issues would be

[15] For further details respecting the statewide program see pp. 44–46 and Chapter IV.

[16] A full report of this meeting was published under the title *Bennington Planning Conference for the Cooperative Study of Teacher Education: Reports and Addresses* (Washington: American Council on Education, 1939). In this will be found documentation for the statements to follow.

identified, that ways and means whereby participants might best discharge their responsibilities would be suggested, that agreements would be reached regarding the nature and utilization of services to be provided by the Commission, and that consideration would be given to how the study might desirably exercise a broad influence in the field of teacher education.

The Commission staff gave a great deal of thought to plans for this opening conference. It was exceedingly eager that there should be complete participation, that everyone present should be assured a thoughtful and friendly hearing, and that the conclusions reached should grow wholly out of the conference process. The staff thought it proper to arrange that certain ideas which it believed important should be presented for consideration, but it desired that these should be fully subject to critical scrutiny. In view of the rather marked difference of experience and occupation on the part of those who were to attend the conference, the staff gave particular attention to methods whereby mutual acquaintance, appreciation, and trust might be fostered from the start. It considered this essential if people were to speak out frankly and listen sympathetically.

Accordingly delegates were first grouped homogeneously according to the type of teacher-preparing institution or the size of school system they represented, and each group set about producing a list of problems in teacher education considered critically important by its members. Later, however, cross-sectional groups including representatives of all types of cooperating units were set up to consider the twelve problem areas of greatest and most general concern. From each of these groups reports were eventually received. At the close of the conference special committees presented general reports on possible patterns of action by participating centers, on plans for the over-all conduct of the cooperative study, on problems of record-keeping and reporting, and on relations with the general world of teacher education. On several evenings during the course of the conference there were presented a series of addresses and panel discussions, dealing with topics which seemed of special importance to the Commission and which were carefully planned in advance.[17]

Problems identified at Bennington

The five lists of problems in teacher education independently produced by the homogeneously grouped delegates during the first few days of the Bennington conference naturally exhibited some interesting differences of emphasis, reflecting the varying backgrounds and interests of their respective authors. But they also showed considerable overlap with the list contained in *Major Issues in Teacher Education* as well as with each other. When they were submitted to the entire conference for vote as to the relative importance of the several items, it became evident that there was widespread agreement on this matter.

It will be worth while to examine the topics in which outstanding general interest was expressed. There was considerable concern with the objectives of teacher education, defined in terms of factors that make for teaching competence. Both pre-service and in-service representatives also stressed the development in teachers of a dynamic and functioning philosophy of education, as well as of a working understanding of child growth and development and of American society as these have implications for the school and the teacher. Continuous evaluation of both prospective and active teachers was also deemed very important.

Conference members were further strongly interested in the question of how the curricula of colleges and universities might best develop teachers of vital personality, with a good attitude toward teaching, facility in child guidance, and ability to make subject matter functional—teachers who would be equipped by their pre-service experience to deal with the practical problems that actual teaching brings. Special note was given to the ques-

[17] All of these may be found in the Bennington report cited above. Two, those of Karl W. Bigelow and Lewis Mumford, were later republished jointly by the Commission on Teacher Education and the Educational Policies Commission in a pamphlet entitled *Cultural and Social Elements in the Education of Teachers* (Washington: American Council on Education, 1940). Mr. Mumford's address was also printed in the *Educational Record* for October 1939; excerpts appeared in *The Education Digest* for January 1940.

tion of how subject matter should be organized in preparatory programs, whether departmentally, or into broad fields such as the humanities, social studies, and natural sciences, or in terms of core courses each of which would draw on various subjects to throw light on some broad life need. The planning and conduct of student teaching was stressed. So was the problem of improving the coordination of the activities of educationists and subject-matter professors as these relate to teacher education.

Two other topics that were judged to be of special importance were the development of an integrated program of school-college relationships calculated to promote mutual understanding and mutual aid, and the general improvement of methods of encouraging and facilitating the continuous growth of all educational workers in service.

Somewhat less response was given to certain other topics, each of which, nevertheless, was of more than average concern. Recruitment, selection, and guidance of prospective teachers came here. So did the program of general education and that of professional education—on both the undergraduate and graduate levels. There was a feeling that relations existing between schools and colleges on the one hand and their communities on the other should be improved; also that understanding and use of community resources, especially as represented by social agencies other than the schools, should be promoted. The importance of developing initiative, creativeness, and resourcefulness in teachers—ability to help shape the direction of education—was recognized, as was the need for the improvement of college staffs through better preparation, selection, and in-service development. Finally in this group of topics were two very explicitly relating to teachers on the job: the improvement of the personnel program—the importance of promoting physical and mental health and of encouraging personal cultural growth and participation in community affairs was specifically mentioned; and provision of more opportunity for participation by teachers in educational planning and policy formulation, both in particular schools and in systems as a whole.

Other topics that were listed but that received less than average response included: placement and follow-up; the number and combination of teaching fields for which secondary school teachers should be prepared; the planning of a three-year, post-junior-college program; general methods courses; preparation for work with limited resources, i.e., in poorly financed and equipped school systems; teacher-pupil participation in continuous evaluation of accepted educational purposes; relations with state departments of education, especially with reference to certification requirements; the role of the supervisor or staff specialist in in-service situations; methods of spreading the influence of the best teachers in a system; the place of workshops and similar devices for in-service education; clarification and improvement of the status of teachers in their communities; and coordination of effort by universities and colleges operating in a given state or region.[18]

Plans developed at Bennington

It should be understood that there was never any intention that the identification and discussion at Bennington of problems in teacher education should lead to immediate decisions as to attacks to be made in the several cooperating centers. The purpose was not to produce a standard list to which all should be committed nor even one from which choices must eventually be made. The procedure employed was viewed as exploratory and was designed to throw light of a general character on the tasks lying ahead both for the Commission and for the associated centers. It was taken for granted that the delegates present could not—or, at least, should not—finally determine what had best

[18] Some readers may be interested to know how the topics that emerged independently at Bennington compared with those listed in *Major Issues*. In general there was striking agreement. The Bennington conferees, however, added and gave considerable emphasis to the needs for helping teachers to understand American society, for more evaluation in teacher education, for improved staff coordination in colleges and universities, and for taking more responsibility as respects in-service education by school system administrators and classroom teachers themselves. On the other hand, certain items appearing in the earlier list were not to be found in the later one: more nearly adequate support for teacher education, the place of experimentation and research in the education of teachers, the probable effects of the junior college movement on teacher education, and the development of professional attitudes. The problem of certification, while listed at Bennington, aroused a surprisingly small amount of interest.

be undertaken at the places they represented, that, indeed, their first job upon returning home would be to engage their colleagues there in planning what should be set about locally.

Accordingly the conference committee on patterns of attack by institutions emphasized in its report that local plans for participation in the cooperative study should be coordinated with existing plans and purposes of the several centers and that the active support and participation of all staff members should be enlisted. While it presumed that the problems listed at Bennington would command attention, it pointed out that local selection of points of attack must also be governed by considerations of local purpose, facilities, readiness of constituency, and the like. The committee urged that the basic considerations in the development of each program should be the needs of the persons to be educated and of those whom they were or later would be teaching, and the perpetuation of the values essential to democracy. Procedures should be such that all participants could be simultaneously teachers and learners, leaders and followers; and continuous institutional self-improvement, rather than either instant or ultimate fixed perfection, should be the goal. Many suggestions were offered as to how the largest possible proportion of personnel in each cooperating center might be informed regarding the cooperative study and drawn into the activities developed in connection with it. Ways and means of effecting relations with other institutions were also proposed. But no standard pattern of operation was recommended: trust was placed in the delegates to work matters out in terms of the special situations that they represented.

The committee that had been asked to advise the Commission as to how it could best make its contribution to the cooperative study approved the already established service division on child growth and development and teacher personnel, but urged its strengthening so far as personnel aspects were concerned. It also recommended the setting up of additional service divisions on general curriculum problems, the American culture, the arts in teacher education, and evaluation. Various types of service that might be rendered by the Commission were considered: provision of consultants, preparation and dissemination of materials, interpretation to the public, stimulation of cooperating groups, carrying out of special studies and investigations, provision of fellowships, support of additional conferences, support of workshops and collaboration centers, direct financial aid to cooperating institutions, and cooperation with other agencies and organizations. All of these possibilities were fully approved with two exceptions: the committee recommended that the Commission continue to devote its main energies to implementation rather than to research of a specialized character, and it was of the opinion that financial aid to particular cooperating units should not, in general, be granted.

In addition to the committees whose work has just been described there were two others that brought in reports at the conclusion of the conference. One of these made recommendations regarding records to be kept locally and reports to be made to the Commission in connection with the study. It was proposed that each cooperating group work out a plan of record-keeping in consultation with Commission representatives but that uniformity be not sought after. It was recommended that descriptive and analytical reports of programs and projects undertaken be made periodically to the Commission, but again in ways suitable to each local situation. The Commission was asked to publish a report of the Bennington conference, to issue periodically for general consumption accounts of programs and projects under way or completed, to express from time to time its own best thinking regarding the problems of teacher education, and to plan the publication of a general report of its experience at the conclusion of the study.

Another conference committee that calls for mention had been asked to consider how the Commission and its associates could be of use to the many teacher-educating interests not intimately associated with the cooperative study. All were eager to share the benefits of the experience as widely as possible while at the same time avoiding even the appearance of assuming a superiority over the other colleges, universities, and school systems that could be counted on to continue doing high-quality work.

The committee recommended that the participating units should seek the active interest and advice of representatives of other institutions and school systems in their areas. To the Commission it recommended the setting up of means of clearing information regarding teacher education; the inclusion insofar as possible of persons from outside the cooperative study in such meetings, conferences, workshops, and collaboration centers as might be arranged; the provision of some consultant service to nonparticipant groups; the development and maintenance of close relations with state departments of education and with educational associations; the provision of speakers for educational gatherings and the preparation of materials for general circulation; and the use of appropriate publicity as a means of keeping the field in touch with the study and stimulating wide interest in teacher education.

Significance of the Bennington conference

The Bennington conference has been rather fully described because of its great significance for the Commission's program. It made that program from the start a participant affair, something thought through and jointly determined by representatives of all the units that had undertaken to cooperate in the national study. It established an esprit de corps that persisted. It constituted a valuable common learning experience, demonstrating democratic methods of group effort that influenced the ways in which delegates later undertook to work in their home situations. It gave the Commission confidence in the practical effectiveness of the operating methods to which it was theoretically committed. Thus it set a pattern that was much relied upon throughout the later stages of the Commission's work.[19]

No explicit agreement as to the goals of teacher education was sought at Bennington. But certain goals were repeatedly mentioned and appeared to command general acceptance. These were the development of (1) traits that make for rich personality and for effective participation in democratic living; (2) attitudes

[19] For a full analysis of conference techniques as employed in connection with the Commission's program see pp. 218–26.

and habits favorable to continuous self-improvement both as person and as professional worker throughout the teaching career; (3) understanding of ways and means of guiding wisely the growth and development of children; (4) skill and knowledge essential to scholarly teaching in a chosen field or fields; (5) understanding of and devotion to democratic values; (6) understanding of the role of education, the school, and the teacher in a democratic society; and (7) the habit of active participation in important activities in the community.[20]

THE COURSE OF THE COOPERATIVE STUDY

With the Bennington conference the period of planning was over so far as the national cooperative study was concerned, and the period of action was begun. For the ensuing three years, that is, through the summer of 1942, the study was vigorously pursued in the field. Other Commission publications have described and analyzed many of its aspects in detail and a major portion of this final report will be devoted to summarizing the chief lessons learned from it.[21]

Immediately after Bennington the several cooperating centers went to work in ways determined locally by each group and in all but a few cases with exemplary energy. In most instances the returning delegates sought earnestly to share their experiences with their colleagues and to bring as many of them as possible into participation in local planning and action. Circumstances made this far easier to accomplish in some situations—the more compact, the more homogeneous—than in others. Planning committees were rapidly developed in most centers, however, study groups were formed, action projects agreed upon and begun.

[20] The reader may wish to compare this list with that set forth in Chapter IV of *Teachers for Our Times*. There listed as "qualities needed in teachers" are respect for personality, community-mindedness, rational behavior, emotional surefootedness, creative power, skill in cooperation, increasing knowledge, breadth and integration of scholarship, skill in mediating knowledge, friendliness with children, social understanding and behavior, effective citizenship in the school as society, skill in evaluation, and faith in the worth of teaching.

[21] See Chapters II and III. A complete list of Commission reports will be found in the appendix.

Staff services

During the first few months the Commission's field coordinators systematically visited the centers assigned to them. These staff members (at first two in number, then almost immediately three, and after the first year four) had general responsibility for representing the Commission in its relationships with the colleges, universities, and school systems associated with it. Contacts originally established at Bennington were maintained through later conferences and by means of regular visits. The field coordinators acted as general consultants; they arranged for particular centers to obtain the services of other staff members and of special consultants; they helped to plan and conduct conferences and workshops and to arrange for participation therein by representatives of the units for which they were responsible; they facilitated intervisitation and recommended support for special projects; they made analyses of their own experience and advised regarding the preparation of reports by cooperating units; and finally they shared in writing two of the reports published by the Commission.[22]

Each associated center designated a local coordinator for the cooperative study with whom the Commission's field coordinator maintained primary relationships. All of the Commission's representatives consistently endeavored to grasp local realities, to bring support to the best of local efforts, and to avoid the exercise of distorting pressures.

The Commission had been able, it will be recalled, to set up a service division on child development and teacher personnel prior to Bennington; soon thereafter a division on evaluation was also established. The staff members working in these divisions began at once to provide consultant and other services. They also shared in the preparation of reports published by the

[22] Charles E. Prall and C. Leslie Cushman, *Teacher Education in Service* (Washington: American Council on Education, 1944), and W. Earl Armstrong, Ernest V. Hollis, and Helen E. Davis, *The College and Teacher Education* (Washington: American Council on Education, 1944). (Dr. Davis was associate in charge of the Commission's clearinghouse services.)

Commission.[23] During 1939–40 and 1940–41 a collaboration center on child growth and development was maintained at the University of Chicago. Thirty-nine persons (twenty-two of them from cooperating colleges, universities, and school systems and seventeen from other institutions) were enabled to spend an academic year or, in a few cases, a semester intensively studying research materials at this center and planning changes to be made in the situations from which they had come. This collaboration center has now been taken over by the University of Chicago.

The original plans to develop other service divisions did not materialize. This was partly because of limitations of funds and partly because of difficulties in locating suitable and available persons to take charge. But much more influential, as bearing upon the modification of plans, was the fairly early recognition of the risks entailed if too much in the way of stimulation should be offered the cooperating units: the temptation to introduce many innovations at once would increase with each new Commission service division and, if yielded to, might result in more confusion than accomplishment. In any case, it soon became evident that the functions originally proposed for a general curriculum division could be satisfactorily performed by the field coordinators and certain special consultants. Such consultants were also employed to some degree in the areas of social understanding and the arts, both of which moreover were invariably represented in the workshops sponsored or supported by the Commission.

Workshops and conferences

The Commission had a good deal to do with workshops. It began by operating one at the University of Chicago for five weeks during the summer of 1940. All Commission staff members as well as a number of special consultants took part and the approximately 160 attendants included representatives of all

[23] Maurice E. Troyer and C. Robert Pace, *Evaluation in Teacher Education* (Washington: American Council on Education, 1944), and Staff of the Division on Child Development and Teacher Personnel, Commission on Teacher Education, *Helping Teachers Understand Children* (Washington: American Council on Education, 1945).

the units in the cooperative study plus a number of persons specially invited. In the summer of 1941 the Commission conducted general workshops, which ran for from four to five and a half weeks, at the George Peabody College for Teachers, Northwestern University, and Stanford University, as well as a special ten-week workshop on human growth and development at the University of Chicago. Attendance totalled 243, of which number representatives of the national cooperative study and the statewide programs accounted for not more than two-thirds. The human growth and development workshop has been repeated annually since 1940, though after 1942 under the auspices of the University of Chicago rather than the Commission.

Beginning in 1940 the Commission also gave encouragement and support to a number of workshops conducted by school systems in the cooperative study chiefly for the benefit of their own teachers. Such were carried on in that year at Denver, Des Moines, Greenville (South Carolina), Houston, Los Angeles, and, by the cluster of North Shore systems, at Evanston (Illinois). In 1941 the Denver, Des Moines, Houston, and Los Angeles ventures were repeated, and new ones were launched at Philadelphia and Spokane. Several of the cities mentioned have continued their summer workshops since. A considerable number of the colleges and universities associated with the Commission began to operate workshops during the period of the cooperative study for the benefit of their summer clientele, the Commission providing special assistance in such connection to the Milwaukee State Teachers College in 1940 and Claremont Colleges in 1941. Beginning in 1941 several of the statewide cooperative studies also arranged workshops in connection with their programs.

But the Commission's contribution to the development of the workshop movement went further. From 1940 to 1942 it conducted a workshop advisory service, continuing and expanding work originally begun by the Progressive Education Association. This was at the suggestion of that association, which also transferred to the Commission certain funds and other valuable resources. The advisory service was accessible to all interested parties. It provided consultants, conducted conferences, circulated critical analyses of workshop problems, and published a directory of all summer workshops of which it was able to learn. For 1941 this directory ran to 170 pages and dealt with over 125 enterprises.

In connection with the national cooperative study, and during its three years of existence, the Commission arranged a variety of conferences. Administrators and coordinators from the cooperating centers were on three occasions brought together with the Commission staff for several days of interaction and deliberation. There were in addition several representative conferences on problems in evaluation, fellowships also being provided in this field; and assistance was given to a number of member groups enabling them to arrange special local and regional conferences. Reports of such conferences were usually prepared and frequently made available for general circulation.

Publications and special grants

Early in 1940 the Commission established a clearinghouse and began the publication of a monthly *Newsletter* of which thirty issues and an index appeared in the course of three years. A considerable body of material developed at the collaboration center on human development was made generally available in mimeographed form. Certain of the addresses delivered at Bennington and at the 1940 workshop were published as pamphlets.[24] Pamphlets were also produced in which were reported the results of special inquiries regarding resources for community study, college programs designed to develop community understanding, and the effects of art programs in workshops.[25] When the United States entered the war the Commission published a timely statement entitled *This War and the Teacher*, which achieved

[24] *Cultural and Social Elements in the Education of Teachers*, already mentioned; and *Culture and Personality*, containing addresses by Ralph Linton, Mary Shattuck Fisher, and W. Carson Ryan (Washington: American Council on Education, 1941).

[25] Stephen E. Epler, *The Teacher, the School, and the Community* (Washington: American Council on Education, 1941); Gordon W. Blackwell, *Toward Community Understanding* (Washington: American Council on Education, 1943), and Ray N. Faulkner and Helen E. Davis, *Teachers Enjoy the Arts* (Washington: American Council on Education, 1943).

a circulation of over 150,000 copies, and a special report dealing with *Teacher Education in a Democracy at War*, written by its chairman.[26] More recently a series of eight published reports, of which this is the concluding volume, have been presented.[27] In addition, articles dealing with Commission-related activities appeared in various periodicals. All of the above was in addition to books, pamphlets, and articles produced by various of the cooperating centers, of which material there was no inconsiderable quantity.

The Commission also adopted the policy of making modest grants to cooperating centers for particular purposes. In this way, for example, the holding of local conferences and the arranging of visits by staff members to other school systems or institutions of higher learning were facilitated. But while the Commission thus provided funds for activities that its associates were not in a position to finance, it usually did so only when it thought that such financing might ultimately be taken over locally if the activities proved their worth. The amounts were never large compared with the budgets of the cooperating centers. In a gratifying proportion of cases local arrangements were eventually made to continue at local expense activities originally sponsored by the Commission. No doubt this development would have been more general had it not been for the disturbing effects of the war.

One grant was made to an institution not included in the national study. This was in support of a joint committee of the faculty of Harvard College and of the Harvard Graduate School of Education. As a result, this committee was able to prepare and publish a report on *The Training of Secondary School Teachers, Especially with Reference to English.*[28]

---

[26] Evenden, *op. cit.*

[27] *Teachers for Our Times, Evaluation in Teacher Education, Teacher Education in Service, The College and Teacher Education, Helping Teachers Understand Children,* and *Toward Improving Ph.D. Programs* have all hitherto been mentioned. The remaining volume is *State Programs for the Improvement of Teacher Education* by Charles E. Prall (Washington: American Council on Education, 1946).

[28] Cambridge: Harvard University Press, 1942.

Impact of the war

The war, of course, both before and after the entrance of the United States, had powerful effects upon the situation in which the Commission and its associates found themselves. Enrollments in curricula for prospective teachers began to fall in 1940 and plummeted after 1941. Both the draft and the attractions of war work were influential in causing this development. Between October 1940 and October 1943 the number of students in state teachers colleges declined nearly 60 percent, and it is probable that the supply of prospective teachers in other types of institutions was similarly reduced. This circumstance contributed to a rapidly mounting shortage of teachers in the schools, which were also losing many experienced staff members to industry and the armed services. Simultaneously all sorts of special pressures were being exerted on the schools and colleges: to modify their offerings along war-indicated lines; to cope with new problems resulting from war impacts on children and youth; and to help with rationing, civilian defense work, and the like. Many staff changes occurred in the colleges, universities, and school systems participating in the study.

Because of these developments early plans for activities in connection with the cooperative study often had to be modified. There was, however, surprisingly little in the way of real disruption. This was largely because it had been assumed from the outset of the venture that the situations in which teacher education takes place are subject to continual change, intelligent response to which is an important test of institutional excellence. The decentralized character of the study and its emphasis upon local integrity and dynamics had been designed to increase the likelihood that adjustments would be made in the light of experience and new occurrences. Had the heart of the study been a series of fixed experimental projects rather than flexible movement guided by emergent purpose and adjusted to changing circumstance, the war would doubtless have undermined much that had been begun. As it was the national crisis provided a severe test of the soundness of the principles that had been adopted, and by that test these principles proved their worth.

Directions of advance had often to be changed and hopes deferred, but the value of what had already been done was not destroyed and new values were achieved. The experience of cooperative study and group action made it easier to rise to new challenges than would otherwise have been the case.

THE STATEWIDE STUDIES

It will be recalled that from the beginning the Commission was interested in the possibilities of statewide cooperative studies as means of promoting the improvement of teacher education. The Commission believed the state to constitute a peculiarly significant geographical unit so far as teacher education is concerned. Each state has a department of education and, with rare exceptions, this body determines requirements for the certification of those who may then be employed as teachers in the public schools. Many of these departments exercise additional influence on teacher education, sometimes through control of the teachers colleges, sometimes through advisory relationships, and sometimes through sheer power of leadership. The state university, the state colleges for teachers and others, and the privately controlled universities and colleges within the state are all usually preparing teachers, the majority of whom hope to be employed in the area. These institutions have, therefore, much in common; yet they often have few contacts with one another and are prone to be more sensitive to their differences than to their likenesses. Competitive impulses are likely to be strong. Moreover, contacts between colleges and universities and the schools are often limited, with employing groups complaining that neither the preparation of teachers nor the services offered to them by the colleges after their employment are adequately suited to the needs of the schools.

For all these reasons the Commission inclined favorably toward the idea of encouraging some statewide cooperative studies in which all the interests just mentioned might take part and which, it was thought, might demonstrate some very substantial values. An additional factor was the belief that whereas the nationwide study could hardly hope to continue as a unit after Commission support ceased to be available, considering its geographic scope, statewide studies might well achieve permanent status.

Accordingly after the national study had been well launched the Commission turned its planning attention to the statewide picture. Preliminary investigation revealed promising possibilities in several quarters and consequently, in November 1939, the Commission voted to seek additional funds to provide substantial support for ventures in three states and more modest aid for developments elsewhere. The necessary grant having been obtained, Georgia, Michigan, and New York were selected to receive chief assistance for three and one-half years in connection with statewide cooperative studies. Later on support was provided for comparable though smaller-scale activities in Alabama, Colorado, Florida, Kentucky, Mississippi, Ohio, and West Virginia.

The all-state wing of the Commission's program was guided by the same principles as were employed in the case of the national study. In each state an interested group came forward which the Commission was prepared to see take primary responsibility for planning and conducting a cooperative program. These groups were, in every instance, representative in character. In New York leadership was exercised by the state's association of colleges and universities, with the friendly support and cooperation of the state department of education. In Ohio the deans of the state-controlled schools of education, and in Colorado the state teachers' association, took the lead. Elsewhere developments centered about the state departments of education. Special full-time coordinators were appointed in Georgia, Michigan, and New York. One of the Commission's field coordinators maintained contact with the various statewide developments, offered counsel, arranged for the provision of special assistance, and encouraged participation in Commission-sponsored conferences, workshops, and the collaboration center. But fundamentally decisions were left to the planning bodies in the various states.

The patterns of state action naturally varied. Some embodied broader, some more limited attacks. The techniques employed were similar to those used in the national study: conferences, workshops, consultant service, intervisitation, publication of reports and recommendations. A detailed description and analysis of what was done and accomplished has been provided in an earlier report from the Commission, and more will also be said about the all-state programs later in this volume.[29] Suffice it for the present to remark that when the possibility of Commission support came to an end, the cooperative relationships established or strengthened were in most cases continued. Usually this was made possible through the earmarking of state-department funds for the purpose; in several instances institutional contributions, direct or indirect, were provided. It ought to be added that in the statewide enterprises the school systems, by and large, were less active than the colleges, universities, and state departments. However, in two of the ten states very effective attention was given to in-service education.

OTHER COMMISSION ACTIVITIES

This general background account of the Commission's experience may be concluded with a brief notice of certain additional activities for which it was responsible.[30] First may be mentioned its concern with the education of college teachers. Problems relating to this matter had been listed in *Major Issues in Teacher Education* and at Bennington and were recognized by the Commission from its earliest days. At one time a substantial special study in this area was projected, but it proved impossible to carry this plan through. However, a series of conferences on the preparation of college teachers was held, in which both colleges and graduate schools were represented, and information was systematically gathered respecting the Ph.D.'s and Ed.D.'s produced by American universities during the decade of the thirties. On these and other bases a staff report was built which

[29] In Chapter IV. The special report referred to is *State Programs for the Improvement of Teacher Education.*
[30] See also pp. 107–12.

the Commission has already published.[31] In addition the Commission's work with the colleges and universities participating in its cooperative studies proved to be fundamentally a matter of the in-service education of college teachers. Through local study-group activities, as well as attendance at conferences and workshops, the growth of many college staff members with respect to professional performance was unquestionably promoted.

Another endeavor of the Commission was to maintain and develop cordial and mutually beneficial relationships with as many as possible of those national and regional educational associations that are focally or even peripherally concerned with teacher education. The Commission also, from the beginning, was concerned to maintain and extend such contacts, and that it should do so was one of the recommendations made at Bennington. The Commission consequently began by promoting annual conferences of representatives of such interested associations as meet normally in February at the time of the convention of the American Association of School Administrators. For several years it also published a special directory of meetings occurring at this time at which aspects of teacher education were being considered.

By 1941 the contacts thus established had proved so valuable that a demand arose that they be provided with some permanent basis. Accordingly in 1942 a Council on Cooperation in Teacher Education was established, under the auspices of the American Council on Education, of which seventeen organizations, in addition to the Commission, became members.[32]

[31] *Toward Improving Ph.D. Programs.*
[32] American Association of School Administrators, American Association of Teachers Colleges, Association of American Colleges, Association for Childhood Education, Department of Classroom Teachers of the National Education Association, Association for Supervision and Curriculum Development, Eastern States Association of Professional Schools for Teachers, National Association of Colleges and Departments of Education, National Association of Secondary School Principals, National Association of State Directors of Teacher Education and Certification, National Association of Supervisors of Student Teaching, National Association of Teacher Education Institutions in Metropolitan Districts, National Institutional Teacher Placement Association, National League of Teachers' Associations, National Society of College Teachers of Education, Teachers College Personnel Association.

It is significant that these associations represented groups of administrators, teachers, and specialists, respectively, and at the school, college, and university levels. Accepting the principles that animated the Commission's work generally this new council has emphasized interaction and cooperation between member organizations rather than the establishment of an independent over-all program. One or two meetings of delegates and ex-officio representatives have been held annually, and in the summer of 1943 a two weeks' conference of some sixty representatives was arranged. In 1945 a special grant from the National Conference of Christians and Jews enabled the Council to launch a college study in intergroup relations. Further expansion of such activities is currently taking place.

In the course of its existence the Commission has also assisted in certain special activities of particular associations, through small grants of funds, consultant services, invitation of representatives to conferences and workshops, or otherwise. The most extended contacts of this sort have been with the American Association of Teachers Colleges. In 1940 representatives of this body were enabled to visit, evaluate, and report on the activities being carried on in the seven institutions belonging to the association that were participating in the Commission's national study. In 1942 the Commission helped plan, staff, and report a novel two-week school for executives conducted by the association and attended by the presidents of 86 of its 173 member institutions along with 45 consultants, speakers, and guests.[33] In 1944 the association and the Commission cosponsored a similar enterprise in which 126 teachers college presidents and deans took part, along with 47 additional university deans, state department officials, school superintendents, high school principals, and other educational officers. Seventeen members of the Commission and its staff also participated, as well as fourteen other consultants and speakers.

Other organizations to which the Commission was able, during its existence, to render special services included the De-

[33] For a full report of this conference, prepared by the Commission, see *The School for Executives* (Washington: American Council on Education, 1942).

partment of Supervisors and Curriculum Development of the
National Education Association, the National Association of Colleges and Departments of Education, the National Association
of Supervisors of Student Teaching, the Teachers College Personnel Association, the North Central Association of Colleges
and Secondary Schools, the Southern Association of Colleges and
Secondary Schools, and the Southern University Conference.

In addition to all the above, members of the Commission and
of its staff, and representatives of the various cooperating centers
and statewide studies, had many less formal contacts with an in-
determinate but large number of persons, groups, and institutions
concerned with teacher education. Visits were paid, personal
conferences held, speeches presented, articles written, and correspondence carried on in response to invitations and in an effort
to share the values of the Commission's work and that of its
associates. In these ways, and through the Commission publications and workshops already referred to, the broader obligations
of the Commission have, within the limits of available time and
energy, been discharged.

SUMMARY

With the background provided up to this point the reader
should be prepared for the chapters to follow. For their understanding and interpretation it is important that he should bear
in mind the purposes for which the Commission was created, the
principles according to which it chose to operate, the methods it
employed, and, indeed, the general nature of its program. The
Commission was never intended to undertake fresh research, to
carry out new controlled experiments, to advance the frontiers
of knowledge with respect to particular aspects of teacher education. Its function was to promote action along lines indicated
by existing knowledge. Thus its task from the outset was basically
one of implementation.

It was for this reason that the Commission sought and obtained the cooperation of colleges, universities, and school systems
where teachers were actually being prepared and employed, and
which were eager to improve their programs for teacher educa-

tion. This it did directly in its national study, indirectly in its statewide studies. Moreover, it deliberately chose to recognize local differences, emphasize local responsibility, and trust local intelligence at every step of the way. It offered, but did not force, its counsel. It facilitated contacts and interaction, but not in the interest of attaining uniformity. It believed in education, that is to say, it believed that increased understanding and insight would lead reasonable beings to improve their behavior, and it was prepared to trust the educational process.

Because of its eagerness to emphasize local planning, and also because the institutions with which it was associated were so heterogeneous in character and representative of so many diverse situations, the Commission never pressed for the formulation of agreements as to what ought to be done in teacher education or how. It will be recalled, for example, that the listing of problems at Bennington was done for purposes of mutual education and not with the design of publication as an authoritative statement. Significantly enough the statewide cooperative studies with which the Commission was associated went much farther in the making of agreements. There were reasons for this. The participants in these enterprises were serving a relatively limited common area. For them to commit themselves to certain principles and policies made practical sense. Yet they, too, avoided the setting up of unnecessary limitations to individual freedom; indeed, they encouraged originality and initiative within a large general framework.

One important consequence of the Commission's emphasis on local action was the notable amount of attention given to ways of working together, to the human-relations aspects of institutional advance. As will be remembered the Commission had begun by strongly desiring to encourage general participation in situations where teacher education was taking place. It was convinced that the human factor—the character and interplay of personalities—is of critical importance for institutional accomplishment. At Bennington, too, sensitivity to the problems of cooperation between educationists and subject-matter people in the colleges, and between administrators and classroom teachers in the schools, had been clearly revealed. As the various studies proceeded the importance of such matters grew, if anything, in recognition. How release personal powers in institutional situations? How control personality factors that lead to self-frustration and group discord? How increase mutual understanding and promote genuine give and take? How enlarge freedom and possibility while at the same time maintaining balance between the parts, and unity so far as the whole is concerned? These came to be seen as basic questions bearing on the improvement of teacher education—or of any other human enterprise.

It is quite possible that the war, and the larger revolution in human affairs of which it is an expression, increased the awareness of the Commission and its associates of these deeper human issues. The crucial problem of our times, despite the novel trappings in which it presents itself, is the great eternal problem of man's relations with man. It is the problem of mutual understanding and mutual trust, of agreement on ultimate ends and respect for different ways of seeking these ends, of personal freedom and social unity, of the rational behavior of men as brothers.

It is essential that teacher education should concern itself with this problem for its task is to provide society with teachers who can help children to share in its solution. And it is essential that teacher education should itself demonstrate how the problem may be democratically solved. If in what this report has to say about the details of teacher education there is less in the way of pronouncement than the reader may have anticipated, let him consider why this is. It is partly a consequence of the Commission's sensitivity to the variations of circumstance that characterize the situations in which teacher education must actually be carried on. Even more it is a consequence of the Commission's urgent belief that improvement in teacher education will most surely result from more earnest self-study by those responsible for such situations and from the development of better and more democratic methods of group action. With respect to these ways of making local progress this report will have more to say.

An analysis of the antecedents and experience of the Commission leads to certain conclusions that may well be listed at this point. These will serve to summarize the nature of the Commission's purposes and program and also to forecast some of the findings to be emphasized later on.

1. The Commission undertook to encourage and support practical efforts for the improvement of teacher education in the field. Its emphasis, in other words, was from the outset on implementation, on the continuous testing in action of well considered ideas as to how improvement might be brought about.

2. In accordance with its basic democratic philosophy it sought to stress local responsibility, group participation, and reliance on rational persuasion. Its program was decentralized though much opportunity was provided for interaction and voluntary cooperation.

3. It undertook to call attention to what appeared to be particularly significant problems of teacher education. But it trusted its cooperating colleges, universities, school systems, and other units to select for their own special attack those problems which, in their particular judgment as affected by consideration of their particular circumstances, were both most pressing and ripest for solution.

4. The Commission did place great emphasis on loyalty to democratic values and reliance on democratic procedures in all situations. It encouraged both the freeing of individuals and efforts to achieve greater institutional unity.

5. The Commission's own services were essentially contributory to meeting locally determined needs. Through such services, however, local awareness of needs was frequently increased.

6. The experience demonstrated the critical importance of human relations and of ways of working together if genuine progress is to be made in the improvement of teacher education. The problems that can be dealt with adequately by single individuals are few and relatively subsidiary. A meeting of minds and a dovetailing of efforts are usually essential.

7. The cooperative study setup proved its value in promoting esprit de corps, giving individual persons and institutions a supporting sense of participation in something of greater than local or immediate importance, and thus enhancing the conviction and courage essential to bold and imaginative planning.

8. The bringing together of colleges, universities, and school systems in the same studies made for better mutual understanding and clearer recognition of how more fruitful relationships of give and take might be established.

9. More time than had been supposed in advance proved necessary for participating units to plan and effect action and to make profitable use of available services. What would have appeared to be more rapid progress could have been brought about through pressures. But the process whereby serious study and democratic deliberation lead to new insights and changed convictions, and thence to substantial advances, could not be hurried too greatly.

10. The Commission's decision to give emphatic attention to the in-service education of teachers, and to approach this problem particularly through the school systems where teachers are employed, proved fully justified.

11. While some disappointments were suffered, the Commission is convinced that it was wise in deciding to stress individual and local responsibility and to trust individual and local purpose, intelligence, and good will. The outcomes, while conceivably less spectacular than might otherwise have been obtained, were genuine and substantial. Unsuspected powers were frequently revealed.

12. Participants in the Commission's program showed major interest in the broad fundamental issues of teacher education, and in the relationships that various parts of the process must bear to one another if unity is to be achieved. Lines of conventional separation tend to become blurred if not erased.

13. At the same time spearhead experimentation was increased —the testing of ideas in action at points where circumstances are favorable without too much fear lest the results prove not

precisely what is anticipated and without too much insistence that great fundamental decisions must first be made.

14. There was a notable spread in participation in responsible planning by workers in the various cooperating units. Opportunity to share in making decisions was extended, and at the same time the area of individual and small-group freedom was increased. The result was more sincere acceptance of generally controlling principles and policies by all concerned, and more vigorous and imaginative action within the realm of individual responsibility.

15. Factors making for unity, aside from wide participation in institutional planning, were found to be common attention to the needs of children and youth—children in the schools, students in the colleges—and to the problems of the immediate community and larger social whole.

16. The Commission is convinced that the spirit of its program and the methods it employed are generally applicable in institutional or other cooperative situations, that they constitute an example of the democratic ways of working that need to be widely practiced in our times, and that they have demonstrated their capacity to effect substantial improvements.

II

Improving the Preparation of Teachers

By DELIBERATE DESIGN the colleges and universities participating in the national cooperative study of teacher education constituted a highly varied group. Geographically they were scattered, which meant that they were affected by differing cultural circumstances, school system setups, and state department requirements. Their student bodies had many characteristics distinguishing one from the other. The institutions also differed widely as to traditions, range and focus of purposes, internal organization, and character of control. In these ways the cooperating centers were reasonably representative of the teacher education scene in the United States.

COLLEGES AND UNIVERSITIES IN THE COOPERATIVE STUDY

Although no two of the cooperating institutions were closely alike the group as a whole was divisible into a number of familiar categories. Thus the state teachers colleges and colleges of liberal arts were, as groups, different in many significant ways. Also readily distinguishable was the participating college of agriculture and engineering. For some purposes it was useful to consider the Negro colleges separately. And finally there were the universities with their characteristic qualities and problems. It will be desirable to examine each of these institutional categories in some detail.

The teachers colleges

The seven teachers colleges in the study had originally been state normal schools, devoted exclusively to the relatively rapid preparation of teachers. By the time the study opened, however, all were established as four-year, degree-granting institutions (though a few continued to offer shorter courses) and most had begun to provide two years of general education for students not planning to teach. One or two were moving in the direction of becoming general state colleges through the addition of four-year curricula for nonteachers. In every case, however, the preparation of elementary school teachers was a major activity. All likewise offered courses preparatory to secondary school teaching, usually in both the academic and special fields—art, music, home economics, and industrial arts being examples of the latter. Distinctly fewer students, however, were enrolled in the secondary curricula. In general, these teachers colleges did not offer graduate instruction, but there were exceptions to this rule—one of the institutions, indeed, had begun to confer the doctor's degree. On the undergraduate level they were, by and large, required by public opinion operating through the legislature and otherwise to be relatively lenient in their admissions policies.

It was characteristic of these colleges that they were and for some time had been on the march: they were less bound by their own traditions than were many of the other institutions in the study, less settled in their characters, more extended in their operations, and more ready to attempt what were for them novel things. At the same time they were somewhat less sure of their status, and in contemplating changes were likely to feel somewhat contradictory impulses, on the one hand to pioneer boldly, on the other to be guided by the example of the older and more firmly established universities and colleges of liberal arts.

All of these teachers colleges, of course, were supported by publicly appropriated funds and under state control. Most had separate boards and maintained a pretty independent existence, even with respect to the state departments of education; but there were those that were more definitely part of a state system with, consequently, considerably less freedom of independent action.

In size the student bodies of these teachers colleges ranged in normal times from about 550 to over 4,000. Some drew their undergraduates predominantly from rural, others from urban areas, while in a number of cases both sources were tapped. For other reasons, too, including the kinds of schools from which they had graduated, their students differed considerably as to cultural background. As has become increasingly true of undergraduate bodies everywhere—especially in state-controlled institutions— the percentage of withdrawal of students prior to course completion was relatively high, though there were significant differences in this respect. The nature of the communities in which graduates would be most likely to work was also a differentiating factor: in some instances placement was predominantly in rural, in others in urban areas. Not many graduates, however, were likely to seek positions outside their own states. All of the teachers colleges were coeducational.

The colleges of liberal arts

The colleges of liberal arts that took part in the study were for the most part of long establishment. There were three entirely separate women's colleges, there was one for men alone, and two were coeducational. In one situation administratively distinct colleges for men and women respectively were part of the same general university setup and shared to some extent the services of the same faculty. One of the women's and one of the coeducational colleges were state controlled; another of the women's colleges operated under Roman Catholic auspices; the remainder were both privately controlled and undenominational. All were four-year institutions unspecialized from the point of view of their students' vocational ambitions, and in only one were as many as 20 percent of the members of a graduating class likely to have prepared for teaching. Thus, it must be admitted, none was as deeply concerned with teacher education as are many other colleges of liberal arts in the country: 50 percent of the graduates of some of these typically will have fitted themselves for the profession. Total undergraduate enrollments in the study's colleges of liberal arts ranged from about 650 to over 2,000.

So far as teacher education was concerned these colleges were mainly interested in preparing for teaching, especially of academic subjects, in the secondary schools, although one gave considerable emphasis to its program for prospective elementary school teachers and several others did minor work in this field. All were primarily undergraduate institutions, although except in three cases programs leading to the master's degree were available and two of the colleges of which this was not true were related, as parts of a large university, to graduate divisions both of arts and sciences and of education. With one or two exceptions these colleges of liberal arts could not be considered particularly experimental minded: they were predominantly satisfied with their traditions and programs. Barring two cases it would probably not be possible to claim anything like widespread positive interest in teacher education—or any other form of vocational preparation, except for advanced scholarship—among the faculties.

The student bodies of the privately controlled colleges of the liberal arts group were drawn from a considerable geographical area and were rather rigorously selected. The same was true to an unusual degree in the case of one of the state-controlled institutions. Student backgrounds were in none of the situations predominantly rural; and culturally the liberal arts undergraduates tended to be somewhat superior. Freshmen were more likely to continue their courses and graduate than was true in the teachers colleges. A considerable proportion of the teachers prepared in at least half of these colleges of liberal arts could be expected to go on for a year of graduate work before seeking a job. Moreover, the positions to which they eventually went were likely to be scattered over several and perhaps more than several states; consequently it was more difficult for the colleges to maintain follow-up relationships. A larger percentage of graduates than in the case of the teachers colleges could expect to receive appointments to city system positions, either immediately or after a relatively short tour of rural duty. There were, however, some differences from institution to institution in all these respects.

Other colleges

The one college of agriculture and engineering in the study was state controlled. Only a relatively small percentage of its graduates prepared for teaching, all of these in practical fields, very largely vocational agriculture. As in the case of the colleges of liberal arts the institutional program was relatively satisfactory to the faculty, and no very large proportion felt any marked responsibility for the work in teacher education. About 160 juniors and seniors out of a total undergraduate enrollment of nearly 2,200 men were registered as prospective teachers. Most of these students, of course, had come from rural communities and would return to and remain in them.

There were two Negro colleges in the study, one publicly and one privately controlled, and both coeducational. The former had begun as a normal school and continued to emphasize teacher education though doing so through general divisions of agriculture, arts and sciences, home economics, and mechanic arts. There was also a small and newly established program of nursing education in this institution. At the time the cooperative study began, a program of graduate instruction had just been established. The enrollment was around 1,200, about 100 more women than men being in attendance. The privately controlled Negro institution had an enrollment of approximately 1,100, with some 200 more men than women. It, too, had always emphasized teacher education and the practical arts. Originally its work had been on the high school level, but after 1923 it had rapidly established a variety of collegiate divisions: agriculture, home economics, business, education, mechanical industries, nurses training, physical education, and music. Teacher education was not, however, limited to the school of education; it permeated most parts of the institution. A considerably smaller proportion of the students completed degree requirements than in the case of the other Negro college.

Both of these Negro institutions, of course, had special problems. They were devoted to the educational service of a minority group. Their students tended to come from underprivileged backgrounds and to have characteristic immediate and prospective needs, yet the staff members, who were outstanding representatives of their race, felt a certain degree of understandable compulsion to be guided by the standards and practices observed in colleges attended by white students. The situation was also influenced by the fact that the social distance between undergraduates and faculty members was likely to be unusually great. Both students and faculty members were, however, strongly interested in teacher education since teaching constituted one of the leading careers available to graduates. On each campus both elementary and secondary school teachers were being prepared, the latter for instruction in both academic and, especially, vocational subjects. Rural education was a leading interest in both colleges.

The universities

The universities participating in the cooperative study—including in that classification one college specializing in work for the master's degree—presented a particularly complicated picture. Of the four that were publicly controlled, three were coeducational and maintained schools or colleges of education, one including a four-year and the others two-year units on the undergraduate level. The fourth enrolled men only and carried on teacher preparation through a department of education in the general arts college. It should be added that in certain of the other state universities, as well as in one of those privately endowed, students preparing to teach might choose to maintain their registrations and earn their degrees in either the school of education or the college of arts and sciences. Of the three privately controlled institutions, all coeducational, one maintained a two-year undergraduate school of education, one was fundamentally a graduate school though it cooperated with related undergraduate divisions in providing for teacher preparation during their junior and senior years, while the third operated exclusively at the master's degree level, combining instruction in education and in the other usual subjects in a single undepartmentalized graduate program. All of the universities, of course, offered graduate work for the benefit of both prospective and experienced teachers.

In general the university schools and departments of education were responsive to new ideas and accustomed to originate them, but ordinarily their freedom of action so far as total programs of teacher education were concerned was limited by the fact that both undergraduate and graduate planning involved other institutional divisions or departments. The educationists had little if any formal control over general education or advanced subject-matter instruction for prospective teachers. And the undergraduate and graduate faculties of arts and science, each with their own centers of attention, were, if not actually unfriendly to teacher education as they saw it, at least likely to feel little responsibility to do more than offer prospective teachers instruction that could seldom be said to have been planned with professional needs much in mind. Moreover, these divisions were not, in general, in a particularly experimental mood. It should be added that there were exceptions to both these statements.

The over-all enrollments of these universities ranged from less than 350 to more than 14,000; the number of undergraduate and graduate students working in the field of education ranged from about 200 to nearly 8,200. The prospective teachers were mostly preparing for positions in the secondary schools. The character of the student bodies varied a good deal. The publicly controlled universities drew heavily, of course, from their own states, with rural areas being strongly represented. Public opinion often prevented them from being very selective so far as matriculants were concerned, and rates of withdrawal were likely to be high. This was an especially significant factor in the case of the university at which registration in the school of education was possible in the freshman year. The privately controlled institutions, by and large, had more cosmopolitan and rigorously selected student bodies and there was less student turnover. As in the case of the other institutions in the cooperative study, placements were in both rural and urban centers, but the geographical spread varied considerably from case to case. In three instances there was heavy emphasis on the inclusion of a year of graduate work in the preparatory program.

Representativeness of the group

The variability just described as so strikingly existent in the case of the colleges and universities participating in the national cooperative study is characteristic of teacher education on the pre-service side in the United States. Teachers are prepared by most institutions of collegiate rank. These differ widely as to history, traditions, general purpose, alertness, clientele, stability of student bodies, levels for which teachers are prepared, demands made upon them by the states and schools for which they are preparing teachers, degree to which teacher education is a substantial part of their total function, and breadth and depth of faculty interest in teacher education. The cooperative study was, therefore, reasonably representative of the national situation. In view of the heterogeneity that consequently marked the study, it evidently would have been foolish for the Commission to expect that the activities and accomplishments of the cooperating centers would fall into some uniform pattern. It would be equally foolish to suppose that detailed plans for the improvement of teacher education could be conceived that would be equally suitable for all teacher-preparing institutions. Principles of local planning and desirable general emphases or directions of movement proved, however, capable of discernment.

WHAT PARTICIPATION MEANT

Following the planning conference at Bennington the several colleges and universities proceeded to organize themselves for participation in the cooperative study. In each case a coordinator was appointed to take the lead in local planning and arrangements and to serve as liaison person so far as relations with the Commission were concerned. Practice with respect to this appointment varied: there were designated two presidents (one university and one teachers college), six deans (three university school of education, one college of liberal arts, one teachers college, and one Negro college), four heads of education departments (two college of liberal arts and two teachers college), a teachers college director of research, a graduate school director of studies, and a liberal arts registrar (the latter two being also professors of history and English respectively), three professors of education (two university and one Negro college), one teachers college professor of psychology, and one principal of a teachers college high school.

The coordinators were ordinarily supported by local planning committees which, however, varied as to size, make-up, and effectiveness. In some instances the committees were small and limited to key administrators; in others, large and completely representative of the staff. The degree of administrative participation or at least backing naturally proved to be an important factor; this degree was large in the great majority of cases. Some institutions made planning for the cooperative study part of the established machinery for institutional planning, while others set it up more or less separately. In the latter cases difficulties usually arose as standing committees began to feel they were being by-passed, and hence changes in arrangements often resulted. The Commission concludes from its experience that when an institution is to take part in a special study it is important that there should be: (1) strong and understanding administrative support; (2) immediate leadership that has established status on the campus; (3) participant opportunities available to all those whose interests are definitely affected; and (4) organic relationship to the regular, ongoing interests and organizational setup of the institution.

Modes of participation

The degree to which the collegiate institutions were caught up in the cooperative study naturally varied: factors of size and complexity made an evident difference in this respect. Several of the teachers colleges seized the opportunity to rethink their entire programs and made it possible for every faculty member to take part in the process. In a number of the university schools of education and in at least one of the colleges of liberal arts, participation in the study was made to relate at a minimum to all professional aspects of the program for teacher preparation. Several of these two types of institution and both Negro colleges made particular efforts to promote cooperative activities in which educationists and subject-matter people might share Because of its sympathy with these efforts the Commission did not hesitate, in this connection, to approve and support local projects designed to improve services to all undergraduates, not merely to prospective teachers alone—for example, conferences devoted to general institutional purposes, or efforts to improve general education or personnel services for all.

One of the university schools of education in conjunction with its related colleges for men and women respectively focused its efforts on the development of an experimental program of teacher preparation that included a graduate year: only a fraction of the three staffs was directly concerned. It should be said that in most places, either at the outset or eventually, attention became centered on particular projects with the result that certain staff members played a much more active role than others.

The Commission had begun by emphasizing the notion of all-faculty responsibility for teacher education and by expressing the hope that in every cooperating institution widespread staff participation in the study could be achieved. Similar views had been voiced at Bennington. On the whole there were substantial and satisfying accomplishments in the way of spreading interest and increasing staff attention to the problems of teacher education; but this required time, patience, and finesse, and the efforts made were not always successful. Faculty members, like other human beings, develop particular patterns of interest and of routine activity for which they are held primarily responsible: if these have never notably included teacher education this is not likely to become incorporated quickly and effortlessly, especially if there is no relief from usual duties. What the Commission learned about how fuller staff participation may be obtained will be discussed later in this chapter.[1]

Starting points

The colleges and universities began their participation in a number of ways, the significant differences having to do with the scope of original attack. Some, at the outset, undertook to

[1] See pp. 109–12.

canvass their entire programs and contemplated efforts to bring about improvements at all points at once. This undoubtedly was in part a response to the breadth of the Commission's interests and to recognition of the importance of all the problems emphasized at the Bennington conference. There was some tendency, as a matter of fact, to use the Bennington report as a sort of blueprint or at least to start the whole local faculty off on a process of identifying problems similar to that employed at Bennington. In other instances a systematic re-examination of institutional objectives appealed as a logical first step, the idea being that general agreement as to objectives would provide a basis and guide for subsequent action.

Of these approaches the first—the effort to use the Bennington report as a blueprint—was quite unsuccessful: local staff members had not shared in the experiences that led up to its formulation and local circumstances had special characteristics that needed to be taken into account. The attempt, of course, was inconsistent with the principle of reliance on local participation and local responsibility on which the Bennington conference itself had been built. The alternative schemes of bringing about a general re-examination of local needs and a reformulation of local objectives proved more effective, provided they were realistic and were not allowed to prevent early action with respect to one or more aspects of the program. The Commission noted that in a few instances these broad and relatively abstract efforts tended to become too long drawn out, too much a matter of verbal manipulation, too preoccupied with blueprinting for its own sake, and thus actually inhibitory so far as action was concerned.

At the opposite extreme from the instances just mentioned were those of institutions that undertook at once to tackle one or more specific problems with little formal reference to the total institutional situation. With rare exceptions, however, colleges that launched early attacks on particular problems bore in mind the relationship of what was being done about them to other aspects of their programs. Indeed such efforts ordinarily served eventually to stimulate thinking about the whole program. In the few cases where specific projects were carried on with slight reference to their relationship to the entire institutional pattern the outcomes were distinctly less satisfactory: the damage to institutional unity more than cancelled the success attending the projects as such.

Approaches of either the broad or specific variety, then, proved capable of resulting in a combination of institutional planning and spearhead action. In many instances this combination was employed from the start. The Commission concludes that progress is most likely to occur when a balance is maintained between institutionwide planning and striking while the iron is hot, that in human affairs blueprints must always be changing under the impact of specific experiences while practical decisions must continuously be guided by such general policies as are currently agreed to, that, in a word, thinking and acting should proceed together, each influencing the other. It believes that arrangements designed to facilitate general and continuous thinking about institutional policies and the relations of parts to each other and to the whole are important; but the Commission considers it to be equally important that the institutional setup should encourage creativeness and experimentation on the part of individuals and small groups that possess ideas and drive, and that cannot reasonably be supposed to be disloyal to or ignorant of the purposes—explicit or implicit—of the institution as a whole.

Techniques employed

The techniques employed by the cooperating institutions in connection with their participation in the study need only be listed at this point. In several instances there was a considerable amount of whole-faculty conferring, sometimes all meeting together and sometimes the staff dividing into study groups. In a number of cases representatives of neighboring colleges and schools were brought into conferences. Particular projects, of course, were usually under committee guidance for both planning and conduct. When, as was occasionally the case, these were of a research character, responsibility for their actual conduct might be delegated to an individual.

The consultant services of Commission staff members and of other persons chosen for special reasons were widely and usefully employed. Sometimes a member of the staff of one institution would act as consultant to others with mutual advantage. There was a good deal of visitation, that is, individuals or groups from one campus would visit one or more others, often but not always those of institutions participating in the study. School systems were also visited a great deal, especially of course those in the immediate neighborhood.

Without exception representatives—sometimes four or five at a time—were sent to Commission-sponsored workshops, and two-thirds of the institutions arranged for staff members to spend a year at the collaboration center on child development. Appropriate representatives were regularly sent to the annual conferences for administrators and coordinators and to a number of special conferences on evaluation.[2]

General accomplishment

The great majority of colleges and universities were well satisfied with what they were able to accomplish during the course of the national study. The Commission shares that satisfaction. Full or exact appraisal, however, is hardly possible at present. The nature and spirit of the study were such that many of its results could not be expected to become clearly manifest for some time. The reader will have to exercise his own critical judgment as he considers the evidence and conclusions presented in this report and in those that have preceded it.

The Commission, it may be said, distinguishes two sorts of accomplishment. First, there were specific changes in particular aspects of programs for teacher education. These represented progress in the direction of better realization of democratic values and fuller satisfaction of the contemporary needs of schools and children. But second, there were changes in the persons who bore institutional responsibilities, changes in their ideas and attitudes and in their ways of working together. The latter were the more subtle but also, as the Commission came to view the

[2] For further discussion of many of these techniques see pp. 155-66 and 218-26.

matter, the more fundamental and fruitful. In this report an effort will be made to deal with both these types of accomplishment.

In the case of a few institutions participation in the cooperative study cannot be claimed to have led to more than slight results along either of the lines just mentioned. The Commission has naturally speculated about the reasons for these relative failures. It is possible in each case to discern local factors that were unfavorable to accomplishment: lack of strong administrative support for participation in the study, sometimes following changes in administration; the assignment of responsibility for local coordination to individuals whose interest in teacher education or whose status with their colleagues was limited; the absence of strong interest in teacher education among locally dominant groups. But the Commission is not disposed to suggest that it should not be held partly responsible. Its staff members, for example, felt that they were less well fitted for establishing successful relationships with some situations than with others. Moreover, the Commission's policy of waiting for local initiative and insight and avoiding the application of outside pressures prevented it from providing the "leadership" that sometimes was expected and would even have been welcomed. Had the Commission deviated from this policy and done so deftly enough, more in the way of immediate results might have been obtained. There would always, however, have been the risk of rousing resentment or of promoting something that would later prove to be inadequately rooted in the local soil. Everthing considered, then, the Commission is convinced that the line it followed was generally well worth while, though it does not contend that its own performance was flawless.

POINTS OF ATTACK

The activities of the colleges and universities associated with the Commission were so varied as to breadth and focus that any attempt to classify them runs the risk of doing violence to reality. Where, for example, deliberate efforts were made to improve several aspects of the program for prospective teachers in definite relation to each other, treating these aspects separately may obscure what was most significant about the situations in question. However, expository considerations seem to require that certain well recognized types of problem be here considered one after the other.[3]

Student personnel: general

There was, in the cooperative study, widespread interest in problems of student personnel.[4] This was especially true of undergraduate counseling or guidance, which tended to be seen as a continuous and integrated process to which selection, the provision of health, speech, employment services and the like, as well as placement and follow-up were to be closely related. What lay at the basis of all this was a mounting and spreading conviction of the importance of giving increased attention to the needs of students. These needs—the academic, the vocational, the personal—were more and more seen as related and, therefore, as necessarily to be treated together. In addition there was increased sensitivity to the dynamics of student development, to the ways in which needs emerge, become modified, or establish their permanence. Such trends were accompanied by a tendency for an ever larger proportion of faculty members to participate in personnel activities or at least become responsive to "the guidance point of view." At the same time there was movement in the direction of better coordination of personnel services. Finally there was a marked increase in efforts to provide the individual student with a more positive role in planning the guidance process, to make of it something in which he responsibly shared.

All of these trends the Commission views with approval. It believes that with growth in size, complexity, and division of labor educational institutions have become relatively imper-

[3] For a fuller account of what was done by the colleges and universities that participated in the national study the reader is referred to *The College and Teacher Education*. Evidence respecting many of the matters to be discussed in the pages about to follow will also be found in *State Programs for the Improvement of Teacher Education*, *Helping Teachers Understand Children*, and *Evaluation in Teacher Education*.

[4] For further treatment of this topic see *The College and Teacher Education*, Chapter II, and *Evaluation in Teacher Education*, Chapter III.

sonalized. Education, however, it considers to be an intensely personal affair, particularly promoted by genuinely personal relations. It is important that teachers should have personal interest in boys and girls and that they should understand how necessary this is for strengthening the educative process. Such interest and understanding is more likely to exist if they themselves, during the period of their professional preparation, have had teachers who possessed these characteristics. The tendency to bring more and more faculty members into the work of guidance, to see to it that this becomes a matter of give and take between the student and his counselor, and to encourage the latter to concern himself with the whole range of the undergraduate's developing needs deserves support and extension.

There is an added reason for welcoming a broadening interest in student personnel. More general attention to the total needs of the student body makes for greater institutional unity. It brings faculty members who differ widely in their subject-matter interests together on a ground of common concern. It provides a basis for determining institutional policy at many critical points. For example, a college or university may with perfect propriety disavow responsibility for meeting certain student needs. But if it does so and if these needs are important either for personal or professional reasons, the institution has an obligation to consider whether they are likely to be met in other ways. If not, it may be the duty of the college to decline to admit or retain certain students on the ground that, should it do so, they would be likely to miss experiences important for their particular development. Moreover, whatever limitations an institution may set upon itself its various services impinge upon total personalities, and questions of curriculum and evaluation have to be resolved in relation to that fact and to each other. What instruction should be offered, and how, must be determined in part, at the college as well as at the school level, in the light of a well rounded understanding of student needs.

Organization of personnel services

Such considerations support the coordination of personnel inquiries, records, and services, as well as emphasis on the general guidance responsibilities of all faculty members. The Commission observed a trend toward both centralization and decentralization with respect to personnel matters. Personnel activities such as selection, guidance, health and employment services, and the like had often developed more or less separately, maintained their own unexchanged records, and operated pretty independently, sometimes with rather confusing consequences so far as students were concerned. Methods of bringing these services into closer relationship varied in degree of formality and otherwise. But the tendency toward coordination and centralization was clear and made for improvement. It was, however, accompanied by an equally evident and valuable tendency toward decentralization—toward the wider sharing of personnel responsibilities already referred to.

In other words better mutual understanding between the various personnel officers and the faculty as a whole was being promoted, personnel records were being brought together and made more generally meaningful, and a common personnel attitude was being developed, but with a broadening, rather than a narrowing, of responsibility. For example, central specialized personnel staffs were more and more endeavoring not merely to coordinate their own activities but to encourage general faculty understanding of and participation in guidance activities. The most successful efforts of this sort were marked by skillful leadership on the part of the personnel experts, by the setting up of responsible personnel councils on which regular faculty members were heavily represented, by relying on volunteers to increase the body of counselors, and by seeing that these persons received expert help with their counseling problems as such came to be recognized. Progress was the result of a capitalization of existing interest and good will, of a give-and-take process of mutual education, and of continuous adjustment of experience increased, rather than of the installation at once as some advanced plan that appealed as ideal to the specialists.

Student participation in guidance

Provision of opportunity for the student himself to share responsibility in the decisions affecting him deserves special attention. Personnel services have not infrequently been largely devoted to sorting and shunting students according to institutional regulations. The recipients of this treatment understand neither the reasons for the rules nor the processes whereby they are applied. The Commission discerned a distinct and advantageous trend away from this sort of thing. Efforts were being made to help would-be teachers to understand what is required for success in the profession, to consider what would constitute significant evidence bearing on their own competence or promise in these respects, to welcome or seek means of obtaining such evidence, and to take personal responsibility for deciding thereafter whether to proceed and, if so, in what direction.

Such practice in self-analysis and self-education the Commission considers particularly desirable for a prospective teacher. It develops his ability to understand his own motivations and work out plans for satisfying them in ways consistent with professional success; it promotes his skill in the identification of problems and the location and use of resources relevant to the solution thereof; and it predisposes him to treat his own students, later on, with the same respect that he has enjoyed. Initiative and self-reliance, rather than docility and dependence, are fostered. In the developments that have been described there was, however, no abdication of institutional responsibility: faculties maintained the right to refuse admission and to specify requirements according to their best judgment though only, so far as possible, after consultation with the individuals affected. The purpose of such consultations was twofold: to make certain that considerations of which the students were most aware would receive due weight and to increase the likelihood that the decisions made would become the students' own because they had shared in making them or at least had come to see their reasonableness.

Selection and recruitment

In a number of colleges and universities with which the Commission had contact problems of selection were being carefully studied.[5] Partly as a result of what it observed in these situations and partly on the basis of other experience the Commission reached conclusions that may be stated here as follows:

1. It is important that persons entering the profession of teaching should be good specimens of our democratic culture, varied in background, talent, and interest, and capable of enjoying success in the work for which they have prepared.[6]

2. Each institution engaged in teacher education has, therefore, the responsibility of selecting from among students who wish to prepare for the profession only those who show reasonable promise of developing into satisfactory teachers.

3. Selective judgments need to be guided by a clear and broad concept of the characteristics of good teachers with due allowance for individual differences and the advantages of variety, by a careful consideration of what the college is capable of contributing to the development of such characteristics, and by a thoughtful weighing of the implications of a wide spread of information regarding each candidate, his history, his present status, and his promise.

4. In judging a candidate various factors need to be taken into account, including physical and mental health, vitality, intelligence, academic accomplishment, other abilities, breadth and character of interests, human quality—especially as it affects relations with children and young people, cooperativeness, integrity, moral character, and the degree to which the individual feels a genuine vocation to teaching.

5. All available evidence with respect to such factors should be pooled and considered as a whole: it is the combination of qualities that is significant, and weaknesses in certain respects may be compensated for by strengths in others; thus all relevant

[5] For further treatment of this topic see *Evaluation in Teacher Education*, Chapter II.
[6] In *Teachers for Our Times*, Chapter IV, the Commission has listed qualities to be sought for in teachers today; these have definite implications for selection.

data, qualitative and otherwise, must be subjected in the end to responsible qualitative judgment.

6. The selective process should be a continuous one: the range and reliability of evidence available when candidates first present themselves are rarely sufficient for very exact judgment, but even when this is least true cases should·be reconsidered periodically in the light of cumulating facts and insights.

7. Selection should be closely linked to guidance and students should participate in both processes so far as possible: each individual should be helped to attain a progressively better understanding of his personal qualifications for a profession, the requirements and opportunities of which he also increasingly comprehends, the hope being that original decisions may be modified, when such action appears wise, through joint agreement.

Recruitment, that is, the attraction of outstanding candidates into preparation for teaching, may either apply to high school students or to those in the early years of college. Its purpose is less to increase numbers—in ordinary times, indeed, this is not important—than to ensure a higher level of quality among those eventually selected for admission to the profession. No special projects with respect to recruitment were carried out in connection with the cooperative study but the Commission is prepared to express some views on the subject, as follows:

1. One of the surest ways of improving the schools of the nation would be to recruit to the teaching profession as large a proportion as possible of those young men and women who are capable of becoming excellent teachers and of finding great satisfactions in a teacher's work. Such recruitment should be systematically engaged in.

2. Institutions preparing teachers should disseminate as widely as possible accurate information regarding the nature, importance, and rewards of teaching, the qualities significant for success in the profession, and the character of the preparatory programs they offer; this work should be done through publications and personal presentation; it should be shared in by

staff members and students already committed to teaching; and it should be aimed at reaching underclassmen and high school students as well as college and high school faculty members (particularly those with counseling responsibilities), and, of course, the parents of promising prospects.

3. College and high school teachers should be especially encouraged to accept definite responsibility for helping to recruit the ablest young persons available for enlistment, at some appropriate level, in their own profession.

4. Closer relations of mutual understanding between high school and college staff members and between educationists and subject-matter professors will increase the likelihood that individuals capable of becoming competent teachers will have their attention favorably called to the possibility.

5. Recruitment activities should always, of course, be carried on with full consideration for the best interests of the individual: particularly to be encouraged are better *general* programs of vocational guidance, at both the high school and college levels, whereby young people may be helped to consider a range of occupational opportunities—teaching among them—and to make selection with reference to their own leanings and aptitudes as well as to considerations of social need.

6. Of fundamental importance is the attitude to life developed in promising young people by experience in American living and general education: deliberate efforts to strengthen the impulse to engage in worthy service to mankind, even at some sacrifice of material well-being, are definitely needed.

7. Since recruiting possibilities must, however, also depend on the other satisfactions that may reasonably be anticipated from the experience of teaching, schoolmen and citizens should try to increase all the legitimate attractions of the profession. The ablest young people can never be expected to accept such salaries as are now frequently provided, submit to excessive community restrictions on their out-of-school behavior, or be willing to repeat routine motions endlessly in a mechanized school system under inadequate leadership.

Placement and follow-up

Special attacks on problems of placement and follow-up were limited in number in the cooperative study largely no doubt because during its time there was a mounting shortage of well prepared teachers.[7] The Commission is prepared, however, to express the following views regarding these matters:

1. The obligation of a college to its graduates and to the schools it serves requires that it should maintain a placement program in which the interests of both are carefully considered.

2. As the result of a good program of selection and guidance a college should possess an educational picture of each graduate, supported by cumulative records, on the basis of which it can intelligently advise both the individual and his possible employers as to his suitability for particular openings.

3. It is equally important, of course, that the college should have a clear understanding of the characteristics—strengths, weaknesses, and needs—of the particular schools that are seeking teachers. Only so can it help bring the right job and the right person together; only so can it protect its graduates from getting into situations where they will be wasted or worse.

4. A beginning teacher's success must depend primarily upon himself and upon the character of the working situation he has entered. It is important that his pre-service experience should have prepared him to meet new problems self-reliantly; it is equally important that each school system take definite responsibility for helping new teachers to become established.

5. A college should, nevertheless, recognize and accept responsibility for continued service to its graduates, especially during the first year or two of active employment. Sound follow-up procedures, viewed as an integral part of the college's program of teacher education, will have the advantage not only of assuring needed and welcomed help to graduates and to the schools in which they are at work, but also of enabling the institution to maintain a constant check on the suitability and effectiveness of its own pre-service activities.

[7] For further treatment of placement and follow-up, see *Evaluation in Teacher Education,* Chapter VII.

6. Participation by college staff members in systemwide programs of in-service education in accessible communities is to be encouraged as a means whereby a species of cooperative follow-up may, along with other and larger outcomes, be accomplished.

Personnel in relation to curriculum and evaluation

In a number of institutions with which the Commission was associated personnel work was very deliberately integrated with other activities. This development clearly reflected the faculty's growing awareness of the extent to which student needs of all sorts interact one upon another—of how, for example, academic accomplishment is influenced by the presence or absence of personal or vocational worries. In one teachers college most staff members were active participants in a highly developed guidance program. As was tending to occur elsewhere, guidance relations established in the freshman year customarily continued throughout the college course, increasing the likelihood of developing genuine acquaintance and mutual understanding. The arrangement also had the advantage of helping each faculty member to observe the total college program through undergraduate eyes, which contributed to carrying out the local plan of seeing to it that curricular decisions were appropriately influenced by personnel considerations. The arrangement had a valuable effect on the supervision of student teaching: because of their regular counseling experience the supervisors were able readily to interpret the personnel records of student teachers assigned to them and also to establish friendly relations rather easily. In another teachers college a striking innovation was the combining of responsibilities for guidance with those of conducting a core program of general education: more will be said of this later on.[8]

By and large evidences of the interrelating of activities in the areas of personnel, curriculum, and evaluation were considerable. The idea that the planning of programs and conduct of courses ought to be influenced not only by subject-matter con-

[8] See pp. 80–82.

siderations and awareness of the requirements of good schools but also by understanding of students and their needs gave greater vitality and deeper meaning to personnel activities. Both personnel and curricular programs tended to draw more and more on the services of persons skilled in evaluation; these, in turn, were more and more eager to be guided, not by technical considerations alone, but also by awareness of the total purposes of the work of guidance and instruction.[9] Specialties in the three areas continued to be recognized and practiced, but with greater interaction. The result was an increase in mutual understanding and respect on the part of the staff and in unity on the part of the entire college program. In the Commission's view this was a clear gain.

One further observation should be made: the general principles of student personnel as here developed—especially those having to do with guidance—are recognized as being applicable to all undergraduates. Indeed while it is possible and appropriate for schools and departments of education to maintain special personnel services, it is better when these can be integrated parts of an institutional personnel program. The Commission did not hesitate to aid in attacks on personnel problems that were intended to result in improvement of services to all college students, not to prospective teachers alone. It believed—and experience has strengthened that belief—that the spread of the guidance point of view and the increase of its influence on institutional policy and action in general would contribute at every point to the improvement of teacher education. It is also convinced that greater and more widespread concern with the developing needs of students can constitute a bond between all kinds of staff members and increase their readiness, in the case of prospective teachers as well as others, to plan instruction so as to enhance the likelihood that it will prove functional for the individuals taught. All this is to be desired.

General education

The Commission never had any doubt as to the importance of all teachers receiving a first-class general education, and the

[9] For a more extended discussion of evaluation see pp. 102–4.

problem of how to guarantee this was one of those stressed at Bennington.[10] All there agreed that teachers should be broadly cultivated persons, competent to perform their duties as private individuals and as democratic citizens, and imbued with the best ideals of our American culture. None of the colleges and universities associated with the Commission were, then, unconcerned about the problems of general education, and several tackled them vigorously during the period of the cooperative study of teacher education. When made by the universities and colleges of liberal arts, however, such attacks were not generally thought of as part of that study. There were obvious reasons for this. In these institutions teacher education was one of many concerns and prospective teachers were a minority among the student body. It was natural, there, that the schools and departments of education should take the lead in connection with the cooperative study and that available energy should tend to be focused on problems exclusively related to prospective teachers. This sometimes resulted in modifications being proposed in the prevailing pattern of general education. But this was a different sort of thing from the efforts at systematic and thorough-going reform that the study of teacher education led to elsewhere.

It was then, in the teachers colleges and Negro colleges that widespread disposition to strive for the improvement of general education, in connection with participation in the cooperative study, was to be observed. In these institutions the preparation of teachers was a dominant concern and hence provisions for general education were more readily thought of as part of teacher education. Moreover, these institutions had not long been operating on the four-year scale; hence, they were in a position to give a large amount of attention to arrangements for general education on the college level. They were still in process of development in this respect. While they were willing to be guided by the wisdom of institutions that had longer experience in the general education field, they were aware that even the colleges of liberal arts were by no means agreed on the subject, that there

[10] For a fuller discussion of general education see *The College and Teacher Education*, Chapter III; *State Programs for the Improvement of Teacher Education*, Part Two; and *Evaluation in Teacher Education*, Chapter IV.

was, indeed, widespread uncertainty and dispute among them.

The prevailing conflict of views regarding general education operated, as a matter of fact, to frustrate a number of hopes that substantial reforms might be instituted. Change in so broad a curricular area called for agreement on the part of the very large proportion of staff members who would be affected, and this often proved difficult to obtain. A number of issues with respect to which marked differences of opinion were noted may be suggested by the following questions:

1. To what extent should a program of general education be prescribed? To what extent should the individual student enjoy freedom of election? How allow for student differences, especially with respect to vocational interests and purposes?

2. Should general education be thought of as something taking place in and probably requiring virtually all the time of the first two years of college, or should both it and more specialized (including vocational) work be more or less spread through the entire four years?

3. Should the planning of a program of general education start with primary attention to the *subjects* about which everyone should presumably know something or to the *needs and interests* of undergraduates?

4. If the former, what should the subjects be? And should a mosaic of departmental courses be developed, should the "great books" approach be employed, or should a broad-fields pattern —with basic divisional courses in the humanities, the natural sciences, and the social sciences—be established?

5. If the needs basis is to be used, how identify need areas and then bring the resources of the several subject matters to bear in connection with them?

6. Ought planning for general education to give greater than usual attention to the development of manual, artistic, and social skills, or should it be exclusively concerned with intellectual and verbal matters?

In two of the teachers colleges in the cooperative study special progress was made in actual experimentation with reform of the program of general education. It is significant, the Commission believes, that in both instances developments had strong administrative support. In one case a small and experimental-minded faculty undertook to go a remarkably long distance, not only in developing a novel junior division program of general education but also in combining instruction with guidance. Committees of instructors representing different specialties undertook to supervise the work of freshmen and sophomores in core courses, some of them meeting for two hours a day five days a week, dealing with bio-social development of the individual, the arts in individual development, man and his natural environment, regional and national socio-economic problems, and the arts in contemporary society. These, plus service courses in English and mathematics, took all but a very small fraction of undergraduate time during the years in question. As was anticipated this revolutionary modification of the curriculum threw up a spate of new problems that required progressive adjustments in the second and successive years of the experiment.

At the second college mentioned there was employed the device of making an experimental broad-fields program available to a limited number of freshmen and sophomores as an alternative to the usual arrangement. This enabled certain staff members to put their ideas to the test despite the doubts of their colleagues. These doubts were at the outset sufficiently strong to threaten the continuance of the experiment, which also suffered from the disapproval of the neighboring state university. Fortunately, careful arrangements were made to evaluate the effects of the experimental program in comparison with those of the normal one. When it was revealed that students in the former compared favorably with those who had followed the usual curriculum opposition was markedly reduced.

It is significant that in both of the experimental developments described there was a marked tendency to provide students with more and more opportunity for participation in planning and for the relatively independent discharge of accepted responsibilities. In both cases, also, programs that remained fundamentally devoted to general education came increasingly to admit to attention the implications of the undergraduates' vocational purposes: more study of the total needs of students revealed that it was unrealistic to consider that those more generally related to their interests and responsibilities as private persons and citizens could remain completely unaffected by their decision to devote their lives to a given profession.

The Commission does not consider that its experience, within and beyond the cooperative study, equips it to speak with authority regarding all of the issues connected with the matter of general education. It believes that many of these must for some time continue to be the subject of debate among educators and that such debate should be encouraged, especially among members of the same faculty. There is no doubt that dissatisfaction with the present chaotic situation with respect to general education is powerful and widespread. Conflicting educational philosophies and the usual preoccupation of individual faculty members with responsibilities that are not general—with, for example, their own departmental specialties—make agreement difficult. At the same time, however, interest in the achievement of greater unity is insistent, as is the desire to make general education more vitally concerned with the related needs of man and society.

The Commission's own judgments respecting the general education of teachers may be summarized as follows:

1. Teachers should receive the best possible general education, not only in order that they may share in what ought to be the birthright of all young Americans today, but also because to them is entrusted considerable responsibility for the general education of all young Americans tomorrow.

2. The aim of general education should be to enable young men and women to meet effectively the most important and widespread problems of personal and social existence; in the case of prospective teachers such education should seek to further the development of knowledge, skills, attitudes, and interests that are fundamentally related to needs and responsibilities shared with contemporaries destined for other vocations.

3. While general education may be usefully contrasted with special or vocational education, it ought not, as conducted, to

ignore the implications of the special or vocational purposes of students; nor should professional education be carried on wholly without reference to students' more general needs: an integration of general and professional education should be sought.

4. At least three-eighths of the college experience of a prospective teacher should have as its primary objectives those properly ascribable to general education.

5. While elements of general education may well predominate during the first two college years they should neither monopolize nor be limited to this period: some educational experiences related to vocational purposes should be provided as soon as the latter are formed; and the idea that general education may be considered as "completed" at some particular time should not be encouraged.

6. The contemporary trend toward balance and integration in general education is significant and deserves support. This implies a basic pattern of broad courses, each developed with the special purposes of general education in mind, each requiring a fairly substantial block of time, and all planned in relation to one another.

7. The trend toward the use of more in the way of nonverbal methods of instruction and student expression also deserves encouragement. Firsthand experience, as well as motion pictures and the radio, should supplement books as tools for learning, and students should be helped to express what they have learned not only in words but through the arts and social action.

8. General education should be concerned with the body and the emotions as well as with the intellect.

9. Students should be given a more active, responsible role in the planning and carrying out of their own general education. This implies that instruction should be flexibly administered to provide for responsiveness to individual differences.

10. A leading aim of college programs of general, or for that matter of professional, education should be to make it probable that graduates will continue their growth in understanding and competence after they have become teachers.

11. The development of superior programs of general educa-

tion on particular campuses requires local group endeavor: faculty unity is prerequisite to curricular unity.

12. Such shared effort should be designed to reveal and clarify existing differences of opinion, to increase general understanding of the needs of students and society, and to obtain open-minded consideration of educational thought and action as expressed and carried out elsewhere.

13. Helpful in facilitating improvements in general education have been faculty group discussions, special studies, interviews with students and alumni, community and service-area surveys, visits to schools and to other colleges, use of consultants, and participation in general education workshops.

14. Willingness to sanction the testing of new ideas respecting general education by experimental-minded staff members working with special groups of students has often helped to resolve differences of speculative opinion and led to an extension of sound reforms.

Advanced subject-matter preparation

In several of the universities with which the Commission was associated special attempts were made to improve the advanced subject-matter preparation of teachers for the secondary schools.[11] These efforts were in each case carried on by committees representing both the schools or departments of education and the appropriate subject-matter faculties. The attacks were invariably made with reference to teachers for particular fields—for example, English, social studies, natural science, or vocational agriculture—but the general implications of recommendations were borne in mind. In most cases, indeed, the committees found themselves concerned with questions of general education before they were through.

These efforts were not unaccompanied with difficulties, and in most instances less progress in the way of reform was made during the course of the study than optimists in the several situations had hoped for; but the work done resulted in dis-

[11] For further discussion bearing on this topic, see *The College and Teacher Education*, Chapter IV and pp. 214–22, and *Teachers for Our Times*, especially Chapters II and IV.

tinctly better mutual understanding, cleared a good deal of ground, brought some significant changes, and laid a substantial basis for further advance. The fact is, of course, that there is ordinarily such distance between educationists and subject-matter professors that it is inevitable that considerable time and energy must be expended before genuine agreement between them as to principles and desirable changes respecting teacher education can be expected. The work of the committees mentioned was successful in greatly increasing the area of such agreement.

It is the striking fact that each of the committees referred to undertook early in their work to study the schools to which their graduates went as teachers, and to receive testimony from such graduates as were in a position to discuss candidly both their preparatory and teaching experiences and the relations they saw between the two. This proved to be a very valuable procedure. It removed the focus of attention from the often apparently conflicting theories of the committee members and rooted discussion in realities the relevance of which all were ready to admit. The suggestions from the field, moreover, bore impartially on all aspects of the preparatory program so that the faculty representatives of no particular department were likely to be made to feel that they were the exclusive objects of criticism. Of course, the committees quite properly retained the right of exercising their critical judgments regarding what they discovered to be going on in the schools and what was urged upon them by the field. Not only did they consider it their final responsibility to decide how their institution might best undertake to meet revealed needs, but they also felt free to be critical of the demands placed upon teachers in some situations. The process was one of give and take.

Those who took vigorous part, through the course of a year or two, in the studies under consideration felt the experience to have been eminently worth while, developed significant new insights, and reached satisfying conclusions. They became convinced that closer collaboration between educationists and subject-matter experts was both possible and desirable in the preparation of teachers and that a broader preparation in fields to be taught, through the medium of instruction more definitely related to a teacher's problems, should be sought after. They proposed a variety of curricular reforms, which may, however, be treated together.

In two situations the designation or appointment of department members to take particular responsibility for matters of teacher preparation was recommended, in one case it being urged that such persons should become liaison professors sitting on both the arts and education faculties. Better integration of the prospective teacher's work in education and in subject-matter fields was declared to be important: in one university where courses in education had been ordinarily concentrated in a fifth, or first graduate, year this existing arrangement was roundly condemned. The committee, three-fourths of the members of which were not from the faculty of education, called it a fallacy to suppose "that training in education is something that can be applied from above at the end of another program; that it is training which in a fifth year can miraculously be clapped on top of a four-year bachelor of arts degree pursued without reference to the vocation of teaching."[12]

The committees became vividly aware of the fact that existing subject-matter courses and concentration requirements were often relatively unsuited to the needs of prospective teachers. They were planned and controlled by subject-matter specialists who tended to think departmentally, to see elementary courses as primarily preparatory for those in advance, to believe that only a relatively large amount of work in their field could provide a respectable knowledge thereof, and to be especially interested in providing preparation for graduate school specialization in their subjects. Prospective secondary school teachers, however, have to look forward to the probability of being required to teach several subjects and to handle them broadly:

[12] The university in question was Harvard, which did not participate in any of the Commission's cooperative studies, but which carried out the investigation described with financial assistance obtained from the Commission. The quotation is from the Harvard committee's report, *The Training of Secondary School Teachers* (Cambridge: Harvard University Press, 1942), p. 124.

they need breadth and integration of preparation. An example of the difficulty that arises can be cited from the case of an institution where teachers of vocational agriculture are prepared. It was evident that they needed to learn something about the care of all kinds of farm creatures, but to do this they had to take an impossible number of separate courses each dealing with its own distinct animal or fowl. A not dissimilar situation faced students who wished to prepare for the teaching of general science.

The committees recognized that there were two courses of action they might follow in attempting to deal with this general situation: they might urge the development and introduction of new courses particularly designed for prospective teachers or they might be satisfied to propose a new grouping of existing courses. Generally the first possibility appealed on logical grounds but was eventually, for practical reasons, not immediately recommended. Where favorable response to the idea could be anticipated it was pressed, but the committees usually concluded that the less radical step had better be proposed to begin with. Even as it was they ran into some difficulties: they often discovered that their colleagues, who had not had the advantage of their study experience, were resistant even to changes which the committee members felt were mild compared with what might sensibly have been suggested.

There were many reasons for such resistance. General conservatism and indifference or even hostility to teacher education played their roles, as did departmental loyalties and unreadiness to agree to reduction of requirements in one's own field. Faith in the virtues of emphatic specialization was an influential element in several situations, as was the related conviction that any needed leeway in the existing pattern could be far more wisely obtained by sacrifices made by the other fellow. In one instance where a divisional committee had ventured to recommend changes affecting the local pattern of requirements in the area of general education, the opposition of the departments that stood likely to lose students and status received support from others who felt that the traditions of a liberal education were being attacked.

But such a candid account of the difficulties that were encountered when efforts were made to reform the subject-matter preparation of teachers should not be permitted to leave an impression of frustration. Progress was made. The university whose committee recommended that courses in education and advanced courses in subject-matter be dovetailed through three years following completion of the sophomore program, and that arrangements be made for the closer and more continuous cooperation of educationists and subject-matter people in planning and supervising preparatory programs, saw these and related recommendations fully accepted by the faculty. This represented a by no means slight advance in this particular setting. Specific changes were also accomplished elsewhere, and setbacks that occurred were not regarded as necessarily permanent. But what is most important is that through earnest group study in which there was representative participation, and through the steady growth of understanding of the real problems of the schools and of the teachers therein, distinct advances were made in the achievement of mutual understanding and in the laying of a reliable foundation for further progress in future.

The Commission may now summarize some of its own general conclusions regarding the role of subject-matter instruction, over and above that which may be considered as falling within the area of general education, in the preparation of a teacher:

1. There can be no doubt that a high degree of scholarly competence is essential in a teacher; such competence requires not only knowledge and personal skill but also the ability to use both effectively in the teaching relationship.

2. It is essential that subject-matter instructors whose students are preparing to teach should be sympathetic to their purpose and informed as to the problems they will face when they enter upon their professional careers.

3. It is also important that such instructors should work more closely and realistically with representatives of schools and departments of education in identifying the needs of prospec-

tive teachers and planning curricula in which both subject-matter and professional elements will be functionally combined.

4. The familiar major-minor pattern of subject-matter preparation is being desirably paralleled in many colleges by arrangements that provide for more integration and greater attention to bearings on personal and social needs. For example, divisional as contrasted with departmental majors are increasingly available to undergraduates. Such arrangements offer particular advantages to students who are preparing to teach in modern elementary and secondary schools.

Professional education: general

There were, of course, numerous attacks made on problems related to the more strictly professional education of teachers in the course of the cooperative study.[13] Some of these were in relation to other efforts: all of the university committees discussed in the preceding section got more or less deeply into a consideration of professional instruction. Some dealt generally with the professional part of the program and some with particular aspects.

There were two subjects of study that received outstanding attention as essential elements in the preparation of all teachers: individual human beings—particularly children; and human beings organized in the mass—particularly the community. It was, in other words, generally agreed that teachers need a special understanding of the young persons with whom they work and also of the society for and in which they work. While these were seen as professional requirements it was also recognized that in part, at least, personal and social understanding had reasonable claims to being considered elements in general education. It is not surprising, therefore, that courses designed to promote these kinds of understanding were variously classified in different institutions.

---

[13] For further discussion bearing on this general topic, see *The College and Teacher Education*, Chapters V, VI, and VIII; *State Programs for the Improvement of Teacher Education*, Part Three; *Evaluation in Teacher Education*, Chapters V and VI; and *Teachers for Our Times*, especially Chapters III and IV.

Child growth and development

Of course, the study of human nature, through courses in general and in educational psychology, has long been considered an indispensable part of the preparation of teachers, but the tendency observable in the cooperative study—partly, certainly, because of the influence of the Commission's leadership—was to substitute a different type of approach.[14] This was characterized by an effort to draw on a variety of disciplines—the psychological, biological, and sociological—in order to provide a picture of human beings as both whole and growing organisms, responding both to internal drives and external influences. It was also usual to balance the study of scientific generalizations about human development and behavior with practice in the gathering and organization of facts respecting actual individual children and covering a considerable period of time. The aim was to develop ability to use the generalizations in interpreting particular cases and formulating plans for dealing with them wisely. The Commission believes that the superior values of these methods of preparing teachers to understand the human organism with which they are to work have been clearly demonstrated.

Social understanding

The Commission is equally impressed by the importance of efforts to develop social and community understanding in teachers.[15] A teacher's behavior should be guided not only by a grasp

[14] For an extended treatment of this topic see *Helping Teachers Understand Children.* This volume describes in detail a three-year study program carried on by experienced teachers, but its implications for teacher preparation are extensive and clear. More explicitly relating to teacher education is a report of a special committee of the American Association of Teachers Colleges made at the conclusion of a year's work at the collaboration center at the University of Chicago: *Child Growth and Development Emphases in Teacher Education* (Oneonta, N. Y.: American Association of Teachers Colleges, 1944). See further the bibliography in the appendix to this report of mimeographed material produced at the collaboration center. Also, *The College and Teacher Education,* Chapters V and VI *passim; State Programs for the Improvement of Teacher Education,* Chapter VII; *Evaluation in Teacher Education,* pp. 137–42; and *Teachers for Our Times,* pp. 92–126 and 165–68.

[15] For additional material bearing on this topic, see *Toward Community Understanding; The College and Teacher Education,* Chapters III, V, and VI *passim; State Programs for the Improvement of Teacher Education,* Chapters III, IV, and V *passim; Evaluation in Teacher Education,* pp. 142–45 and 203–18; and *Teachers for Our Times,* Chapter II and pp. 139–41, 158–59, and 168–71.

of the needs and capacities for response of his pupils, but also by an informed awareness of the needs and expectations of the culture of which the school is an expression. Knowledge of the immediate community is important. This will increase the teacher's understanding of the children and their opportunities, will sensitize him to local problems and resources, will help him to perform his professional role effectively.

The good teacher will know how to adjust his behavior sensitively to a particular school situation, taking intelligent account, for example, of the differences between an urban and a rural environment, or a homogeneous upperclass community and one marked by tensions related to poverty, and to differences of nationality, race, and religion. Such considerations have evident implications for the preparation of teachers. Not only should they learn the importance of community understanding for their profession but they should be taught how to develop it. They should learn, through practice as well as precept, how to study a community and how to make use of what is learned in developing teaching procedures. Nor should the preparatory experience fail to impress prospective teachers with a sense of obligation, personal as well as professional, to take a responsible part in community affairs. Again, the how as well as the why should be taught, and experience as well as classroom instruction provided.

Of course, the focus of attention should not be limited to the immediate community. In teachers, more than in most other classes of citizens, it is important that there should reside a considerable understanding of their region, their country, and their world. As has been emphasized, a teacher's broad social responsibility is fundamental. He can scarcely discharge it wisely in ignorance of American and other cultures. The implications for preparatory programs are clear.

In the cooperative study various means were employed to develop in prospective teachers such elements of community and social understanding as have been stressed. In some situations special courses were created, in others elements of social and community study were included in professional core units, and in both of these cases direct community contacts, preceding as well as in connection with student teaching, were often provided. The goals differed: general understanding of the values, structure, and functioning of society—especially our own—skill in community analysis and evaluation, ability to adapt oneself to a new community environment, skill in discerning community resources and in utilizing them for educational ends, and predisposition to enter responsibly into community affairs.

The Commission considers that continued effort along such lines is essential to the improvement of teacher education. It believes that reading and discussion should be strongly supplemented by firsthand experience—by opportunities to observe community and broader social realities directly and under skilled guidance, to practice techniques of social inquiry, and to participate responsibly in community life. Contacts should be made with social-service agencies, with libraries and museums, and with neighborhoods and homes. Travel should be encouraged. With proper advice and guidance many prospective teachers can make rich educational use of vacation periods for the extension of social understanding, even—and perhaps particularly—in connection with earning opportunities. Such guidance should be provided.

Creative expression

A further element that the Commission considers important in the preparation of teachers (though it cannot claim that it was widely emphasized in the colleges participating in the cooperative study) is education in the expressive arts.[16] It would be possible to urge the value of this as a part of general as well as of professional education. The case for the arts in teacher education rests, indeed, on both foundations. First of all, artistic activity offers a unique means of emotional release and creative expression that is particularly valuable to personality in our tense and mechanical times. Then such activity, because

[16] See in connection with this topic, Ray N. Faulkner and Helen E. Davis, *Teachers Enjoy the Arts* (Washington: The American Council on Education, 1943). This is a report on art experiences had by teachers who were attending workshops, but it possesses definite implications for teacher preparation. See also *The College and Teacher Education*, pp. 174–77, and *Teachers for Our Times*, pp. 77–81 and 137–38.

it does not call for the use of words and is a matter of putting parts together with emphasis on the emotional content and effectiveness of the whole, provides a greatly needed balance to the intellectual, verbal, and analytical elements of experience with which teaching is ordinarily so predominantly concerned. Furthermore, acquaintance with the arts and some even minor skill in artistic expression help a teacher to enrich instruction in many ways and to understand and establish communication with children who are more responsive to other than verbal symbols. Finally, an appreciation of the arts is certainly to be considered a characteristic of any well educated person.

Direct experience

The reader will have observed the suggestion in the discussions of child study, social study, and art activity—all three —that direct experience should be included.[17] Children and communities should be studied, not merely studied about, and actual artistic creation, however amateur, should be attempted. Such attempts at the mingling of theoretical inquiry with active contacts with reality were markedly displayed in the cooperative study. Prospective teachers were enabled to begin observation of children relatively early in their preparatory careers, and opportunities were provided whereby they might work with young people responsibly and under guidance in varied school and other situations. They were also led to study communities at first hand and to take part in their affairs. Such direct experiences were designed to serve a number of purposes: to extend the basis upon which students and their advisers could check the wisdom of tentative vocational choices; to enable the students to comprehend and judge better for themselves the theoretical formulations that were being presented in class; to sensitize them to the uniqueness of individual human beings and communities and help them to guard against using mechanically generalizations regarding either; and to develop in them feelings of ease, security, and competence in real situations.

[17] For additional material bearing on this topic, see *The College and Teacher Education*, pp. 174–79 and 304–5, and *Teachers for Our Times*, pp. 135–37, and *Toward Community Understanding, passim*; also the reference relating to student teaching, pp. 100-1 of the present report.

Direct experience was arranged for in a variety of ways. Laboratory schools, art studios, and student organizations provided readily accessible opportunities on the campus. Relationships were also established with nearby public and private schools, with social agencies of various kinds, and with other institutions in the immediate or more extended community. These relationships were of such sort that advantages accrued to outside bodies as well as to the prospective teachers and the college programs. A number of colleges and universities undertook systematically to help students to use their vacation periods in ways calculated to contribute definitely to their well rounded development as teachers. Counselorship in summer camps made possible growth in the understanding of children. Jobs in trade or industry or on the farm enabled prospective teachers to increase their grasp of the nature of important aspects of American life. Travel provided opportunities for the expansion of horizons and the reduction of provincialism. One university arranged for most of its sophomores to spend the three-week period before the beginning of college classes in the fall giving full-time service to various public schools scattered through the state that it served. Many of the activities listed had always been available to undergraduates during vacation periods, but the deliberate effort of college faculties to see to it that their educational possibilities were well realized represented a relatively new and a very important development.

Larger instructional units

One marked trend in the cooperative study was in the direction of combining the elements of professional education into a few relatively large and inclusive units; there was a distinct movement away from reliance upon a great number of short, specialized, and quite distinct courses.[18] The purpose was to assure greater continuity of experience and closer attention to interrelationships of various kinds, and at the same time to make possible more flexibility and variety. The development was

[18] For further treatment of this topic, see *The College and Teacher Education*, Chapters V and VI *passim*, and *State Programs for the Improvement of Teacher Education*, Chapter IX.

closely tied up, it should be added, with the tendency to provide for more direct experience, which was, indeed, facilitated by the arrangement in large blocks of time.

At one university where two undergraduate colleges were cooperating with the graduate school of education in conducting an experimental three-year program, three-hour seminars in the junior and senior years were succeeded in the graduate year by a three-hour central seminar, a two-hour divisional seminar (in the humanities and language arts; the social sciences; science and mathematics; art and music; home and community life, health, and recreation; or elementary education), and three to four hours of student teaching. The work of these seminars— planned to constitute a unified but flexible whole, and supervised by committees of educationists and subject-matter specialists—combined the integrated organization of subject matter, curriculum planning, teaching methods, and evaluation. Continuous guidance was also a function assigned to seminar leaders. A close relationship was maintained with the work of student teaching.

Student participation

One important advantage—and indeed one definite purpose —of the large blocks of time arrangement in professional education was the opportunity provided for more participation by the prospective teachers themselves in planning the details of the educational experiences enjoyed.[19] As a matter of fact the idea that students should be worked with, rather than on, affected college practice in many ways. In student personnel programs, as was previously noted, the aim increasingly was to encourage personal responsibility by helping the individual to estimate his own strengths and weaknesses and reach his own judgments as to what he must undertake to do in order to attain an adequate level of professional competence. In programs of general education as well faculty members found it advantageous to arrange for undergraduates to share in planning and evalu-

[19] For further treatment of this topic, see *The College and Teacher Education*, Chapters II, III, V, and VI *passim* and pp. 302–4, and *Evaluation in Teacher Education*, Chapters III-VI *passim* and pp. 4, 14–15, and 364–65.

ating details of the course of instruction. The same was true of professional courses, even when not consolidated, and of student teaching. The participation occurred not only in connection with particular courses or other types of educational experience, but sometimes on the higher level of institutional planning: there was, for example, experimentation with the inclusion of student representatives on faculty committees with large responsibilities and even in general faculty meetings.

There were several reasons for this very striking trend toward provision for more responsible participation by undergraduates in the determination of their educational programs. Basic was the desire to realize the implications of democratic theory. Belief in the worth and potentialities of the individual required that he should be not merely permitted but actually stimulated to share in choosing a course of action in the light of his personal goals. Conviction as to the importance of group methods, in which all give and take according to their several powers and needs, urged the employment of such methods in educational planning. Adherence to the idea that self-guidance according to the dictates of one's own reason should receive all possible encouragement further demanded that students be not relieved of the responsibility of choice.

All such considerations, it will be observed, are as applicable to college students who are not preparing to teach as to prospective teachers. They also have implications for the conduct of education in the secondary and elementary schools. While the manner and degree of student participation in educational planning will appropriately vary with age, experience, and other individual characteristics, provision for such participation cannot properly be neglected even in the earliest grades. Because this is true it follows that there is a special, professional reason for such provision in programs of teacher education. A teacher whose own education has been mostly a matter of passive acquiescence in programs and procedures predetermined by his instructors is not likely easily and effectively to lead his own pupils to share responsibility in the planning of their educational experiences. Prospective teachers particularly, therefore, should be treated as persons, as capable of participating intelligently in the determination of their own educational courses.

But it is not only because of the experience it provides in pupil-teacher planning that more student participation is professionally advantageous to prospective teachers. As it works out—or can be made to work out—in practice it brings the individual into closer and more significant contact with the whole process of institutional planning. The sense of what the faculty as a whole is driving at is heightened and the values of continuous cooperation in thought and action among staff members become evident. Thus the teacher-to-be begins to see how important it will be for him to take part in the affairs of his own school and system when he enters upon his professional work. And he begins to develop skill in democratic group work of the sort that it is desirable he should be able to help carry on at that time.

For all reasons given, the Commission strongly favors the trend toward increased student participation in programs of teacher education. It hopes that more and more will be attempted in this direction. From its experience, however, it offers two warnings. The first is that no efforts can succeed that are not genuine, that do not actually provide students with influence. Better an honest dictatorship than a false democracy. Students who are likely to make good teachers for our times will not long be deceived by merely being permitted now and then to hold the reins. Of course, they will make some mistakes if they are given real responsibility, but they can learn from such mistakes. And it is at least an open question whether the faculties might not have made even worse mistakes without them.

But in any case student participation does not imply at all that the faculty should not participate. One of the values of the process is the experience it brings in learning how to assess and accept the contributions to a group process of classes and individuals representing special resources and responsibilities. This brings us to the second warning. It is possible for faculties newly enthusiastic over the idea of student participation to ask more of undergraduates than their experience has prepared them to perform. The Commission observed a few examples of this sort which might easily have resulted in unjustifiable discouragement with the whole idea of student participation.

Both pitfalls mentioned are likely to be avoided when certain conditions are present. The process should be seen as a potentially significant means to larger and very important ends; then the temptation to employ it in dogged mechanical fashion, rather than with human artistry, will be avoided. An experimental temper should be preserved: results should be evaluated by students *and* faculty and procedures modified in the light of experience. Perhaps most important of all a relationship of mutual friendly confidence should be cultivated: genuine participation requires give and take which is really possible only where personal relationships have been established.

Student teaching: related arrangements

Trends with respect to student teaching in the cooperative study further exemplified the movement in the direction of program integration.[20] With increasing emphasis on direct experience, moreover, not only did the character of arrangements for student teaching tend to be affected, but these also came to be viewed as culminating rather than as standing more or less alone. There was a marked tendency to provide for considerable precedent experience with children in school and other situations.

The colleges equipped with campus schools were particularly well situated to enable students to observe children and participate in their guidance in connection with various courses beginning fairly early in the preparatory program. The accessibility of such schools, as well as the fact that they were under college control, greatly facilitated the working out of such advantageous arrangements. Some institutions, without campus schools of their own, were able to provide substitute facilities through agreements effected to mutual satisfaction with public schools located in their immediate neighborhoods. In either case instructors in various courses found it desirable to comple-

[20] For further details respecting student teaching, see *The College and Teacher Education*, Chapter V *passim* and pp. 180–211; *State Programs for the Improvement of Teacher Education*, Chapter VIII, and *Evaluation in Teacher Education*, Chapter VI.

ment and strengthen their classroom programs by bringing their students, both in groups and individually, into direct contact with boys and girls in a variety of real school situations.

Another type of arrangement, calling for close contacts with children at a fairly early stage, should also be mentioned. According to this, sophomores or juniors gave an afternoon or evening a week during a quarter or semester to assisting in the work of local youth-serving agencies. These experiences with boys and girls in nonschool situations proved to have many values. They were often helpful in connection with selection, demonstrating to certain underclassmen that work with young people was unlikely to yield them personal satisfactions, while strengthening the vocational purposes of others. They also tied in effectively with courses in child growth and development. The fact that the contacts provided were away from school had its own advantages: children are never merely *school* children, and teachers who have come to understand what they are like when they are elsewhere are better equipped than those who lack such knowledge.

An ingenious arrangement, already mentioned, was that whereby a considerable proportion of the prospective teachers at one university was enabled to spend several weeks just prior to the opening of the sophomore year helping out full time in various public schools. In this way an unusually early concentrated experience with school and community realities was provided. Students were prepared for the event during their freshman year, plans were worked out carefully in advance by faculty members and school administrators working together, and the students' experiences were definitely drawn on in connection with courses immediately following. Of course, the work assigned in the field was very different from that given when, toward the end of their preparatory course, the undergraduates undertook responsible student teaching; but it proved possible to find many things for them to do that were educationally valuable to them as individuals as well as useful to the host schools.

Increased use of direct experience prior to student teaching proper had, as has been seen, the valuable effect of leading more course instructors to familiarize themselves with real school situations. This strengthened the likelihood that their instruction would provide a realistic foundation for student teaching. A related development was the tendency for these instructors to play an increased role in the planning and oversight of such teaching, to provide counseling services for undergraduates while in the field, and to share in the conduct of seminars after teaching experience, focused on problems met by students while in the schools. Many values of early direct experience to the students have already been mentioned. Here one more may be specified: prospective teachers with such experience came to responsible student teaching with much more self-confidence and ease than those whose prior contacts with flesh-and-blood youngsters had been slight.

Student teaching proper

The arrangements made for actual student teaching varied widely in the cooperative study, notably reflecting differences in local circumstance. There was a distinct tendency, however, to lead up to culminating full-time experience, throughout periods ranging from three to nine weeks, in more or less typical off-campus schools. The colleges and universities that possessed campus schools or adequate substitutes therefor customarily used them for beginning student teaching, but even these were tending to send their students into the field for at least part of their professional practice. The full-time arrangement made it possible for prospective teachers to get the feel of whole-school situations and often of community situations as well. Moreover, it made it easier to ensure student teaching experiences in rural and other situations similar to those in which the prospective teachers were likely to find employment after graduation.

Relatively concentrated and extended student teaching in typical school situations proved to have a variety of related values. It enabled prospective teachers to get really acquainted with at least a few children, to observe them fairly closely in different situations—often including their homes—and to discover for themselves the significance of teacher-pupil relationships. It also made possible getting the feel of a school as a whole, of the relations existing among teachers and between them and administrative officers and parents, all this yielding some sense of the significance for educational accomplishment of the degree of institutional unity existing. Finally, it provided opportunity for community study, for finding out at first hand something about the school-community interplay and its significance for the teacher's work. Experience in rural communities, frequently especially arranged for, had particular advantages for the large proportion of students who could look forward to beginning their active careers in such settings.

Often during such practice-teaching periods students returned to the campus on Saturdays for seminar discussions with their instructors. Thus was provided prompt opportunity to consider the implications of new experiences and to receive guidance as to how to handle troublesome situations. Of course, students likewise had continuous supervision from particular directing teachers in the schools and were ordinarily also visited on the job by representatives of the college. Finally, it was normal practice to set up a special seminar during the semester or quarter following full-time field experience, in which questions growing out of the students' contacts could be carefully considered. Faculty members representing the various academic fields as well as the more professional subjects took part in these seminars. One frequent result was that the ideas of members of both groups as to how their earlier courses should be conducted were significantly affected.

Time allocations in teacher education

One of the problems that continually recurs with respect to programs of teacher preparation is that of the allocation of available time to the various elements. It is usual for every faculty member to feel that more attention might advantageously be devoted to his particular specialty. This view tends to grow stronger with the steady cumulation of knowledge and the consequent tendency for each subject to be broken down

into more and more subspecialties, the proper teaching of each
of which seems to call for more and more time. It undoubtedly
gains further support from the tendency of each specialist to
identify with his subject. Nor is the competitive influence of
departmentalism to be overlooked.

The Commission has already expressed the opinion that joint
study by faculty members of the needs of students and communities, and of the problems of the schools, in each case
broadly viewed, is likely to help bring agreement as to the
pattern of teacher preparation. It has also taken the position
that at least three-eighths of the total time of a four-year program
should be given to work designed primarily to promote the ends
of general education. It believes that from one-eighth to one-
sixth of that total time will ordinarily suffice for strictly professional instruction. But it is impressed by the fact that many
courses, especially those of newer type, are not easily assigned
to some particular category: for example, a course on the
community has implications for both general and professional
education and in the case of prospective teachers of the social
studies for subject-matter equipment as well. The Commission
does not believe that nationwide agreement as to the allocation
of time in programs of teacher education is desirably to be
sought; for it prefers to emphasize the values of more genuinely participant and realistic local study of the problem, as
well as of cooperative study in which state departments of
education and representatives of the state's institutions of
higher learning democratically share.[21]

Evaluation

Encouraged and aided by the Commission, the colleges and
universities cooperating in the national study gave considerable
attention to programs of evaluation.[22] The objects of such
appraisal were the students who were contemplating becoming
teachers and the processes of selection, orientation, guidance,
instruction, and student teaching as employed by the various

[21] See Chapter IV, pp. 192–218.
[22] For an extended treatment of this topic, see *Evaluation in Teacher Education.*

institutions. The values of continual efforts along such lines were clearly established.

Evaluation begins with an identification and clarification of purposes defined in terms of the specific behavior these imply. It moves on to determine sources of evidence that may be employed in establishing the extent to which such behavior occurs, and then to select or develop methods of gathering such evidence. It concludes by making use of the methods in question and interpreting the results in the light of the goals or objectives that have been agreed upon. The immediate aim of this process is to reveal both where individuals stand, what progress they have been making, and also the effectiveness of the educational program, in whole or in part, that has been provided for them. But the ultimate aim is improvement, made possible by a clear demonstration of strengths and weaknesses.

There should, therefore, be a close relationship between evaluation and instruction. Instruction presumably reflects the purposes of the institution, which ought to be determined with due regard for the purposes of the student. It is with such purposes that evaluation must begin. Furthermore, what is revealed by the evaluative process will frequently suggest the need for instructional reform. But there is more to the relationship. Evaluation can itself be a learning experience for those evaluated provided they see in it an opportunity to find out something they genuinely want to know about themselves. For this to occur they must, of course, understand the process and share in the interpretation of its results.

The evident implication of what has just been said is that evaluation ought not to be an intermittent mystery carried on exclusively by specialists but rather a persuasive activity participated in, though with expert assistance, by all faculty members and students. Only when the latter is the case are the results likely to be fully influential on those, improvement in whose behavior it is the ultimate aim of evaluation to bring about. Only through provision for participation, moreover, can a democratic respect for personality be manifested. Only thus, finally, can the practice of self-evaluation be developed.

A soundly conceived and widely shared-in program of evaluation can have exceedingly valuable integrating consequences for teacher education. Emphasis on self-evaluation under guidance, continuous throughout the preparatory program, will help the individual to integrate himself and the institution to integrate its services. Appraisal of the institutional program as a whole will result in faculty cooperation in the clarification of objectives and consideration of the degree to which the various parts of the program fit together and support each other. Thus, through democratic action, order, sequence, and unity will be increased.

A further advantage of a college program of evaluation in which students participate is the effect it is calculated to have on their own practice when they become teachers. When they have experienced the satisfaction of learning to appraise their own strengths and weaknesses and of being treated democratically by their instructors as these have carried out their evaluative responsibilities, it is likely that they will wish and know how to provide similar satisfactions for the children with whom they eventually work.

The Commission is impressed by the values of evaluation in teacher education such as have been described above. It saw those values clearly demonstrated in the cooperative study. It believes that evaluation of this sort should be regularly carried on in colleges and universities where teachers are prepared.

Five-year programs

The Commission sympathizes with the tendency toward the establishment of five-year programs of teacher preparation and considers them to be as justifiable in the case of elementary as of high school teachers. [23] It cannot believe that the teaching of little children is any less socially important or that it calls for any less professional skill than the teaching of adolescents. Nor does it accept the assumption implicitly underlying most con-

[23] For further discussion bearing on this topic, see *The College and Teacher Education*, pp. 119–25, 146–64, and 214–22; and *State Programs for the Improvement of Teacher Education*, pp. 28–43.

temporary practice that children, young or older, in rural areas do not deserve as well prepared teachers as those provided for youngsters in the cities. The case for a five-year program of teacher preparation is as strong for any one of these categories as it is for any other.

That case rests, in each instance, on a proper recognition of the social significance of the teacher's function and of the range and complexity of understanding and skill required for the adequate exercise of that function. Five years of collegiate and university experience is certainly not too much if a teacher's general education is to be adequately advanced, if a sufficient grounding in particular subjects is to be attained, if the necessary understanding of child growth and development and of society and the community are to be achieved, and if a suitable amount of direct experience in conjunction with classroom study is to be had. This is all the more true in a world of rapidly advancing knowledge and one marked by changes and complexities that make sound teaching a matter requiring increased understanding and skill.

Of course, the Commission does not assign any virtue to time of preparation apart from the use of that time. A good four-year program will produce better teachers than a poor one of five years' duration. Moreover, there are dangers accompanying the extension of the preparatory period that ought clearly to be recognized. Chiefly to be opposed is any tendency—and such exists—to postpone all professional elements in teacher education to the fifth (or first graduate) year. In the Commission's judgment the ideal would be a five-year program in which the professional and other elements were continuously intermingled. It would, of course, take the same position with reference to the more customary four-year program. In neither case, certainly, should professional instruction be begun any later than the third college year. In the case of five-year programs a three-year integrated unit may desirably be begun at this point.

Another danger to be avoided is that of still further delaying direct contacts of prospective teachers with children and community life. The Commission has already stressed the importance of direct experience as an integral element in teacher education and has stated its belief that such experience should come early and last throughout the preparatory period. Serious harm can be done by holding prospective teachers too long at the stage of purely abstract consideration of the realities with which they eventually must responsibly deal. The Commission considers, therefore, that the lengthening of preparatory programs not only permits but requires increased provision of opportunities for direct and responsible experience with children, schools, and communities.

The Commission understands, of course, that five years of preparation for teaching is a goal the prospects of attaining which vary from place to place in this country. Some states and municipalities have already established the requirement for secondary school teachers. In some sections, at the other extreme, a three- or even a two-year requirement would represent an advance. Economic factors and the degree of public enlightenment regarding what good teaching calls for are key elements accounting for the variety of practice that exists. Consequently advances toward the goal recommended must depend on the mounting readiness of communities to reward teachers for having undertaken superior preparatory programs and on the increasing willingness and ability of prospective teachers to meet the added expense. The implications both for salary schedules and for arrangements designed to lighten the costs of college and university attendance, especially by superior candidates for teaching careers, are obvious.

The manpower shortage which was a consequence of the war had the effect, of course, of checking and even reversing the trend toward lengthening the period of teacher preparation. The conditions following the war, however, are likely to prove favorable to new advances. With the ending of selective service and a reduction in the demand for labor, college enrollments may be expected to reach new heights very rapidly. Under these circumstances the number of states requiring five, or at least four, years of pre-service teacher education will again increase. This will prove socially advantageous *provided* selection is simultaneously improved and more effective programs of educational experience are developed.

The College Faculty and Teacher Education

The Commission based its cooperative study, it will be recalled, on the assumption that local faculties must, in the last analysis, be relied upon to bring about improvements in the preparation of teachers. Its experience confirmed this belief. Yet it became more sharply aware of the need for reforms in the preparation of college teachers and of the importance of procedures designed to facilitate their growth in service.

The established pattern of graduate éducation in the United States is not calculated to develop in any prospective faculty member much skill in cooperative endeavor. Rather narrow subject-matter specialization and highly individualistic endeavor are the rule. The usual scheme of staff organization in the colleges also encourages separatism. Divisional and departmental lines are sharply etched, and individual professors are not accustomed to discussing with others what they should do in "their" courses. Curriculum committees and similar bodies are likely to be more concerned with smoothing over clashes between various special interests than with achieving new creative integrations. Moreover, prestige and promotion for any given professor tend to turn more upon status achieved in his particular field than upon his effectiveness as a team worker on his own campus. All this militates against that institutional unity upon which the Commission has come to place very great value. Some positive suggestions may, therefore, appropriately be made. While faculties concerned with teacher education will, of course, be particularly in mind, it should be said that the comments have many implications for colleges devoted to other ends.

The preparation of college teachers

It seems clear that graduate schools need to reconsider their functions and procedure. That they should continue to develop research specialists is beyond question. But it is equally clear that a large proportion of men and women to whom doctor's degrees have been awarded will devote their lives chiefly to college teaching.[24] It is essential that these persons should be soundly trained in scholarship. But it is also important that their graduate experience should contribute to their growth in teaching skill and in ability to function effectively as faculty members. It is not enough that they should develop loyalty to their specialties and ability to communicate persuasively with their fellow scholars. They should come to college teaching with an interest in young people and with an understanding of them; equally, they should come with an interest in the college as an institution and a grasp of its functions. And they should be eager and able to understand and be understood by their students and their colleagues.

There are clear implications here for the modification of graduate school programs. It may be said that pressure for such modification is mounting, that presidents and deans—of junior colleges and colleges of liberal arts as well as teachers colleges —are increasingly calling for such modification. That prompt response on the part of the universities can be anticipated is, unfortunately, by no means as clear. Graduate school practice is determined by graduate faculties (deans and university presidents have surprisingly little influence at this level) and these faculties are predominantly made up of research specialists whose interest in the problems of college teaching and college-faculty membership is limited. Moreover, during the next five or ten years the demand for holders of the customary doctor's degree may be expected to be unprecedentedly heavy. The war reduced the flow of new recipients of the degree to a trickle; its conclusion finds scientific research more esteemed than ever before in our history. In these circumstances graduate faculties may feel disposed to continue the familiar patterns of graduate education. On the other hand the anticipated rapid increase in college enrollments, especially in institutions relatively new in character, may well work in the opposite direction. The need for functionally trained teachers for such institutions may force

[24] For a fuller treatment of this topic, see *Toward Improving Ph.D. Programs*.

appropriate response, particularly by graduate schools of education and by universities not hitherto notably active in the field of graduate work.

The in-service growth of college teachers

In any case there is today special reason for attention to procedures likely to improve teaching and skill in faculty membership on the job.[25] Of central importance is the employment of group methods designed to promote staff participation in local educational planning. Leadership should be particularly concerned with promoting such group action as may result in the democratic formulation of over-all policies and in the emergence of support for experimental activities. The substantial improvement of program can in ordinary circumstances be brought about only through a process of mutual in-service education on the part of the whole staff. Responsible, cooperative working together on specific but seminal problems by representatives of various interests—departments, for example —is an indispensable means of advance.

In the promotion of such cooperation factors of personality and human relations will require much attention. The improvement of college education, whether of teachers or of others, will not result automatically from the adoption of superior plans: the plans will have to be made to work. If they are to work effectively the actors in the situation must understand and believe in the plans and must be eager to work together for their success. They must also understand and believe in one another. All this calls for general participation in making the plans.

Also called for, the Commission believes, is emphatic attention to those elements in the college situation that faculty members have most in common, that can most readily provide ground on which all may stand together. The students constitute one such element. This is one reason why emphasis should be laid

---

[25] For further treatment of this topic, see *The College and Teacher Education*, Chapters VIII and IX; *State Programs for the Improvement of Teacher Education, passim*; and *Evaluation in Teacher Education*, especially Chapters I and IX. Chapter III of the present report, while dealing explicitly with teachers in elementary and secondary schools, also has implications for staff arrangements and action in the colleges.

on studies of the student body and its needs, on personnel programs in which a large proportion of the faculty participates, and on giving students a share in the planning of educational experience.

Another element held in common is the community or service area or—to put it in its largest terms—the social order. Group consideration by staff members of the educational implications of social developments can promote a sense of joint purpose and suggest means of developing a more functional educational program. In this connection it should be repeated that the planning and conduct of programs of teacher education can benefit only if college representatives maintain close contacts with real schools in real communities. Shared acquaintance with such schools adds to the common ground. Moreover, it checks the tendency of faculty members to make educational decisions on the basis of abstract and unrealistic ideas as to what a teacher needs.

Factors making for in-service growth

The generalizations and recommendations offered in the preceding paragraphs rest upon the Commission's experience and observation. It saw colleges moving along the lines suggested and benefiting from such movement. Something should now be said about how these developments were encouraged and implemented locally.

Skillful administrative leadership was invariably important. Qualities that proved particularly valuable were an understanding of people, responsiveness to human values, grasp of the unfolding situation, and a keen sense of timing. Together these made for judgment as to what sort of stimulation the faculty was ready to respond to, and how that stimulation could most effectively be provided. Leaders with these qualities understood that there was no point in driving for action until the situation was ripe. And they had patience, once something was started, to trust those who had taken up the challenge.

Planning committees proved exceedingly helpful where wisely developed. The best of them, invariably representative and often appointed by administrators from panels nominated by the staff, avoided legislative or administrative functions and devoted themselves to matters of strategy. They undertook to analyze local needs, throw the spotlight on problems of key importance, encourage attacks on such problems by as many faculty members as were interested or affected, and facilitate the provision of resources in support of those attacks.

For development of institutional unity it proved important that administrators and planning committees should give special support to activities that were capable of attracting and influencing staff members from various departments and of various ranks: in this connection the value of studies of students, society, and the schools has already been mentioned. It was also found desirable to give a good deal of thought to maintaining adequate channels of communication, to seeing that the faculty as a whole was kept well informed of what was going on. For this purpose written reports proved to have distinct limits of effectiveness. The greatest spread of common understanding came when the largest proportion of the faculty was participating in the developments. But it should be added that several institutions found collegewide conferences of several days' duration, held, usually, just before the opening of the fall semester, to be very effective for purposes of communication.

Faculty study activities yielded the greatest satisfactions to participants, and the greatest results, when they were focused on problems that seemed significant to group members and when thought about them led fairly readily to action. It was important, therefore, that arrangements for making legislative decisions should be efficient and integrally connected with the planning and study program. In some colleges legislative bodies were so organized at the outset of the cooperative study as to make action exceedingly difficult to obtain. Efforts to get around these situations by a species of bypassing were attempted in some instances, but only succeeded in making for more disunity. Patient working with existing agencies and steps in the direction of frank reform of prior arrangements were more successful.

Two comments remain to be made. In the first place it should be said that the cooperative study revealed a very widespread attitude among college staff members favorable to movement in the direction of greater unity. This no doubt was an expression of a feeling the emergence of which seems characteristic of contemporary society. Not merely in the international sphere is the isolationist principle being discredited. The second comment is to the effect that participation in the cooperative study or in the statewide studies clearly helped in bringing about such movements as have here been considered. The sense of being part of an enterprise that transcended institutional boundaries and the natural desire to see one's own institution play a worthy role in such an enterprise, encouraged the further development of a sense of we-ness.

It will have been observed how much stress has been laid on the significance of the human factor and of personnel considerations. Good human relations are no less important for the success of educational enterprise than for industrial production, in which field their value has now been abundantly demonstrated by research.

SUMMARY

The chief conclusions of the Commission respecting the preparation of teachers may be summarized as follows:

1. The improvement of teacher preparation depends immediately on the capacity, understanding, and cooperativeness of those charged with its conduct at particular colleges and universities. Every effort, then, should be made to strengthen faculties, extend participation in the realistic study of the job jointly to be done, encourage coordination of effort, and support the continuous evaluation of programs as well as experimental efforts to better them. This implies the employment of democratic procedures calculated to facilitate the steady in-service growth of the teachers of teachers.

2. Whatever increases a faculty's sense of shared responsibility for teacher preparation, and its stock of common understanding of the factors to be considered, is likely to increase the

unity of an institution or program and lead to added effectiveness. In the cooperative study the development of personnel programs in which many instructors learned how to counsel students respecting personal, academic, and vocational problems —all three—helped in this connection. So did firsthand study of the schools and teachers in service and their actual problems, study participated in by both subject-matter professors and educationists. Joint study of the communities served was also helpful.

3. The use of consultants—including college and university experts, state department officials, school administrators, and experienced teachers—proved helpful, as did visits to schools and to other colleges where outstanding practices might be observed. Also of definite value were participation in work conferences, workshops, and statewide cooperative studies.

4. The most effective way of making steady improvement was that which combined continuous attention to fundamental institutional purposes and policies with the use of concentrated spearhead attacks at a succession of particular points. The latter were especially fruitful when they had broad implications and when these were carefully developed.

5. The most effective and justifiable recruiting and selective processes are those that consider a variety of factors together, that concern themselves with the guidance of the student as well as with the welfare of children and of society, that enable the individual to share in the responsibilities of decision, and that provide for periodical reconsideration of the wisdom of previous decisions. Prospective teachers should be superior specimens of the culture, but it ought to be recognized that good teachers may represent various combinations of talent, background, and interest.

6. Teachers adequate for our times cannot be prepared in less than four collegiate years. The trend toward five-year programs for both secondary and elementary school teachers deserves encouragement where practical considerations permit it to operate, and this without distinction as to whether these persons are to teach in urban or rural communities.

7. So far as possible all educational experiences provided as elements in a program of teacher preparation should be planned with reference to each other so that they may combine to meet effectively the personal, social, and vocational needs of students. Unity and continuity of program should be striven for.

8. The primary objectives of at least three-eighths of the undergraduate work of prospective teachers should be those properly ascribable to general education. It is undesirable that this part of a student's work should be concentrated in the freshman and sophomore years on the assumption that general education may be "completed" during this period, or with the consequence that attention to professional concerns must be postponed until a later time. Instruction primarily designed for general education should give attention to any implications of its subject matter for professional development. The reverse holds equally true.

9. Advanced subject-matter instruction for teachers should exhibit the highest standards of scholarship. Offerings in a particular field should, however, be planned and conducted with informed reference to the tasks that prospective teachers eventually will be called upon to perform. This should result in more attention to the interrelations of departmentalized subjects and to practical implications for personal and social well-being.

10. The study of human growth and development, particularly during childhood and adolescence, should constitute one of the basic elements in the professional preparation of teachers. This implies attention both to a synthesis of materials drawn from various biological, psychological, and social sciences and also to the cases of particular individuals.

11. Of comparable importance in teacher education is the study of the nature and problems of community and broader social existence. Instruction should aim not only at comprehension but also at developing the impulse to share in social action and skill in so doing. Informed social purpose and intelligent social participation are particularly desirable in teachers. Acquaintance with rural communities and their problems is especially indicated when teachers are likely to begin their professional work in such communities.

12. Understanding of the arts and facility in nonverbal expression should also receive greater emphasis in teacher-preparatory programs.

13. The organization of general education and of the professional part of the preparatory program into relatively large blocks of time, with a conscious effort to increase integration, continuity, and flexibility, is more likely to prove effective than the use of a larger number of separately specialized short courses.

14. With the lengthening of the customary period of teacher preparation the importance of providing students with direct experiences in relation to classroom study has increased. Special attention should be given to enabling prospective teachers to study children, schools, and communities at first hand, not merely to observe them but to work with them with some appropriate degree of responsibility. Such opportunity should begin fairly early in the preparatory program and be continued in complementary relation to a variety of classroom experiences. Campus-school facilities and those that may be provided through suitable arrangements with nearby public schools should be fully capitalized in this connection. Available opportunities for prospective teachers to work with children away from school should be employed.

15. It is particularly important that programs of teacher education should contribute throughout to the development and strengthening of democratic powers. These notably include the ability to think, feel, and act for oneself and also capacity to work effectively as one of a group. Consequently, professional preparation should consistently enable prospective teachers to share responsibly in planning and carrying out their own educational programs and provide them with regular experience in cooperative endeavor.

16. Student teaching is a most important part of the preparation of teachers. It should come near the close of the college or university course, and should be carefully prepared for by faculty members acquainted with the prospective student-teaching situations. Such preparation will be facilitated when a campus school is available or, alternatively, a neighboring

public school over which the institution shares control whereby proper supervision and direction can be guaranteed. However, it is most desirable for prospective teachers to have a culminating experience of full-time work in representative off-campus schools, especially in rural schools if that is where first regular teaching experience is likely to be. Up to eight or nine weeks may profitably be so employed.

17. Student teaching should provide opportunities not merely to carry on instruction but also to become acquainted with the children, the staff, the life, and the problems of the whole school in which the experience is had. Students should live in the community if possible and have time to study it and participate in its activities. The college should provide students with guidance during their time in the field, and on their return they should be enabled to compare their experience and to discuss its implications with various staff members.

18. The entire program of teacher preparation, including extracurricular experiences, should be designed to facilitate the balanced growth of the prospective teacher as a whole person. Fundamental concern with assuring his professional effectiveness is far from justifying neglect of other aspects of his total development. The effective teacher is an effective citizen.

19. Strictly professional elements should be allocated from one-eighth to one-sixth of the time available in a four- or five-year program of teacher preparation. It is to be recognized that there will be doubt as to whether some important elements should be classified as general or as professional education, and that acceptable integrations may be worked out that cause the professional block to *appear* to exceed or to fall short of this proportion.

20. Evaluation should play an important role in pre-service teacher education. Prospective teachers should learn to evaluate their own strengths and weaknesses and to help children and young people to do the same. They should learn to appraise the effectiveness of teaching procedures as a means to the continuous improvement of their own work. And college staffs

should be constantly employing evaluative techniques for the same reason.

21. The placement of graduates is a responsibility that should be jointly shared in by the colleges and universities, the students themselves, and the school systems. The same is true of planning follow-up arrangements. Both, therefore, call for the cultivation of cordial cooperative relationships between schools and colleges as well as full respect for the individuals involved.

22. The importance of continuous give and take between college faculties and the staffs of representative schools is so great as to deserve special emphasis. In this way the college program can be checked at every point as to its effectiveness for teacher preparation. In this way, also, the schools can be kept in constant touch with valuable resources for the steady improvement of their own programs and the systematic facilitation of professional growth on the part of their personnel.

III

Improvement of Teaching in Service

THE QUALITY of teacher preparation is exceedingly important. But no matter how excellent, it cannot by itself determine what kind of job will be done by a given graduate, either at the beginning of his professional career or as that career continues. Many other factors operate in this connection, of which a large and significant proportion represent the working situation. How teachers behave, how they affect the boys and girls with whom they are associated must depend very considerably upon the material and human circumstances that characterize the schools and communities in which they are employed. These may or may not be favorable to a teacher's full realization of his existing powers or to his exerting himself so as to increase these powers. Other influences also, of course, operate to affect professional efficiency: the presence or absence of intimate personal problems, for example, or the emotional impact of national and international events. But these are not susceptible of direct control by professional forces. The working situation, on the other hand, can be so controlled, at least within significant limits. And since work is a major element in adult experience, the character of working circumstances makes a profound difference with respect to professional satisfactions, professional accomplishment, and professional development.

Moreover, our times demand a rethinking of the functions of schools in our society and a modification of school patterns to make them more effective in meeting contemporary personal-social needs.[1] Such rethinking and modification call for a pooling of the powers of thought and action of all educational

[1] For an extended development of this view, see *Teachers for Our Times*, especially Chapters II and III.

118

workers. It is not enough that university professors and school administrators should devote attention to these matters: the participation of classroom teachers is essential. These teachers, close to the children and engaged in the task of working directly with them, have access to insights and opportunities for experimental action that must be capitalized. Improvement of working situations is needful, therefore, not merely in order that teachers may better enjoy their work but even more that their capacities may be fully used in the process of creating better schools.

SCHOOL SYSTEMS IN THE COOPERATIVE STUDY

It was for reasons such as have just been suggested that the Commission chose to include in its national cooperative study as many school systems as institutions of higher learning. Its basic concern, of course, was with the quality of teaching being offered to the children of the United States. That quality was evidently quite as dependent on the in-service experience of teachers as on their pre-service preparation. Moreover, the advantage all around in bringing together in a single enterprise units representing both phases of teacher education seemed clear. In this way mutual understanding might be promoted as well as a more effective dovetailing of efforts. Besides, the Commission thought it logical that attempts to encourage professional growth on the job should center in the systems where teachers were actually at work.

Advantages of including school systems

It is only honest to report, however, that at the outset the Commission did not see the full implications of the step it was taking. Indeed, the Commission began with the limited concept of in-service education that focuses attention on maintaining and increasing the professional competence of individual teachers by continued study. It was impressed by the mounting importance of such education. The average period of active service was steadily lengthening so that it seemed obvious that a teacher's original preparation needed to be supplemented if newer knowledge of subject matter, of children, of techniques was to be attained. Moreover, social changes such as those related to depression, war, peace, and the like were calling for educational adjustments that could not be intelligently made except by teachers who kept up in their understanding of such matters. The Commission saw teacher education as properly a continuous process whereby individuals grew steadily in their ability to serve the best interests of society and to help boys and girls satisfy their personal-social needs.

Of the services of colleges and universities in providing educational opportunities for teachers in service the Commission was fully aware and appreciative. But it felt that the kind of general in-service growth that it saw as needful especially required leadership and activity where the teachers were regularly employed—in the school systems themselves. There teachers spent most of their time; there were at hand the communities and the children whom it was their duty and privilege to serve; there were the actual problems they must solve if improvement was to be attained. It was, moreover, to help solve such problems that the Commission thought colleges and universities should direct their activities for the in-service education of teachers. All of these considerations justified establishing direct relations with a group of school systems.

The Commission's experience with selected school systems considerably broadened its views as to what ought to be emphasized about in-service education. In the first place, it came to be more sensitive to the extent to which conditions surrounding the job influence a teacher's ability to function up to the limit of his existing powers. The attitudes and behavior of fellow teachers, supervisors, administrators, and the community in general may either restrict and discourage or release and support. To consider such factors as part of the in-service education of teachers may appear to stretch that term unduly, but certain it is that they greatly affect the degree to which the aims of teacher preparation and the hopes of teacher growth will be realized. The Commission has, therefore, no hesitation in emphasizing the significance of those elements in the working situation that permit and stimulate teachers, individually and as team workers, to perform up to the peak of their powers. Such conditions and such performance are strongly conducive to further growth in competence.

The second not wholly anticipated conclusion reached by the Commission, as a result of its experience with school systems, was that much professional development in service can best be attained by indirection. Self-conscious attempts by active teachers to identify their professional weaknesses and then to set up and follow study programs specifically designed to correct these weaknesses were not widely successful. On the other hand opportunities to improve the educational program—to move in the direction of doing more effectively important jobs for which the teachers felt personal responsibility—met with remarkable response. Where such opportunities were developed the basic competence of the teachers was more or less taken for granted, and the increase in that competence became a sort of byproduct of activity focused on enlarging services to children and to the community. While some teachers said, "We need to know this," and benefited from study definitely designed to be preliminary to action, more said, "We need to do this," and gained increased understanding and skill incidental to their activity in modifying educational practice.

With these preliminary comments offered, a description and analysis of the Commission's experience in relation to teachers in service may be presented, together with conclusions of importance. The work of the school systems with which the Commission was associated will naturally receive major attention, but the activities of colleges and universities relating to the in-service education of teachers will also be brought in at appropriate points. Particular attention will be paid to the procedures whereby, according to the evidence, teachers were helped to do the best job of which they were capable at any given time, and furthermore to grow steadily in professional stature. The relation of both developments to program improvement will be emphasized.[2]

Representativeness of the group

As in the case of colleges and universities, the Commission selected school systems for participation in the national cooperative study with the intention of ensuring as high a degree of representativeness as possible. Geographical distribution was wide, ranging from Massachusetts to California, from Michigan to Texas. Size and type of organization were also varied. Very different sorts of communities were served by these schools. Three systems were located in great metropolitan cities (with populations ranging from 1,500,000 to nearly 2,000,000); four in cities which, while smaller (122,000 to 385,000 inhabitants), were nevertheless well up in rank of size for the country and dominant, in this respect, in their sections; and twelve in still less populous cities or school districts (3,000 to 82,000 inhabitants), some being relatively independent but most satellites of great metropolises. Of those last mentioned a few were manufacturing centers but the majority were residential suburbs. In addition to the above there were included four county school systems serving predominantly rural populations, the schools of a rural supervisory union, a small system in a TVA town, and a private country day school.

Of the whole twenty-six units, sixteen were grouped so as to constitute four clusters on a basis of contiguity, common interests, and, in one instance, service of the same population at different age levels. It may be added that of the twenty-six systems one operated a high school only and five limited their attention to elementary education. The rest included both elementary and secondary schools and, in four instances, municipal junior colleges or universities.

[2] For a fuller account of what was done by the school systems in the national cooperative study, see *Teacher Education in Service*, and for special topics see, *The College and Teacher Education*, Chapter VII; *Evaluation in Teacher Education*, Chapters VIII and IX; and *Helping Teachers Understand Children*. Significant statewide approaches are described in *State Programs for the Improvement of Teacher Education*, Part Four.

As will be readily understood the systems varied in many significant ways besides that of serving communities of differing size. The characteristics of the children taught covered the widest range. Few races, nationalities, and religions in the composite of the United States were nowhere represented. The range as to occupational background and social-economic status of parents was equally wide. These children reflected the impacts of quite different sectors of American life. They were looking forward to very different educational and vocational futures. In some systems, say those of the fashionable suburbs or those of the rural districts, the school populations were relatively homogeneous in character; but in others—those, for example, of the larger cities—the children of one school building presented problems differing markedly from those existing elsewhere in the same system. Student needs and community needs of the greatest variety were thus represented in the systems in the cooperative study. These differences challenged the teachers who participated in the Commission's work.

Variety among teachers and administrators

The teachers who were affected by their system's membership in the cooperative study also exhibited the variety that marks the practitioners of their profession in the United States. Some of the systems were noted for the high quality of their professional personnel. By reason of good salaries and satisfying working conditions—one or the other or both—they had been able to attract and retain the services of superior teachers. In other localities, however, the personnel situation was only ordinary or even inferior. In the rural districts, as is usual, opportunities were often not attractive to the ablest and best educated beginning teachers, and when these did accept employment they were apt soon to move on to positions offering better pay and more prestige. In some systems, therefore, the problems of in-service education were notably affected by the rapid turnover of staff, while elsewhere a factor of particular importance was the high average age and established position of the teachers. In the latter type of situation traditional incentives to continued study and experimentation were often proving ineffective.

The systems in the study were further varied with respect to character of administrative leadership and provision of supervisory and other services to the teaching staff. Some of the superintendents enjoyed national reputations because of the activities they had initiated or supported that had encouraged teachers to make progressive improvements in their work. Others, less well known, had similar accomplishments to their credit. All, of course, were sympathetic with the purposes of the cooperative study; otherwise, they would not have brought their systems in. Most of the superintendents had held their offices for a considerable period, but some were quite new. Several changes occurred during the course of the study.

Central-staff provisions varied a good deal: in some of the smaller systems there were no specialists in supervision; elsewhere these were available, sometimes in considerable numbers in proportion to the total teaching personnel. The usual pattern was to have supervision organized according to grade levels and particular subjects, but in several places a trend toward giving supervisors broader assignments had begun.

Variations in roles assigned to teachers

Some of the systems with which the Commission became associated had already gone a considerable distance in the direction of providing for participation by classroom teachers in educational planning and for assistance to them in this connection. In certain instances, however, this was more true of particular schools or divisions than of the systems as a whole. Worthy of special mention is the fact that one or more high schools in several of the cities had been members of the Progressive Education Association's eight-year study or of the comparable study of the Southern Association of Colleges and Secondary Schools. Many of the teachers in these situations had been particularly active in curriculum revision and not a few had attended summer workshops. But in most of the systems teacher participation was not far advanced. The custom of appointing classroom teachers to committees working on educational problems was fairly common but the percentage of the staff thus affected was usually small and the influence they exercised was often slight.

From what has been stated it will be seen that the cooperative study included a very considerable range of in-service situations. These were reasonably representative of the diversity characteristic of the American school scene. Because of that diversity the Commission's policy of encouraging its associated school systems to take individual responsibility for planning their participation in the study was clearly justified. No proposals it might have made of activities to be undertaken in the interest of local in-service education could have been universally suitable and acceptable. Thus, practical considerations supported those more theoretical ones that inclined the Commission to rely on local initiative, local judgment, and local good will. Consequently, what happened in the various systems in the course of the study varied a good deal. Nevertheless, as will appear, principles of general usefulness relating to ways and means of increasing teachers' accomplishments on the job proved discernible.

WHAT PARTICIPATION MEANT

Local organization for participation in the cooperative study was effected by the school systems in much the same general way as was done by the colleges and universities. At or about the time of the Bennington conference, for example, local coordinators were designated to represent the systems in their relations with the Commission and to head local activities. In seven instances superintendents of schools undertook this responsibility, though in one such case a classroom teacher later succeeded. Central-office representatives served in five cases. These representatives bore such titles as director or supervisor of curriculum, associate director of elementary education, assistant director of child accounting and curriculum, and divisional director of instruction. In this group two changes were made in the course of the study, but the new appointees were persons of the same general status. In one center the coordinator was the high school principal, and in another, the director of graduate studies and head of the department of education of an associated university. The four clusters of school systems were each represented by a single coordinator.

In most systems the coordinators had associated with them planning committees which came to exercise significant functions of leadership. These will be treated in some detail later on in this chapter.[3] Coordinators and committees ordinarily enjoyed strong and intelligent administrative support, a factor of great importance for the success of the enterprise. The Commission had emphasized its hope that developments in connection with the cooperative study would be integrated with the ongoing programs of teacher activity in the several systems— should not be set up as temporary "projects"—and this hope was very well satisfied. In a few instances the relating of cooperative-study activities to those already established caused some difficulty, but the problems that arose were usually acceptably ironed out.

Modes of participation

By and large the size of a school system proved to have considerable bearing on the ability of leaders to bring a large proportion of teachers into active participation in the study. It was, for fairly obvious reasons, generally easier to do this in the smaller centers. The cities of intermediate size, however, were often remarkably successful in reaching large percentages of their staffs. But even here (and, of course, much more in the case of the very largest systems) the problem of maintaining lines of communication between the planning bodies and the teaching group as a whole was one that required a good deal of thoughtful attention. Later references will be made to devices effectively employed for this purpose.[4] It should be added that the very largest systems tended, no doubt wisely, to focus their

[3] See pp. 136–41.
[4] See pp. 140–41.

efforts in particular schools or on activities designed to appeal to particular groups of teachers.

Everywhere the central emphasis was on group activity. This is partly to be explained by the Commission's encouragement of cooperative endeavor as originally exemplified at Bennington and later continued in other ways. But a trend toward increasing the opportunities for responsible participation, groupwise, in educational planning was already clearly visible in the school world when the cooperative study began. At any rate limited, or at least only incidental, attention was given to purely individual actions designed to result in increased teaching competence. This was not because such action was deemed unimportant. Certainly the Commission, with its strong views regarding individual freedom and responsibility, does not underestimate the values of personal study and experimentation. Moreover, it is pleased to believe that the group activities that characterized the participation of school systems in the cooperative study stimulated many individuals to much independent work. However, the group emphasis tended to divert attention from individualistic incentives to continued study and similar matters. With increasing group activity, indeed, reliance on such incentives as promise of personal promotion or salary increase came to be seen as inappropriate.

Ways of getting started

The methods of attack employed by the different school systems, at the outset and as time proceeded, varied in a number of ways. On the whole the more elaborate, systematic, and "logical" approaches proved less rewarding than those that simply enabled many teachers to get to work on specific jobs where study could fairly promptly lead to action respecting the educational program. Efforts to begin by formulating an educational philosophy for the system or by deciding just what kind of school should be worked toward tended to bog down in verbal dispute, at least when concrete implications were not carefully developed. On the other hand, surveys of teachers' concerns—of problems they sensed in the working situation that called for earnest attention—usually proved helpful in pointing the way toward the establishment of successful study groups. The fact that activities directed at the improvement of the educational program met generally with a better response and led to more substantial outcomes than activities more self-consciously designed to improve the teachers, that is, to *prepare* them to undertake program improvement, has already been emphasized.

Of equal value, experience shows, was the widespread practice of maximizing the individual's responsibilities in participation and the related reliance upon the voluntary principle. Administrators, coordinators, and planning committees that focused on facilitating spontaneous efforts rather than on pressing for universal participation in some centrally determined program were satisfied that their policy proved its superiority. The welcoming and support of good ideas from every quarter led to increasing activity, the emergence of much valuable new leadership, and thoughtful changes in actual teaching practice.

Some apprehension was felt lest the degree of decentralization just described might result in chaos, and the existence of such a danger cannot be denied. The problem of balance in any educational situation between policies and actions individually determined and those to be agreed upon by groups representing successively larger areas is a fundamental one. Obviously there are certain matters with respect to which a given teacher (or given building staff, or the representatives of a given school level) cannot properly act without reference to others. The school systems in the cooperative study, however, demonstrated two things: first, that much more decentralization than has been usual is possible without serious risk of confusion and with an increase in challenge and response all along the line; secondly, that through the development of democratic arrangements for general participation in policy formation at successively higher and more inclusive levels, the danger of action at cross purposes can satisfactorily be avoided.

As in the case of the colleges and universities in the cooperative study, the school systems generally came to see the advantages of a combination of over-all planning and spearhead action. Central bodies, such as planning committees and policies councils, essentially representative in character, proved their worth in thinking continuously about matters with systemwide implications. They found it possible to guard against too much dispersion of effort and to watch the relation of parts of the program to each other and to the whole, without operating oppressively or dictatorially. Indeed they were notably able to open doors for those who wished to try new experiments, and to stimulate such wishes, as they themselves came to be sensible of promising opportunities. Thus the expression of sound creative impulses, the emergence of new voices, was encouraged. Details with respect to procedures found useful in this connection will be presented further on in this chapter.

Points of attack

In the preceding chapter it was noted how various were the focuses chosen for special attention by the colleges and universities participating in the cooperative study. Yet despite this diversity it was readily possible to arrange the report of their activities under headings corresponding to the customary aspects of programs of teacher preparation, for example, student personnel, general education, professional education, student teaching, and the like. The topics and their arrangement reflected both what is generally considered essential in the pre-service education of teachers and also the order in which the various elements achieve prominence in the four or five years devoted to such education. To a considerable degree what the prospective teacher needed to learn provided the organizing principle of the presentation, and the conclusions as to how that learning might best be promoted was subsidiarily developed.

Experience with the school systems in the study does not lend itself to analysis along corresponding lines. The development, by systems themselves, of programs for the in-service education of teachers is as yet a relatively new thing, and patterns are still in the process of formation. The focus of interest, moreover, tends to be on concerns growing out of situations, rather than subjects in the usual academic sense. And it is on ways and means of satisfying such concerns that the experience of the Commission throws its most helpful light. Hence, it is to a description and analysis of such techniques that this chapter will turn shortly. This is of especial interest since the same methods proved useful over the widest range of interests.

Something should, however, here be said about the character and range of concerns to which teachers in service proved ready and often eager to devote their attention. There was the greatest variety. Quantitatively the most important focus of interest in these school systems was child study, which was felt to be needed as a guide to curricular development and which appealed to all sorts of staff members.[5] No doubt the special consultants and other resources available from the Commission also help account for this emphasis. The usual aim was to increase the understanding of the nature and needs of children in general and in specific instances and thereby to heighten the ability of teachers to meet such needs, both through the use of subject matter and also through handling all kinds of individual and group relations. Some study groups specifically undertook to improve guidance activities. Several carried out illuminating comparisons as to abilities, interests, attitudes, and purposes, of themselves and groups of their pupils.

A second major focus of great interest was the community. Groups of teachers surveyed community needs in order to check on the adequacy of curricula and to get leads for change in program offerings. They studied the resources of their communities with a view to making more effective educational use thereof and in order to determine their adequacy for meeting the out-of-school needs of children. They developed plans for encouraging and helping teachers, new and old, to enter more fully and satisfactorily into the group life of the communities in which they were working.

[5] An extended account of such study in one system is given in *Helping Teachers Understand Children*. See also, with respect to this and all other points of attention listed here, *Teacher Education in Service, passim; The College and Teacher Education*, pp. 229–52; *State Programs for the Improvement of Teacher Education*, Part Four *passim;* and *Evaluation in Teacher Education*, Chapter VIII.

Studies of children and studies of communities had great uni-
fying value: they dealt with objects of common concern to all
teachers. Moreover, the two approaches supported each other: the
child could not be studied without reference to his environment,
and the environment was being studied for the benefit of the
child. This was particularly clear where groups of teachers
undertook to examine time pressures on children or to look more
carefully into their home conditions.

A good many study groups naturally focused attention on
specific curricular matters of greater or less magnitude. Some
set as their goal the achievement of broad changes such as the
development of new terminal curricula for high school students
or the introduction in junior high schools of integrated core
programs. Others dealt with questions that individual teachers
or groups of teachers might act upon without the prior necessity
of policy changes, for example, reading difficulties, homeroom
practice, activity periods, the development of patriotism and
other desirable character traits, the promotion of better habits
of health and recreation, auditorium programs, failure reduction, and the use of audio-visual aids. Groups were frequently
formed by teachers concerned with the same subject matter. A
recurrent object of attention was increase in understanding
between teachers operating at different levels in a system and
better articulation of curricula as between these levels. The
subject of marks and of reports to parents was studied.

There was much interest in the improvement of school-community relations, in increasing the public's understanding of
what the teachers were about, in sensing and appraising its ideas
as to what the schools should be doing, and in achieving greater
cooperation with parents and other laymen in serving the needs
of children. Nor were relationships closer to the scene of professional action neglected. One center dealt rigorously with the
personal difficulties that arise among teachers and between them
and administrators and that often interfere with professional
efficiency. The problem of helping new teachers to become
oriented and achieve a secure sense of belonging was considered
in a number of places. Elsewhere the character of relationships

existing between teachers and pupils was studied with a view to improving the effectiveness of learning.

No little interest was displayed in issues relating to the working situations in which teachers found themselves. Matters of salary and tenure were studied. A frequent concern was how to deal with pressures of various sorts—pressures to introduce this or that new subject or slant into the curriculum, pressures to undertake specified tasks in the community or engage in more professional activities. It may be noted that teachers who originally looked upon the Commission's program as threatening one more pressure often discovered that it rather provided a means of dealing fairly satisfactorily with existing pressure problems.

Finally, the quite personal interests of teachers were by no means neglected. In many systems groups were formed for the study of art, crafts, literature, current events, or personal typing. That such activities might directly or indirectly contribute to professional effectiveness was recognized, but the opportunities were provided without particular reference to such considerations. It was accepted as appropriate that a program designed to assist in the in-service development of teachers should endeavor to meet personal as well as professional needs. With the coming of war many groups were naturally formed to study first aid, civil defense, and similar subjects.

Enough has been said to indicate the general character and range of the interests that teachers employed as a basis for in-service study and action in connection with the Commission's program. The evidence is clear that if the concerns strongly felt and voluntarily experienced by teachers are used as starting points, a program of in-service education can be developed that will relate to matters of genuine importance and exhibit adequate scope. It is not necessary—it is not even desirable—that some logically complete program should be thought up for the teachers in advance by administrators or outside experts.

Following the teachers' leads increases the likelihood that action will accompany study. Moreover, it must be remembered that teachers are continually accessible to new ideas. As they read and study for one purpose new concerns will develop. Contact with administrative leaders and consultants, and participation in conferences and workshops will provide additional stimulus. And planning committees are always in a position to stir up interest in problems that, when a system's needs are viewed in the large, appear to have been overlooked. The Commission's experience convinced it, however, that taking the cue from the teachers themselves is a productive procedure. It should be added that the consequences will be most likely to lead in the direction of significant program improvement when two conditions are present: first, that a rich association is maintained between the teachers and the children and adults of the community; and second, that the teachers have a similar association with important social ideas and ideals. Administrators are in a strong position to see to it, if they will, that such conditions exist.

General accomplishment

The gains made in most of the school systems with which the Commission was associated provided solid ground for general satisfaction. Of course, as in the case of the colleges and universities, full appraisal must await the passage of time during which the consequences of various innovations have an opportunity to develop fully. What can be said here, however, will provide the reader with a basis for exercising considerable judgment respecting accomplishments.

As was true of the institutions of higher learning some school systems achieved a great deal, while at the other extreme were a few that made only limited gains. The Commission must share responsibility for this latter result. But the character of local leadership and traditions was also of evident influence. Local uncertainties, due, for example, to administrative changes or insecurities, always operated as adverse factors, and a high degree of centralization, with a large proportion of critical decisions made at points remote from the action front where the teachers were operating, undoubtedly had disadvantageous consequences.

In general, however, the progress made was extraordinary, especially considering the novelty of the challenge with which the cooperating school systems were presented. That major responsibility for promoting the continuous professional growth of teachers on the job reposes in such systems is not as yet generally understood. The Commission believes that the story of what was accomplished in the cooperative study should and will increase recognition of this responsibility, and action in accordance with such recognition.

TECHNIQUES FOR SHARING DECISIONS

The Commission did not attempt to present the school systems in the national study with any recommended pattern of procedure. Local judgment was relied upon although that judgment, of course, was influenced by discussions in which Commission representatives participated. Such discussions occurred in the home situation but also at conferences that, beginning with Bennington, brought teachers and administrators from all participating units together. The patterns that were developed varied. However, certain elements so generally emerged and proved so valuable that a somewhat extended description of each is called for. It will be seen how they fit together and support each other. The elements to be considered have been grouped as techniques for sharing decisions (including planning committees and policies councils) and techniques for study and exchange (such as study groups, use of consultants, workshops, and one or two others). The analysis will be presented in this and the following main subdivisions of this chapter. But first brief attention must be given to certain considerations that apparently controlled developments in the various centers.

Controlling considerations

Fundamental in the school systems participating in the cooperative study of teacher education was, as has been stressed, the desire to maximize the scope available to teachers for the exercise of initiative, and also the opportunities at their disposal for participating in group study and group decisions. One aim was to encourage full expression of individual powers as well as activities calculated to enhance such powers. Another was to increase such understanding and agreement as are essential to achieve and maintain an atmosphere of dynamic unity in the system as a whole and in its several parts, especially the so-called "building groups." This was to be sought after by spreading participation in policy making and planning. A third aim was to ensure sensitive response to new needs and to new ideas as to how needs might be met: to enlarge the likelihood that programs and procedures would be promptly modified in ways that would result in improved educational services to boys and girls and to the communities they represented.

All this called for the working out of a neat balance between centralization and decentralization. The desire to manifest faith in individuals and small groups, to provide them with the greatest possible opportunity to exercise their own judgments and take responsibility for consequent action, required guarding against tight controls at the center. But such a policy was seen to involve the risk that developments at various points within the system might be inconsistent, if not conflicting. This would inevitably lead to a swing back toward stricter controls. Such an outcome could be avoided, it was thought, only by emphasizing common concerns and by developing instrumentalities representative of the entire system that would so operate as to preserve and promote what was essential to the maintenance of the right kind of unity. It was assumed that individual members of a system staff could be counted on to give due weight to considerations broader than those relating to their more immediate and specialized interests, providing such considerations were well understood. And it was believed that properly constituted central bodies could find ways both of encouraging widespread participation in activities designed to promote program improvement and teacher growth, and of guarding acceptably against cross-purpose developments and the occurrence of dangerous imbalances in the system as a whole.

It was further thought that those working at the center might perform a specially useful function by facilitating the spread of ideas first developed and tested in practice by pioneering teachers. The time usually comes when such teachers are eager for help in evaluating their accomplishments, and, if the results prove favorable, in conveying to others the values demonstrated. At about the same time, teachers who have not been sharing in new developments are likely to become curious as to outcomes and as to how they themselves ought to be affected, if at all. At this point central authorities are presented with a special opportunity to assist in spreading any improvements. Conferences may be arranged for wide consideration of the implications of such pioneer efforts for the over-all program. With the aid of consultants a revised course of study for general experimental use may be developed. The formation of study groups may be encouraged and needed books and other materials provided. Eventually revised statements of objectives may emerge, and a new and carefully worked out curriculum may win general approval and adoption.

The above statements undoubtedly suggest a clearer and more universal grasp of the problem, by the Commission and its associated school systems, than existed at the beginning of the study. Possibly it would have been wiser to present them as conclusions. However, the views expressed were at least implicit in the earliest thinking and, if there were plenty of false moves made in the course of developments, these were usually corrected as they were recognized.

Planning committees

In most instances the school systems began by setting up local planning committees in connection with their participation in the cooperative study.[6] Original ideas as to the exact functions to be performed by these bodies naturally varied, as did their composition. The experiences they had also differed from place to place, as well as in the degree to which they achieved success and status. But by and large they proved themselves to be important elements in the programs of which they were parts,

[6] For a fuller treatment of this topic, see *Teacher Education in Service*, Chapter II.

and comparative study has revealed certain principles respecting their operation that may be confidently set forth.

At the Bennington conference the school system representatives, almost all of whom were administrators, had exhibited great sensitivity to the desirability of ensuring full participation by classroom teachers in planning and supervising the program of in-service activity about to be launched. The setting up of planning committees soon thereafter was ordinarily designed to support this purpose. Membership was customarily determined, eventually if not immediately, by election. Considerable thought was usually expended on making certain that the body would be highly representative. Classroom teachers frequently predominated: in one instance they occupied twenty out of twenty-three places on the committee. But principals and persons from the central office were, of course, also regularly included. The principle of rotation in office was ordinarily applied. A committee of twenty to twenty-five members was usually established in cities with several hundred teachers or more.

These newly created planning bodies faced many problems. First of all they had to achieve some unity of their own. Often they were made up of persons who at the outset were 'relative strangers to one another: it took them some time to get acquainted, to learn to communicate successfully, to develop an esprit de corps. This was made the more difficult because individual members came from different backgrounds of experience which were often rather specialized in character and sometimes thought of themselves primarily as representing particular interests. As time passed it became clear that an essential requirement for success was that committee members should learn to think together in terms of the needs and welfare of the system as a whole. Because of this recognition, and because these committees came to exercise less and less power of decision affecting individual and group interests, ideas as to how they should be composed tended to be modified. It became evident that membership in excess of ten or twelve persons made it very difficult to develop a genuine common mind. More than proportional representation of the central staff—members of which were most likely to be in touch with the whole system's problems—came to be seen as advantageous. The importance of electing principals and classroom teachers on the basis of individual competence for the committee's planning functions rather than according to some elaborate scheme of exact representation for all levels, subjects, and buildings came to be recognized. It also became clear that too swift rotation could seriously interfere with unity and effectiveness.

Planning committees had to learn what it was appropriate for them to do and what it would be wiser for them not to attempt. In the beginning there was a certain tendency among them to study problems themselves or to arrange for such study through subcommittees and then to issue pronouncements or recommendations. This proved unwise. It tended to limit participation in the local program for the cooperative study and to stir the suspicions of those staff members who were not intimately connected with what was going on. With experience, then, there was a general abandonment of such efforts. The emphasis turned to stimulating and aiding study activities on the part of others. Opinions were collected regarding local matters calling for group attack, interested staff members were helped to organize and arrange times and places for study-groups, and resources for the aid of such bodies were marshalled. Moreover, local conferences and workshops were set up, the participation of key representatives in such affairs elsewhere facilitated, and arrangements worked out for visiting other systems or institutions of higher learning.

In such ways a number of important contributions were made by planning committees: local participation in efforts to improve program and develop competence was increased; opportunities were provided for hitherto silent voices among the professional staff to be heard and hitherto unsuspected leadership to emerge and function; local experts were helped to make contacts with groups of teachers ready for their assistance, and outside experts were used to stimulate interest and render services at points of felt need; continuity and integration of efforts were encouraged without being decreed; and mutual acquaintance and interaction were promoted.

As the number of study groups in a system grew the planning committee customarily found itself faced with a mounting problem of coordination and even of keeping informed concerning what was going on. It was obviously impossible for a body of ten or even twenty regular members to keep in close touch with the activities of 100 to 200 working bodies. Two helpful discoveries were, however, made. The first was that it was not essential to maintain a fully coordinated pattern of group work. Especially as experience developed more understanding of group methods among the teachers in general and more grasp of systemwide factors, problems, and purposes, the risks connected with letting people go pretty much on their own proved not too serious. Certainly it was concluded that such risks were fewer than those inherent in a policy of strict centralized control. It was learned that any effort to ensure logical completeness and precise articulation of the working activities was likely to have the effect of frustrating the enthusiasms of some persons and of bringing pressure on others to do things for which they were not yet ready.

The second discovery that planning committees made was that much coordination could be achieved through intermediary bodies. In one city with over 2,000 teachers, for example, the central planning committee found three "level" subcommittees —elementary, junior high, and senior high respectively— extremely useful. In the same community citywide study groups served a coordinating function among groups in separate school buildings dealing with similar topics.

The impression should not be left, however, that here or elsewhere the central committees gave up completely their efforts to influence the developing pattern of group activities. They took the lead in getting new groups started. In doing so they were guided by often very careful appraisals of system needs, of teacher concerns, and of available resources. In the smaller systems they tended wisely to use their influence to prevent too wide a dispersal of activity: here successive focusings of interest and effort seemed most profitable. In the larger situations, on the other hand, planning committees found it advantageous to encourage the development of an aggregate of working groups, the individual units of which offered a variety of attractions to different staff members.

One problem with which planning committees, especially in the most sizable centers, had to struggle was that of maintaining effective communication with the professional personnel generally. It was felt to be highly desirable that there should be widespread understanding of the program that was developing but it was not easy to discover how to bring this about. Written reports proved useful, but only within rather strict limits: it is very difficult to convey to nonparticipants the flavor and significance of the experiences enjoyed by others. However, the several systems that developed periodically published "house organs" during the course of the study found them effective for promoting mutual good will and common unity. These seldom attempted to cover thoroughly all that was being done in connection with the developing in-service program: highlights of past events were reported and notice of forthcoming events was given, but considerable space was also devoted to personal items and the like.

Planning committee members were, of course, able to communicate a good deal through various personal contacts. As more and more teachers became active in various aspects of the work these also shared helpfully in word-of-mouth explanation of what was afoot. Faculty meetings of building groups, for example, provided opportunities for formal or informal reporting. Moreover, interchange of information was made easier as more and more teachers tended to take part in two or more study groups. In fact, as the programs grew, as participation became more widespread, and as decentralization increased, the need for systematic communication by the planning committee appreciably declined and the task of doing what remained important, along this line, became simpler. In one system annual or semiannual "open house days" proved exceedingly effective for the purpose. On these occasions entire system staffs came together and devoted most of their time to small group meetings, each of which enabled interested but relatively uninformed teachers to discuss what was going on with others who had been actively participating. The informal give and take that ensued proved more effective in developing understanding and good will than did set speeches delivered in general meetings.

Some of the planning committees began with a practically clear field: they were unique in their systems as representative bodies with systemwide responsibilities and they did not inherit much in the way of a pre-established in-service program. Elsewhere this was not the case, and in such situations the newly created bodies had the special problem of working out their relations to others already in existence. This required time, patience, and mutual adjustments. Since the cooperative study was by agreement committed to the promotion not of temporary projects but of developments viewed as part of the ongoing system program, planning committees were properly concerned to find an appropriate role in the permanent setup. It proved satisfactory, however, to let this matter work itself out with experience. Focus of attention on worthy jobs to be done (of which there were always more than enough to go around) tended to make eventually possible the amicable ironing-out of any problems of relationship. The authority of the situation came to resolve the conflicts, existent or potential, between personal authorities.

Policies councils

It has been explained that planning committees connected with school system programs for professional development found it desirable strictly to limit their powers of policy making and action so far as the system's educational program in general was concerned. This was a matter of practical restriction of function to a manageable assignment. It represented no reduction, among the systems participating in the cooperative study, of interest and belief in the further sharing among the entire professional personnel of policy making and even administrative responsibilities. Such interest and belief, indeed, generally increased during the course of the cooperative study.

It is the Commission's view that professional service suited to democratic schools can only be fully rendered when teachers are free to participate in the process whereby the planning and administration of educational policy are carried forward. It believes, as a matter of fact, that teachers always do and must plan and administer. But it thinks such behavior should be given more recognition, encouragement, and status, and that this is particularly true as respects its group expression. Participation, directly and through chosen representatives, in the making of fundamental decisions bearing on school policy and practice is an essential means of developing institutional unity and of broadening the opportunities for the responsible exercise of personal freedom. Both outcomes are essential if educational programs and teacher-pupil relations suited to the needs of our times are to be created.

Conventional notions of school organization and administration correspond poorly both with reality and with democratic ideals. They predicate a hierarchical arrangement with policy-making authority centralized in the board of education and administrative authority in the superintendent. Below these, other staff members are seen as occupying various levels of subordination, with the classroom teachers or perhaps the school secretaries or custodians at the bottom of the chart. The implication is that power—of ideas, of judgment, of executive authority —originates at the higher levels and operates in one direction only, that is, downward. Actually this is unrealistic. Good educational ideas may be originated or promoted in any quarter of a school system, and able administrators are accustomed to taking full advantage of this fact. The best of them do so openly, encouraging and recognizing contributions from wherever they may come. This accords with the democratic belief that all men must be presumed capable of creativity and that group advance and accomplishment is promoted when the powerful flow of ideas is multidirectional.

Much the same may be said with respect to the exercise of

judgment respecting policy and to the administration of policies explicitly or tacitly adopted. No board of education has ever determined all of the policies that significantly influence the character of an educational program and its effect on the children in whose interest it is established. Many such policies are matters of uncritically and even unwittingly accepted tradition. Many are the consequences of decisions made by the superintendent, by various other individuals, including classroom teachers, and by groups of various sorts within the system. What the board actually reserves to itself reflects local custom and the impact of dynamic factors in the local situation. The administrative function is also actually widely distributed, being significantly shared in, in practice, by classroom teachers who are the persons acting at the point of contact with the children.

Wise school superintendents and principals understand perfectly that the teacher's appraisal of policy and administrative conduct is of key importance in determining program effectiveness. What is to be aimed for must be both understood and believed in by those working with the student body if much success in the attainment of professed goals is to be expected. Moreover, considerable administrative power must be freely allowed to classroom teachers if policies are to be executed wisely in situations basically human in character, hence varied and changing. The mechanical application of fixed administrative rules has strict limits of efficiency where personal relations are of the essence; and this generalization applies to situations involving principals and teachers as well as to those in which teachers and pupils are the actors. None of this is to deny the importance of certain principles, rules, and agreements, but it does argue for the practical necessity of participation in decision making and of leeway in administrative application.

Again, the practical conclusion is supported by democratic theory. Respect for personality requires that all members of a school system staff should be presumed capable of contributing to the determination of policies designed to achieve program excellence, and of sharing responsibility in the carrying out of such decisions as may be made. Furthermore, there is an assumption that group enterprise will be most successful when there is general participation in planning and in the execution of plans. When classroom teachers share in policy formation two advantages may be expected: first, decisions unsuited to the realities at the points of teacher-pupil contact will be less likely; and, second, understanding, acceptance, and suitable behavior on the part of those upon whose actions the success of policy agreement so largely depends are more likely to ensue. Democratic procedures make for greater and surer progress.

Teacher participation in policy formation and teacher responsibility for policy administration were markedly advanced in the school systems participating in the cooperative study.[7] In several of the larger of these, formal policies councils were established or further developed. These bodies were designed to provide official means whereby all system employees might share in suggesting and considering matters of major import for the improvement of the educational program. Their function was both to recognize existing interest in such general questions and also deliberately to encourage, strengthen, and spread that interest. Such councils, being charged with decisions of concern to every class of employee in the system, were organized with a careful eye to guaranteeing their representative character: even when all administrators were included, classroom teachers constituted a large majority of the membership and these were elected by particular building or other homogeneous groups; sometimes the clerical employees and the custodians were represented. The number of delegates was relatively large—over 300 in one metropolitan center and 165 in a city of 325,000 inhabitants. Consequently, the executive or steering committee had important functions to perform; and a good deal of spade work was ordinarily assigned to special committees, some of which included persons not regularly members of the councils.

Customarily proposals might be made to these policies councils by an individual or group. As observed, such proposals related to curricular questions, administrative issues, and mat-

[7] For a fuller treatment of this topic, see *ibid.*, Chapter III.

ters affecting teacher welfare. Among topics dealt with, for example, were the following: pupil grouping, treatment of controversial issues, use of community resources, articulation, serious disciplinary cases and truancy, counseling and guidance programs, home study, teachers' meetings, teacher rating, community-chest drives, salary schedules, status of employees released for service in the armed forces, promotion and retirement. The existence of the council made it possible for doubts and dissatisfactions with the existing situation to achieve free expression; it provided a means of clearing up misunderstandings and bringing about needed reforms; and it enabled persons with new ideas to obtain for them a hearing and possibly influential support. The continuous re-examination of the existing policy situation was facilitated with two results: the sloughing off or correction of old policies no longer fitting, and the adoption of new ones consistent with developing reality and thought. In both ways, incidentally, opportunity for the exercise of initiative by individuals and small groups within the system was enlarged.

The relation of policies councils and comparable arrangements to the improvement of teaching is clear. They can contribute greatly to the development of a sense of we-ness in a school system, to the attainment of a superior degree of institutional unity. They provide means of general participation in policy formation, increasing the likelihood that policies will be wisely chosen and widely understood and accepted, and that a sense of personal responsibility for making the whole system program go will be generally shared. These are consequences calculated to lead to greater and more willing effort as well as to better and more vital accomplishment on the part of the whole personnel.

TECHNIQUES FOR STUDY AND EXCHANGE

Policies councils served, in the school systems with which the Commission was associated, to spread participation in basic decision making and to develop human situations conducive to self-realization and growth. Planning committees were effective in facilitating widely shared-in attacks on particular problems of teachers. But membership in such bodies was available to only a small fraction of the total staffs. It was the study groups that provided the greatest and freest opportunity to all persons to have a part in the programs developed in connection with the cooperative study. Group study, indeed, must be considered to have constituted the heart of such programs, to have proved itself indispensable to local activities for in-service education. It was an outstanding feature of the work done in every center.

Study groups during the school year

The most pronounced method of group study engaged in was that of small working groups that met regularly throughout term time.[8] As already indicated, the setting-up of such study groups was facilitated and promoted by planning committees. In a considerable proportion of the school systems in the cooperative study, these committees began by surveying teacher opinion as to matters calling for attention. This procedure proved valuable in revealing those concerns to which teachers might be counted upon to devote serious effort.[9] With respect to topics thus brought to the fore, however, there was need to exercise certain judgments. Thus, suitability to group methods of attack had to be considered, as well as the need for and availability of special resources for the benefit of those who might undertake the proposed study. Finally, account had to be taken of the likelihood that circumstances were conducive to the making of satisfactory progress. Nothing can harm group procedure more than the repeated experience of failure to achieve results, either because the group bogs down or because its recommendations fail to be acted upon.

Another conclusion, one that has already been touched upon, stands out clearly. While some teachers were interested in study directly designed to increase their personal competence, the

[8] For a fuller treatment of this topic, see *Teacher Education in Service*, Chapters IV and VI-IX; *The College and Teacher Education*, pp. 229–52; *Evaluation in Teacher Education*, Chapter VIII and pp. 307–21; and *Helping Teachers Understand Children*, especially Chapters VI and XII.

[9] For subjects actually selected for group study, see pp. 129–32.

considerable majority responded more readily to the chance to tackle the improvement of the educational program. Group study of the kind here discussed evidently will thrive when it gives teachers the opportunity to share responsibly in efforts to do better those tasks which they consider both important and properly their own. As their views broaden about what is important and what is their responsibility, new study groups will naturally be formed.

Several principles operated to control the composition of these study groups. Almost universally emphasized was the principle of voluntary participation, and this proved its value over and over again. It ensured the interest of group members and increased the likelihood that each could play a positive role. It respected the right of individuals to choose not to engage in such activities. Moreover, it put planning committees and others under the necessity of promoting only those study groups for which there was genuine demand. The proportion of teachers responding to available opportunities was always satisfactorily high.

With the voluntary principle operating, the kind of person participating in a given study group depended, of course, on its appeal. Some topics attracted classroom teachers from a particular grade, or school level, or subject. There were groups limited to principals or supervisors. Other groups drew from the entire faculty of particular schools—the so-called "building groups." But there were also many cross-sectional groups, quite heterogeneous so far as subject, school, or level represented was concerned. Experience showed that the important thing to watch for, beyond interest, was capacity to contribute to group deliberation and action.

Many different methods of working were successfully employed. Discussion was universally an element, of course. Much relevant reading was done, and original inquiries were often planned and carried through. Information was gathered, for example, regarding practices in different parts of the local school system and elsewhere. Rather intensive study of particular children or groups of children was frequent. Some members also made firsthand contacts with the community: in certain instances lay persons worked with them regularly, in others these were brought in for special purposes.

Group leadership was usually self-developed, and it was strikingly demonstrated how much in the way of leadership ability is available on the staff of the normal school system. However, resources at hand in the shape of specialists of various sorts were also freely drawn upon. Supervisors and other members of the central staff found new and unusually rewarding opportunities to be of service to different groups. Principals and classroom teachers with special knowledge and skills—sometimes as a result of experience at workshops or the collaboration center —were also in demand as consultants. Very fruitful use was made of the services of outside consultants, as will be considered in more detail later on.[10] Individual members of particular study groups often increased their powers of contribution by workshop attendance or comparable activities.

The frequency, place, and length of meetings held by these study groups and the period of time during which they found it profitable to continue their joint activities naturally varied, depending upon such circumstances as their purposes, composition, and progress. Building groups tended to meet in their own buildings before, during, or after school; cross-sectional groups suited their schedules to the jobs they had tackled and the convenience of their members. In one school system where many groups were in operation most meetings were eventually called at one place in the late afternoon or early evening on alternate Thursdays. This arrangement limited the possibilities of participation somewhat, but it also protected individual teachers from the temptation to engage in too many activities. Distinctly advantageous was the fact that it made for increased mutual acquaintance and good fellowship, a large proportion of the group members eating their evening meal together in the cafeteria of the school where the meetings were held.

One lesson clearly taught by the experience of the cooperative study was that it is of great importance that groups be free to

[10] See pp. 150–55.

modify their purposes and methods as they proceed, and to dissolve without embarrassment if it becomes evident that the job tackled is not susceptible of successful treatment. A self-propelling group, formed by the voluntary action of its members, must expect to feel its way along. It often takes time for the members to become acquainted—to become a genuine group. Some leads tentatively taken may fall through rapidly, while others will prove unusually fruitful. Often the problem originally chosen for study proves, upon examination, to be too large, and must be broken down if satisfactory progress is to be made. This may or may not suggest subdivisions of the original group.

In all such circumstances the maintenance of flexible plans is important, as is the practice of periodical self-evaluation.[11] Groups that are faltering should, of course, be given whatever help may be available, but when it becomes clear that they cannot expect to achieve satisfying results they should be encouraged to disband, without any feelings of guilt, so that the members may individually turn their energies to more rewarding tasks.

Reference has been made to the matter of getting acquainted. The importance of the human-relations aspect of group study deserves further emphasis. Genuine participation on the part of all members is essential if the educational consequences are to be at a maximum, and this requires that all should feel at ease in the group situation. This takes both time and usually some deliberate effort on the part of group leaders and of persons of superior status in the professional hierarchy. Leaders can do much to promote an atmosphere of friendly equality and to help each participant to find something positive to do. Study groups are at their best when participation is most general and when the members appraise each other's contributions in terms of their quality and without reference to irrelevant distinctions as to source.

One exceedingly important point respecting this kind of group study remains to be made. It is essential that ease of

[11] For a discussion of relevant evaluative practice see *Evaluation in Teacher Education*, Chapter VIII and pp. 307–21.

movement back and forth from the deliberative to the action stage be maintained. Teachers become discouraged if their thoughtful suggestions for the improvement of the educational program do not result in practical experimentation. This implies the importance of making certain that study groups are kept realistically aware of administrative or other difficulties that should be given due weight when proposals are being formulated. It further implies the value of a considerable degree of administrative decentralization and a willingness to approve experimental deviations from "standard" practice. The school systems in the cooperative study generally concluded that the advantages of enabling study group members to test out matured ideas promptly overbalanced any difficulties due to lack of uniformity. Of course, there were always limits to the degree of deviation from modal practice that was safely permissible, and the development of certain inclusive agreements on this point was required. Moreover, the central authorities found it desirable to aid in the evaluation of pioneer efforts and in the study of their results by many teachers. In these ways successful innovations were helped to have rapid and widespread influence.

Use of outside consultants

The school systems and indeed all units cooperating with the Commission had a great deal of fruitful and instructive experience with outside consultants, especially in connection with group study.[12] Commission staff members served regularly in this capacity but special consultants were also often employed in relation to particular problems. Various services were appropriately provided by such persons, often, of course, in combination. The needs differed from situation to situation. Sometimes inspiration, building local self-confidence, or lending authority to local decisions seemed particularly called for. More frequently expert assistance in planning or in evaluation was chiefly requisite. In any case the consultant, not a regular member of

[12] For further treatment of this topic see *Evaluation in Teacher Education*, pp. 321–27; *Helping Teachers Understand Children*, especially Chapters IV, XII, and XIII; and *State Programs for the Improvement of Teacher Education, passim.*

the group by which he was brought in, was expected to prove especially helpful through his contribution of unusual knowledge, insight, and skill.

The selection of a consultant calls for thoughtful consideration of the qualities needed if he is to meet the requirements of the situation to which he is to be brought. Presumably some special expertness is what is wanted, for example, outstanding competence in some particular field of knowledge, or wide acquaintance with foremost practice in certain places, or technical skill in evaluation. Sometimes—though by no means always —it may be important that the consultant be a person of considerable prestige. It is relatively easy to identify individuals who will meet such requirements as these.

It is less easy to make certain in advance that skill in the art of consultation is present; the importance of so doing is, indeed, not infrequently overlooked. That importance is here deliberately emphasized. For to be effective, a consultant must be quick in comprehending the nature of the situation in which he has been invited to participate, skillful in adjusting his own thinking to the realities of that situation, and able readily to establish a relation of mutual trust between himself and those with whom he is to work. He must have a practical turn of mind and believe in the process of give and take. He must be skilled in grasping what others are trying to communicate— sometimes, indeed, what they may be trying to conceal. And he must have the power of expressing his own ideas in ways that will successfully convey his true meaning to the particular persons who have sought his help. Experts committed in advance to particular answers, slow to grasp the essence of new situations, unable quickly to establish rapport with others, unaccustomed to group methods, or satisfied to win verbal assent to proposals not readily understood and hence unlikely really to be put into practice, do not make good consultants.

It makes a difference when and by whom a consultant is summoned. Consultants have been known to be invited in for quite inadequate reasons: because the idea seemed fashionable or because the local group vaguely hoped for *some* sort of inspiration. The results in such cases were not always fruitless but success was far more usual when more definite needs had been identified. To be sure, the need might be a fairly general one, as for help in analyzing a situation and determining specific points for attack. Often, however, such focuses had been already selected and the need was for assistance in planning an appropriate program of action. Such situations proved particularly ready for the sort of service a consultant can render.

It was always helpful when the need for consultant services was genuinely felt by the group with which the guest was to work. Local leaders were often influential in developing this sense of need. But when such leaders moved too rapidly the prospects for success were reduced. Groups were resentful when they felt consultants were being foisted on them. It proved advantageous, accordingly, in order to make certain that the consultant was really wanted, to consider carefully the sort of help that was hoped for, to discuss possible names with the group before a selection was made, and to arrange matters so that it would not be embarrassing to discontinue the relationship if it failed to prove satisfying in practice. Such preparatory measures increased the likelihood that the consultant would be given not only a friendly reception but also one in which his ideas would not be uncritically accepted.

Since the purpose of consultation is to bring the expert's powers to bear upon a particular situation, it is important that he should be helped in every possible way to size that situation up quickly and accurately. This means that he should be given as much information as possible before his visit and that the use of his time should be intelligently planned. The prospective consultant should be well supplied with background materials. He may properly be sent minutes of the group's meetings and formulations already agreed upon or under consideration. In addition he should receive a special statement respecting the matters on which his help is particularly wished, the local factors especially relevant thereto, and the possibly conflicting trends of local opinion about the action to be taken. Needless to say a competent consultant will welcome such information and study it carefully.

Planning the use of a consultant's time is an art not as yet too well understood, but one the cultivation of which invariably proves rewarding. The number, character, and sequence of events to be arranged need to be considered carefully. With which key individuals should the expert have a chance to talk, and when? What places, buildings, or equipment ought he to see? How many meetings with what groups should be scheduled, and what plans made for conducting these? May it be important to schedule some general address? Should provision be made for periods of informal contact, and what should be the character of any such? Answers to questions like these should be arrived at only after full consideration of the local situation and with due regard for the working style of the particular individual to be invited.

Ordinarily it is best to get to the stage of group discussion as soon as possible after the consultant arrives. Specifically, an extended opening speech by the visitor is risky business: he may give an impression of premature commitment to some position or other and thereby set up equally premature resistance. Getting acquainted is essential to genuine reasoning together, and the give and take of discussion is conducive to such acquaintance. Incidentally, it may be added that this requires time and it is consequently wise to anticipate a period of fumbling before minds can really begin to meet and true agreements emerge.

Experience shows that leeway for unanticipated arrangements and relaxation is important. As the period of consultation proceeds the need for certain unplanned interviews or other activities may become exceedingly evident, and it is unfortunate when no time is available in which to meet such needs. As to informal breaks in the schedule, these often contribute powerfully to the promotion of mutual understanding and trust, to the development of friendliness and the attainment of significant insights.

Everything that has hitherto been said has implied the desirability of allowing sufficient time for the visit of a consultant. Two days may yield three or four times the result of one, especially when a consultant is new to a given situation. Yet the cost, considering the element of travel expense, will ordinarily not be anything like doubled. Three or four days or even a week may, indeed, prove most economical in the long run. A word may be in order about the values that attach to repeated visits by the same consultant. Such an arrangement, when the visitor has initially demonstrated his capacity to be helpful, has several advantages. Mutual understanding originally attained can be capitalized and increased. The second and succeeding consultations can pick up promptly where the preceding ones left off. Moreover, the prospect of a consultant's return increases the likelihood that any given visit will conclude with definite agreements as to next steps and that these agreements will be carried out.

It should be said that in any case such agreements may well mark the conclusion of a consultation. They should ordinarily constitute the goal toward which discussion is directed. What does it seem best to do next? Who should do it? When and how? With what hoped-for results? If the local situation has really been ripe for consultant help, and if the consultation has been skillfully participated in on both sides, agreement respecting these matters will be a normal outcome. If the consultant is to return at a set date, that date becomes a useful deadline for specified action.

It has been found helpful to take special notes on group meetings in which a consultant participates and to draft a statement of agreements reached as to principles to be relied upon or actions to be taken. Frequently, moreover, reports prepared by the visitor after his departure have proved very valuable. In this way it has been possible to obtain the consultant's considered and systematic analysis of the situation with which he has been asked to help, and a careful formulation of his suggestions. It is desirable that all such documents should be explicit as to what the next steps should be, when they should be taken, and by whom. In cases where the same consultant is repeatedly employed, it will be natural, at each fresh visit, to review these commitments, evaluate their consequences, and formulate further plans accordingly.

The Commission's experience convinced it of the great value of consultant relationships of the sort described above. It saw that value demonstrated not only among school systems but also in situations at the college and university level. Consulting provided a peculiarly effective means of getting practical advantage from the special knowledge and understanding of persons not regular members of a working group. It stimulated, helped bring about local agreement, served as a spur to considered action. The cost was slight compared with the results—or with other investments more hallowed by tradition but frequently less productive.

To the consultants themselves, and to the institutions they represented, many advantages accrued. Close contact with practical situations, for example, provided the experts with opportunity for the continual testing and correction of theoretical formulations. The teaching and writing of such individuals accordingly benefited. Moreover, some of those consulted were stimulated to arrange for more intensive work with the visitors at summer sessions or more lengthy attendance at the colleges or universities where the latter were active. When this occurred it was found that previous contacts had laid the basis for unusually fruitful relations.

The Commission believes, accordingly, that the use of outside consultants and the provision of consultant services should be extended. It recommends definite budgetary allowance to this end and facilitation by the colleges, universities, state departments of education, and other agencies from whose staffs effective consultants are most likely to be drawn. These institutions might well encourage the development of requisite skills. It would also be helpful if some means might be found of aiding groups that want consultant assistance to locate persons of demonstrated capacity for such work.

Workshops: setup and administration

Study groups during the academic year and the use of outside consultants have great value, but they suffer from one inescapable limitation: that of available time. The summer workshop, a complementary device widely employed in the cooperative study, overcomes this difficulty.[13] It enables teachers to work intensively on their problems over a period of weeks when school is not in session and with expert assistance continuously available. The workshop in a variety of forms has convincingly demonstrated its value for the education of teachers in service.[14]

A workshop is planned to provide a situation in which teachers may work intensively on problems growing out of their professional situations and so make progress toward the more effective discharge of their professional functions. The focus on problems implies a considerable degree of individualization and a definite pointing toward change of practice. Learning about is related to planning to do. The problem that serves as a starting point may be essentially individual: for example, how to improve a course over which the particular teacher has a high degree of personal control. Or it may be a larger matter, a question, say, of some general curricular adjustment, decision respecting which must be participated in by members of a group. In the latter case individual workshop participants naturally consider themselves representative of others who expect to benefit at second hand from their experiences. Frequently, however, delegations from a given school or system have come to a workshop bringing with them a common problem for joint attack, and on occasion whole school staffs have attended. In such instances the likelihood that plans developed at the workshop will be promptly acted upon in the working situation is naturally enhanced.

[13] For further treatment of this topic see *Teacher Education in Service*, Chapter V; *The College and Teacher Education*, pp. 222–29; and *Evaluation in Teacher Education*, pp. 327–48; and likewise K. L. Heaton, W. G. Camp, and P. B. Diederich, *Professional Education for Experienced Teachers* (Chicago: University of Chicago Press, 1940).

[14] The term "workshop," which has achieved great popularity in educational circles in the course of the last ten years, has been applied to events widely varying in character. The unfortunate result has been a considerable degree of confusion and misunderstanding: it would be helpful if the use of the term could be limited to occasions similar in their characteristics to those about to be described and analyzed. It was to such occasions that the term was originally applied by the Progressive Education Association, whose leadership in workshop development was inherited by the Commission's workshop advisory service. To say this is not, of course, to imply that other types of educational event that have called themselves workshops have not been valuable educationally.

Nearly half of the school systems in the cooperative study organized their own summer workshops and all sent representatives to those operated on various university campuses. Each type had its advantages. For example, the home workshops made possible the participation of larger proportions of local teachers, while those elsewhere provided for more contact with representatives of other situations. Campus workshops promise to become regular features of college and university summer sessions, increasing in number. But only the larger school systems can hope to maintain their own workshops year after year; smaller systems could not annually attract sufficient attendance.

In the cooperative study four to six weeks was the usual workshop period, though there were variations in both directions. It is doubtful if the briefer ones were able to realize all of the potential values of workshop experience. Sometimes the appeal of a given workshop was limited to particular groups or attention was restricted to particular topics; in other instances attendants constituted a more heterogeneous body and the problems studied varied a great deal. The same is seen to be the case when workshops other than those directly sponsored by the Commission are examined. There have been those arranged solely for elementary, for secondary school, or for college teachers; some have dealt exclusively with the problems of principals. There have been others concerned solely with child growth and development, with some particular recognized field of high school instruction, or with such special interests as intergroup relations. But there have also been workshops (and this was usually true in the case of those sponsored by the Commission) that attracted people from various teaching and administrative categories concerned with a wide range of subject matter and other educational problems. Each type has proved to have advantages for particular purposes. All have had certain common characteristics that justify generalization.

Workshop staff members should possess wide knowledge, theoretical grasp, and practical understanding. Equally important, and harder to obtain, is experience in working on a genuinely give-and-take basis. To a considerable extent, a workshop as a whole has to be created as it proceeds, by staff and student members cooperating. Moreover, in working with individuals and small groups of attendants it is essential that the staff be able to find common ground, establish a friendly atmosphere conducive to a two-way flow of ideas, and enlarge the willingness of those they aid to trust themselves and act courageously upon their convictions. Staff members who have been accustomed to operating more or less independently within predetermined and familiar patterns, to offering "their own" courses, to presenting their own systematic and often highly theoretical formulations of subject matter and leaving it largely to their students to make applications to their particular situations, often find workshop methods trying and even confusing. Many have successfully made the adjustment, however, and, as a result, have found new and greater satisfactions in a teaching-learning situation which is more participant, more dynamic, and more influential upon action than that with which they have been familiar. Persons who have been successful as consultants have, for obvious reasons, proved particularly successful as workshop staff members—the reverse being equally true.

It has been found valuable to bring a staff together several days before the formal opening of a workshop. Opportunity is thus provided for study of the records and statements of purpose of those who are to participate, for discussion of general workshop policy and further development of plans, for laying foundations of mutual understanding and regard, for checking and preparing facilities, for getting set to go. However, the preliminary character of this activity is customarily recognized, and responsibility for continuous planning is transferred, as soon as possible, to a committee on which workshop attendants as well as staff members are represented. The members of this planning committee keep their ears to the ground, hear complaints, receive suggestions, consider ways and means of effecting improvement, convey proposals to individuals, and make decisions bearing on general matters. Of course, separate staff meetings are also held at frequent intervals during the workshop period. On these occasions progress is evaluated, suggestions for improvement are weighed, individual difficulties are reported and suggestions for overcoming them are offered, and the needs of particular participants and ways and means of better serving them are considered.

Workshops: program and methods

The first few days, even the first week, of a workshop are likely to be devoted to orientation and exploration. Small groups of individuals with similar purposes are formed under staff leadership. Here, and also in personal conferences with one or more staff members, working problems are described, available resources are examined, and plans for individual and group activities are refined. Invariably some participants are hazy about the tasks they wish to tackle, while others have too limited vision. It takes time to deal thoughtfully with all such considerations, to look into them together, and to agree upon the best possible aims under all the circumstances and the best possible procedure for attaining these aims.

The pattern of activities designed to forward professional concerns naturally varies from workshop to workshop and from individual to individual within a particular workshop. The most usual elements, however, are group meetings, individual conferences, and independent study. Special-interest groups sometimes find it helpful to hold daily meetings with their leaders throughout the entire workshop period, but sometimes it seems better to meet less often, or to subdivide, or even after a time to disband. Moreover, it is always possible to form new groups after the workshop is under way if further contacts among participants, further definition of needs, and increased understanding of available resources reveal the advantage of such procedure. The flexibility that all this implies is an essential element in good workshop practice.

Ordinarily each participant is assigned to some one staff member for continuous guidance. But others are available for conference purposes, and sometimes more work may be done with one of these than with the official adviser. Not infrequently a participant finds close association with some fellow attendant —some person of more or differing experience or of greater insight and analytical powers—to be particularly valuable. Indeed, the character of a successful workshop is such that all present, students and staff alike, may teach as well as learn.

As has already been implied, workshops have seldom offered courses of systematic lectures or comparable formal instruction. A few, however, have found it profitable to make something of this character available or to advise certain participants to take advantage of opportunities of this nature offered in the regular summer session on the same campus. This has been true at the workshop on human growth and development at the University of Chicago, for example, where several short series of lectures presenting basic scientific concepts proved useful. It seems clear that such experience may be the most effective means for some teachers at some times to increase their ability to perform their professional tasks well. The main thing here, as with all other aspects of a workshop program, is that each participant's personal share of responsibility for identifying his own problems, recognizing his own needs, charting his own course, framing and carrying through his own plan of professional action should be understood and, indeed, emphasized. Thus, his independent activity is of central importance. It will be influenced (but not thereby made less his own) by the friendly advice and criticism of others and by stimulating contacts with records of thought and experience.

This leads to reference to the importance of nonhuman resources at workshops. While personal contacts are emphasized, this does not imply any idea that they are all that is necessary. Library facilities are essential. A great deal of reading is done, more, many workshop members have testified, than at usual summer sessions. Such reading feeds discussion in groups and conferences, where it is critically treated. Staff members and fellow students offer suggestions for its extension. The range is customarily from theoretical treatises to simple accounts of actual practice in particular teaching situations.

Films and recordings are also often available. In many cases, moreover, opportunity is provided for observation in adjacent schools and for excursions to surrounding communities.

During the workshop period a series of general meetings is usually held. Some of these are devoted to the consideration of questions of workshop operation, some to good fellowship, and some to listening to speeches and panel presentations or to the general discussion of matters of professional or broader concern. Numerous problems are involved in planning meetings of the last type, for example, selecting subjects, deciding how often meetings will be held, and choosing speakers and panel participants. It is perhaps well not to arrange very many in advance. The workshop planning committee, once established, can best gauge the demand, and speakers are ordinarily not too difficult to obtain. The workshop group itself provides a first resource, the staff of the host institution another, and there are often present distinguished visitors who may be drafted. The traditional notion that higher education is chiefly a matter of listening to lectures needs to be guarded against. On the other hand, occasional addresses, especially those of the stimulating, sight-lifting sort, have proved very worth while.

As a workshop draws to a close, participants are ordinarily expected to evaluate their experience and formulate their views regarding the progress they have made. Since most of them will have been engaged on problems growing out of their regular working situations, documentary evidence of accomplishment in the way of course units developed or other types of written plan for action to be taken in the fall is likely to be available. These may be individual or, in the case of committees of colleagues working together, group products. In any case, such papers, as well as impressions formed in the intimacy of workshop relationships, provide participants and staff alike with the means of estimating quantity and quality of accomplishment. Such evaluation is important both to those responsible for the conduct of the workshop, in that revealed strengths and weaknesses may lead to improvements another year, and to individual participants. It is worth while for each attendant to be able to estimate his progress, and to the staff this is necessary if questions of granting credit must be considered.[15]

The novel character of much in workshop practice has caused some issues to be raised regarding graduate school credit for such experience. These issues seem now to have been settled favorably by most of the outstanding graduate schools, although it is still customary to place some limits on the amount of workshop credit that can be counted toward fulfillment of requirements for advanced degrees. The testimony of most participants has been that their workshop experience has contributed more to their professional growth than other comparable forms of in-service teacher education. If we believe such contribution to be the test of workshop education, and if we are prepared to trust the judgment of the individuals most concerned—confirmed, it may be added, by the later judgment of their colleagues and administrative associates—university recognition of the value of such work seems wholly justified. It is worth mentioning that a surprisingly large proportion of workshop attendants have not been interested in credit.

Workshops: other aspects

Something should be said of the significance of some of the seemingly less serious characteristics of workshop practice. Planners of workshops have deliberately sought locations where comfort and beauty were assured; they have concerned themselves with provisions for recreation and informal social contacts; they have arranged things so that getting acquainted would be easy and natural. All this has been done with a purpose. The relationship essential to cooperative accomplishment is that of mutual understanding and trust. The achievement of such a relationship is more likely when conditions are conducive to friendliness. Observers have noted that workshops often breed informality of garb and of address. These things are by no means essential to successful workshop experience but they may be a natural consequence of the relations that should be established.

[15] For further treatment of evaluation at workshops see *Evaluation in Teacher Education*, pp. 327–48.

The reader will recall what was said in the preceding chapter about the role of the arts in teacher education. In all of the workshops with which the Commission was associated provision was made for art activities. There were various reasons for this. It was felt that activities such as painting, modeling, weaving, dancing, music making, and the like would provide a superior type of recreation and contribute to the process of getting acquainted. It was believed that teachers, in common with most contemporaries in other fields, are skewed on the analytical and verbal sides, and that experience in creation through the use of media other than words would tend to restore the balance. And it was thought that many teachers would benefit professionally from learning at first hand what children experience when they attempt artistic expression, thus gaining understanding that would enable them to assist such children even though they were not art teachers. This aspect of workshop programs proved very popular. An informal appraisal established the value of the experience for the release of tensions and promotion of friendly acquaintance.[16] While other outcomes were not so demonstrable the Commission has no doubt of the desirability of continuing to promote art interests at workshops.

Workshops with which the Commission had most to do fitted with great success into the patterns established by other procedures for the facilitation of teacher growth in service. Indeed, they were essential to the full development of such patterns. It was customary, in the cooperative study, for key members of local planning committees, policies councils, and study groups to give a summer to workshop attendance. Often, as has been noted, delegations would attend bringing with them shared responsibilities. During the regular school year matters calling for more intensive study than was possible while classes were being conducted were earmarked for attack at workshops. An effort would then be made to select the most appropriate persons to devote their energies to such affairs. Thus, workshop activities tended to grow out of term-time activities. Thus, too, they tended to contribute definitely to activities planned for the

[16] See *Teachers Enjoy the Arts.*

ensuing year. Continuity of thought and action was promoted. Such continuity was increased when the same college and university representatives served both as consultants to given school systems and as staff members at workshops serving those systems.

One of the very significant consequences of workshop experience has been the development of new leadership. Recognized leaders have increased their powers of helpfulness. But teachers who had previously exercised limited influence in their home situations have also returned from workshops with ideas, enthusiasm, and skill in group methods that have resulted in their rapidly becoming stimulating forces making for general improvement. There is no doubt that on almost every school system staff there are unrecognized persons who, if their imagination could be touched and their courage kindled, would emerge as new and challenging voices. The fact that so many former workshop members have attained this role is one convincing evidence of the value of workshop experience.

Other techniques employed

The most generally used elements in the in-service programs developed by the school systems that participated in the cooperative study have now been described and analyzed. Certain other techniques that proved their usefulness will be more briefly dealt with. These are conferences and the sending of staff members to the Commission's collaboration center on child growth and development. It will be seen how these activities, too, fitted into the sort of pattern that has been presented above.

A considerable number of the school systems in the cooperative study held conferences of various sorts. A number of the smaller systems arranged for their total staffs to come together for several days before the opening of school in the fall. One large city experimented successfully with a three-day conference held during the school year and attended by 20 percent of the teachers, chosen by lot. These were general-purpose conferences. But there were others that were related to particular concerns. Five affiliated systems, for example, sent some 250 classroom

teachers, principals, supervisors, and other administrative officers to a resort hotel for several days to consider a variety of
problems relating to personnel. Perhaps the day-long meetings
in one system that were devoted to keeping the entire teaching
staff in touch with the work of the local planning committee
and with the developing program of in-service education might
also be classified as conferences.

A detailed consideration of conference procedures will be
offered in the succeeding chapter.[17] Although the conferences
there treated will differ in certain respects from those employed
by single school systems the technical principles set forth will be
highly relevant to the latter. It need only be noted here, therefore, that these principles will prove to be similar to the ones
that have already been set forth as sound in the case of study
groups and workshops. A good conference will have definite
purposes, bear a clear relation to other activities, be carefully
planned, provide for a maximum of participation, have its lighter
moments, and avoid pressing prematurely for formal commitments. Such a conference can make a very useful contribution to
an ongoing program of teacher education in service.

The Commission's collaboration center on child growth and
development provided a very intensive study experience, during
the course of the cooperative study, for a necessarily limited
number of college, university, and school system representatives.
This center was established at the University of Chicago under
the direction of a Commission staff member. Gathered together
there was an extensive collection of research materials bearing
on the growth and development of human beings and representing the results of research in various of the biological,
psychological, and social sciences. These materials were intensively studied, during each of two years, by a group consisting
of several staff members and approximately twenty collaborators
annually.

The aim of study at the center was threefold: first, to attempt
a synthesis of the contributions of the various sciences as they
related to child growth and development; second, to tease out

[17] See pp. 218–26.

the implications of these findings for the educational process; and finally, to enable collaborators to work out plans for improvements in their own working situations. Group methods of study were relied upon. Presentations were made to the whole body of collaborators by various of its own members, by regular staff members, and by outside scholars invited in for the purpose. Committees were organized to work on problems of synthesization and to develop statements respecting educational implications.[18] Individuals worked vigorously on the tasks they had brought with them from their places of employment. College and university representatives were likely to be developing plans for new courses or curricular reorganization. Collaborators from school systems were usually central-office persons, occupying key positions and preparing to extend and strengthen their services to classroom teachers upon their return from the center. Such persons naturally became leaders in local child-study groups and in curricular reorganization.

The collaboration center was in many ways similar to a workshop. It differed from many workshops, however, in that it had a single focus and a dominant element of advanced subject-matter analysis. It was not designed for classroom teachers but for college professors and key administrative figures in school systems. It proved a very effective device for the purposes for which it was designed, and would appear to the Commission to be capable of adaptation to other fields than that of child growth and development—say to social understanding.

The collaboration center in child growth and development has now become a central element in a program whereby the University of Chicago is aiding in the further development of programs of child study in an increasing number of school systems. Other elements in that program are a summer workshop and an extensive consulting service. It is to be hoped that similar programs will be developed at other universities.

[18] For publications emerging from the collaboration center, see the bibliography in the appendix.

SIGNIFICANT TRENDS

The Commission believes that it is possible to identify a number of broad trends respecting the in-service education of teachers, trends that deserve encouragement. The similarity of many of these to developments in the field of teacher preparation is not surprising.[19] The education of teachers, pre-service and in-service, is properly a continuous process. It is natural and desirable that at both stages of the process the same general aims should be recognized and the same basic ideas respecting ways of working employed.

The school systems in the cooperative study were, like the colleges and universities, striving to increase institutional unity. They were seeking to achieve a better balance of centralization and decentralization. Democratic participation in the determination of general policies was being fostered and, at the same time, more opportunity for freedom of experimentation by individuals and groups was being provided. Group methods were being increasingly employed. Cooperation in related thought and action was being emphasized, with the focus of attention being the recognized need in the working situation.

Sensitivity to the importance of the human factor was mounting. Respect for personality and an understanding of human needs were seen as essential to program improvement. For a teacher to make the most of the powers he already possesses and to seek to increase those powers, he must have a sense of being respected as a person and of being able to contribute to the improvement of the common enterprise. Teachers in service respond to opportunities to pool their ideas and to act responsibly as free men voluntarily bound by agreements in the formulation of which they have shared.

Another striking trend was that toward using jobs recognized as needing to be done as the starting points for study leading to action. The very nature of these tasks, complex and dynamic, makes for cooperation and for thinking that focuses on process rather than drives for abstraction from reality. In this way the

[19] Compare Chapter II, pp. 109–12.

traditional conflict between the intellectual and practical approaches tends to be resolved. Practitioners, dissatisfied with things as they are, are encouraged and helped to utilize all available thinking power to the end of improvement; those who are gifted in speculation are required to submit their ideas and principles to the impartial test of practical application.

All this is relevant to the further trend toward seeing the school system itself as the focal center for the in-service education of teachers. Such a view recognizes the capacity of the individual teacher for continuous professional development and the significance of the working situation as stimulus and field of operation. The Commission is fully convinced that school system leaders must and will increasingly see the significance of this trend, and act to further it. Superintendents should accept leadership in the development of programs of the sort described in this chapter as one of their most important responsibilities. This statement has obvious implications for the education and selection of school administrators.

The development of system-centered programs of in-service education calls for appropriate budgetary provisions. In the past such education has been viewed as fundamentally an affair of the individual teacher. Costs were to be borne by that individual, though encouragement in the form of salary increases conditional upon the achievement of a bachelor's or master's degree was provided. This system has become less efficient as more and more teachers have met the requirements. But it is subject to more fundamental criticisms. It carries the implication that there is a point at which teacher education may be considered completed. It ignores the importance of group endeavor as a means to program improvement and professional growth. It determines who shall do what in terms of individual financial capacity rather than of personal suitability for the experience and of prospective advantage to the system.

The precedent for the sort of development that is recommended is the provision of supervisory leadership. This is customary, and it is accepted as proper that the expense should be provided for in city, county, and state educational budgets.

It is quite as justifiable that similar provision should be made for such purposes as the following: the release of teacher time for participation in important group activities; the purchase of books, supplies, and clerical aid for the benefit of planning committees, study groups, and workshops; the employment of consultant services; the operation of local conferences and workshops; the sending of teachers to significant conferences and workshops held elsewhere; the sending of key persons to collaboration centers or other places where their capacity for local leadership can be enlarged. The Commission has noted with approval a definite tendency (and not only in the school systems with which it was associated) toward the increase of budgetary provisions for purposes of this sort. It believes and hopes that this tendency will continue. Such provision may be expected to pay impressive dividends. It should be noted that a great increase over what is at present customary for such purposes would still affect total school budgets to only a minor degree.

Something should now be said respecting the emergent role of the colleges and universities in programs for the in-service education of teachers.[20] The Commission does not believe that the taking of increasing responsibility for such programs by school systems will weaken that role. It will unquestionably modify it but it will also almost certainly increase its significance. It will make for a greater degree of functional relationship between the schools and the institutions of higher education. Thus, a trend already noted in the chapter on teacher preparation will receive further support. The consequences can only be to the advantage of teacher education, both pre-service and in-service.

It is not being suggested that the traditional methods of the colleges and universities in the in-service field are likely to be wholly abandoned, or that this would be desirable. As the holding of a bachelor's degree comes closer and closer to becoming a universal requirement for admission to teaching the

[20] See also *The College and Teacher Education*, Chapter VII and pp. 310–11, and *State Programs for the Improvement of Teacher Education*, Part Four.

number of experienced teachers taking summer, evening, and extension courses in order to complete undergraduate programs is, of course, bound to dwindle. The demand for graduate instruction leading to the master's degree, however, is likely to increase. A proportion of this instruction, varying according to the needs of the particular teacher, can certainly be given better on the campus. It will undoubtedly be desirable for some of this to be organized in course units, although it may be hoped that more courses can be organized in clearer relation to the professional needs of those who take them.

But it seems evident that experience of the workshop type is destined to receive growing recognition as a ·desirable and, indeed, essential element in programs of graduate study for teachers in service. This will be true not only in the case of the summer workshops organized by the universities on their own campuses. School systems that set up local workshops have found it possible to arrange with neighboring institutions for assistance in planning the program and for granting credit to participating teachers to whom such credit is important. Moreover, mention needs here to be made of the development by several universities of field services to school systems with in-service programs. These involve the organization of study groups by a particular school system or cluster of systems in conjunction with some nearby university. Meetings are held periodically for a semester, sometimes every week, sometimes every other week. A four-hour period on Saturdays has often been selected. University staff representatives have served continuously as consultants. Decisions as to what teachers should participate, what problems should be dealt with, and how programs should be planned have been cooperatively arrived at by methods already described in connection with earlier discussion in this chapter. Costs have been borne by the school systems or shared between them and the teachers concerned. The universities have endeavored to keep their charges at a minimum.

It is to be hoped that a movement will develop to provide assistance in in-service programs by universities at reduced charges. During the war, when enrollments at institutions of higher learning were sharply reduced, some states adopted policies whereby field services by staff members in state-controlled colleges and universities were made available without or at a minimum charge. Continuation of such policies should be carefully considered. So far as privately controlled institutions are concerned, it should be noted that these have traditionally been accustomed to allocating income from endowment exclusively to the support of undergraduate and other on-campus term-time programs; summer-session and extension courses and the like have been expected to pay their own way. This has meant relatively high charges for services that have constituted a major portion of university work in the in-service field. While the historical reasons for this discriminatory practice are clear enough, it is hard to see that it has any logical justification. Some tendency to correct the situation is discernible, and this tendency deserves encouragement. It may be added that there is also a distinct trend toward charging at a lower rate when academic credit is not desired. This seems a wholly logical arrangement. When universities provide noncredit services at less than cost, when school systems pay the resultant charges, and when individual teachers make up the difference required if credit is to be granted, a reasonably fair division of burden would seem likely to have been achieved.

No question of academic credit emerges when college and university faculty members provide consultant services to study groups and at conferences. Such services, however, constitute an important contribution by institutions of higher education to programs of teacher education in service. This importance, together with the values of the experience to the consultants and hence to the institutions they represent, justify deliberate attention to the development of consulting skill.

The promotion of in-service programs by school systems tends to make for clearer and more continuous relations between those systems and particular colleges or universities. Teachers who have had a rewarding experience at a campus workshop, for example, tend to seek further help from its staff members in the form of consultant service, and if distances are favorable a formal field-service arrangement may be worked out with the university. A more effective integration of the various parts of the program may then readily come about. It must evidently be advantageous when workshop participants have had a chance to think out their plans in advance with staff members who are familiar with the working situations from which the participants come.

A school system may, however, properly be hesitant about putting all of its eggs in the basket of one particular institution. It may feel that better help for certain purposes is available elsewhere. Its teachers may have associations in many places or be eager to experience new contacts. There are thus valid reasons for avoiding too exclusive a commitment in any one direction. Institutional rivalries may also constitute a factor of some importance in the situation. Difficulties, for example, have arisen when teachers who are working for an advanced degree at a given institution have wanted to transfer credit granted for activity at summer workshops or in field service carried on under other auspices. One reason for this, of course, is that activities of this nature are still relatively novel: an institution that is accustomed to recognizing credit granted for course work done elsewhere may be hesitant about workshop credit if it itself has not developed this sort of program. Such problems are steadily being ironed out.

There is some prospect, indeed, that a new degree of cooperation between colleges and universities will develop. For example, a certain school system that relied chiefly upon the services of a neighboring university felt that it needed to turn to a far distant institution for help on one particular set of problems. In order to facilitate this arrangement the nearby graduate school arranged to designate the chief consultant from the distant campus as a visiting professor on its own staff. There may, then, be a trend in the direction of increasing interinstitutional cooperation of this sort in the interest of meeting with maximum effectiveness the growth needs of particular school systems and their teachers.

SUMMARY

The Commission's conclusions, based on its experiences with the in-service education of teachers, may now be summarized as follows:

1. If the full potentialities created by proper selection and preparation of teachers are to be realized, and if children at any given time and place are to receive the best teaching possible, it is essential that the conditions under which teaching is done should be conducive to the full realization of each teacher's existing powers. If these powers are to increase steadily —as it is both possible and desirable that they should do—the working situation should be further conducive to continuous personal and professional development. The school system is central to the in-service education of teachers, and provisions for such education are essential to a good system.

2. Democratic theory and practical experience both point to the conclusion that the improvement of teaching on the job requires that teachers share responsibly in planning and carrying out program improvements. Group activities designed to bring about such improvements have proved particularly effective in leading to teacher growth.

3. Such group activities today deserve particular encouragement and support as complements to more familiar, and more individualistic, means of teacher education in service. Individual efforts at personal and professional self-improvement, through continued study (formal and informal), travel, summer work experience, participation in community affairs, and the like, remain important. Contemporary circumstances, however, justify special attention to cooperative endeavors.

4. A better balance of centralization and decentralization in school systems—democratic determination of fundamental policies at the center coupled with maximum freedom within the resultant framework for particular teachers and schools—is required if teaching is to be most effective throughout a system. If through sharing in their determination teachers understand and accept basic policies and a broad framework for operation, they can be trusted independently to act in ways consistent

therewith. Through such action all available power for program improvement can achieve expression.

5. Every effort should be made to attract as large a proportion of teachers as possible to participation in group activities designed to improve the local educational program. This means that tasks that seem both appropriate and important must be available; opportunities must be present for each participant to make a positive contribution; participants must feel free to modify goals or even abandon their efforts if experience indicates the wisdom of such steps; a spirit of friendly equality must be developed within each group; and conditions must be favorable for a relatively easy movement from the thinking to the doing stage.

6. Participation in group activities should be voluntary; if conditions conducive to volunteering exist, response will be satisfactorily general; if not, forced participation will fail to yield successful results.

7. Wise administrative leadership is of key importance for the development of effective local programs of teacher education in service. Essential in leaders are human understanding, a clear grasp of the dynamics of the local situation, a keen sense of timing, ability to distinguish between stimulation and driving, and faith in the democratic process.

8. Representative school policies councils have demonstrated their value as devices for the sharing of policy-making and administrative functions. They have enabled good ideas to obtain a hearing, whatever their source; they have prevented unrealistic decisions; they have increased understanding, acceptance, and suitable behavior on the part of those through whose actions policies must be implemented.

9. Planning committees have proved very effective for guiding the strategy of in-service programs of teacher education. It has not been found satisfactory, however, for them to attempt to serve as legislative or administrative bodies. Their best function has been to stimulate and facilitate the activity of study groups, workshops, and conferences with due regard both to pressing local needs and to the concerns particularly felt by the teachers.

10. Such committees have been most effective when their members have achieved esprit de corps and ability to think readily in systemwide terms. It has not proved essential that they should be strictly representative or that there should be rapid rotation in membership. A membership of ten to twelve appears to be ideal.

11. Successful planning committees have not found it necessary to exercise control over all in-service activities, or even to maintain close contact with them. Decentralization has proved more effective. Intermediary bodies, representing school levels, for example, have sometimes been useful.

12. An important function of planning committees has been the maintenance of channels of communication. Written reports have proved less successful as means of keeping all teachers informed about in-service programs than have occasional meetings of the entire staff organized into small groups.

13. Planning committees and central-office personnel can perform a valuable service by facilitating the spread of ideas and practices introduced and tested at particular points. Opportunities for general consideration of outcomes may be helpfully provided, and steps looking to widespread adoption given approval and support.

14. Study groups during the school year are the most important feature of any system-centered program of in-service education; they provide an ideal means for widespread participation by teachers.

15. Such groups, in the Commission's experience, successfully served many different purposes: they studied child growth and development, local communities and the broader social scene, curricular and instructional problems, articulation between levels in a school system, teacher welfare and staff personnel, teacher-pupil relations, school-community relations, and also subjects of personal interest. They led to changes that represented program improvements.

16. Such program improvements were most significant when the participants in group study had rich association with the

children and adults of their community, and with important social ideas and ideals.

17. According to their purposes study groups may properly be variously constituted. Some in the cooperative study were made up of classroom teachers from particular grade levels or of particular subjects. Groups consisting of teachers from a given building were often especially effective. Sometimes cross-sectional groupings proved most fruitful. Principals, supervisors, and other representatives of the central office often took part in groups of these several sorts, on occasion formed groups of their own. Laymen were sometimes included and proved valuable members.

18. Effective group study invariably involves reading and discussion and may include the gathering of special data, direct work with children or the community, or comparable activities.

19. Leadership resources can usually be developed satisfactorily by each group, with supplementation from elsewhere within the school system. Supervisors and other local staff members, including classroom teachers with special knowledge or skill, have proved to be valuable resources, serving in consultant fashion.

20. Outside consultants too have been very helpful to study groups. Such persons should be carefully selected because of expertness relevant to local needs and because of their ability to work effectively in consultant capacity. This latter includes skill in sizing up local situations, capacity to operate in terms of that situation, and effectiveness in the rapid establishment of good human relations.

21. It is important that the decision to employ a consultant should be made, or at least honestly approved, by the group that he is to serve, that his visit should be carefully planned and prepared for, and that he should be given full preliminary information. Adequate time should be allowed for any visit. Repeated use, at intervals, of the services of the same consultant have often proved of particular value.

22. Self-evaluation is an important part of the group-study process, and groups should be free to modify their directions in the light of evaluative findings.

23. Successful group study requires that good human relations within the group be developed and maintained: the emotional climate should be conducive to general participation and to free exchange and examination of views. Group members of superior status have special responsibility for the creation of such a climate.

24. It is essential that groups find it possible to move fairly easily from discussion to action. It is important that administrators should provide groups with information that will protect them from reaching impractical conclusions, and that on the other hand they should give groups all possible assistance in putting carefully thought-out conclusions to experimental test.

25. Local conferences, when arranged to focus on topics of concern to teachers and to provide these with maximum opportunity for participation, have demonstrated their value as parts of in-service programs. Some have proved helpful in spreading understanding of such programs to all staff members. Others have usefully been limited to particular problems, with attendants appropriately selected. Conferences of several days' duration, held just before the opening of school, have been particularly valuable.

26. Summer workshops have been outstandingly helpful as elements in programs of in-service education for teachers. They make possible intensive work on tasks drawn from teaching situations by individuals and groups of teachers, through an extended period of uninterrupted time, in stimulating circumstances, and under expert guidance. Such workshops have been successfully organized locally by particular school systems and, also, by colleges and universities, on state, regional, and nationwide bases. They may be limited to particular topics or types of educational worker, or they may be set up to meet a wide range of needs and appeal to a considerable variety of attendants.

27. Good workshop arrangements are marked by flexibility whereby plans are subject to continuous modification, by staff members and attendants working together, as dictated by the latter's needs, the availability of resources, and emergent insights. Group discussion, individual consultation, and inde-

pendent study are chiefly relied upon; formal presentations are rarely used and then only for special purposes.

28. Workshop staff members need to couple expert knowledge and broad experience with skill as consultants and as group workers.

29. The most successful workshops have had strong library resources, access to relevant films and recordings, available opportunities for direct experiences in schools and communities, studios where attendants could engage in art activities, and attractive and comfortable, if simple, living conditions conducive to the ripening of friendly acquaintance.

30. Workshop participation has proved particularly effective when it has been related to other in-service activities, when, for example, attendants have come as representatives of study groups in their school systems and have been expected to return with new powers of leadership. Consultants to study groups have had certain advantages as workshop staff members.

31. Evidence of the value of attendance at properly conducted workshops is overwhelming, and the practice of granting graduate credit for such attendance has proved wholly justified. To prevent abuses, however, it is important that staff members observe individual progress carefully, and that both they and the attendants evaluate workshop accomplishments thoroughly.

32. The Commission's collaboration center in child growth and development demonstrated the effectiveness of an adaptation of workshop technique during the regular academic year, with reference to a particular body of scholarly research findings and for the benefit of college and university professors and school system leaders. This technique appears to be wholly adaptable to other fields of study related to teacher education.

33. Colleges, universities, and their staff members have important roles to play in the in-service education of teachers. In addition to offering on-campus instruction at the graduate and —decreasingly—undergraduate levels they are developing workshops and other new services related to in-service programs promoted by particular school systems. A commendable example would be field consultant services. All such tendencies to

provide help in relation to and at the point of need deserve encouragement.

34. System-centered in-service programs raise new problems of financing. The logic of the development points to the appropriation of additional funds by school boards. A substantial and rapid movement in this direction is, indeed, eminently desirable. Simultaneously, universities should move to reduce charges for their services to teachers and school systems by increased appropriations for such purposes in the case of state-controlled institutions and by the reallocation of endowment income in other cases. It will remain appropriate, however, for individual teachers to share costs where credit toward degrees is being sought.

35. The tendency toward developing closer working relations between school systems, on the one hand, and the colleges and universities, on the other, in connection with the in-service education of teachers deserves all encouragement, not least because it promises to influence pre-service programs desirably. Experiments in cooperative relations whereby particular school systems may draw on the resources of several graduate institutions are particularly worthy of support.

IV

Improvement through
Interinstitutional Cooperation

TEACHERS ARE PREPARED in particular colleges or universities; they work in particular school systems. In each instance there exists a corporate entity with a limited geographical base functioning through a definite body of persons. The quality of teacher preparation and the degree to which teachers realize and develop their powers on the job depend immediately upon the character of these entities. Particularly significant is the effectiveness of the persons who staff the preparatory institutions or occupy key positions in the schools. In the preceding chapters the importance of such persons creating an institutional unity received particular emphasis. Much attention was given to ways and means whereby faculty members might work more closely, understandingly, and effectively as a team. In the case of school systems the importance of such teamwork was equally stressed. The values of respect for personality, of group methods of operation, of a balance between centralization and decentralization, and of a common focus on the needs of persons, schools, and communities were repeatedly noted.

The Commission has emphasized the fact that improvements in teacher education ultimately require changes in the particular institutions or systems where teachers are being prepared or are engaged in the pursuit of their profession. It believes that if such improvements are to be substantial the changes will have to be the consequence of joint study and action on the part of the staffs of those colleges, universities, and school systems. Hence its special insistence, throughout its work and this report, on local responsibility, local study, local integration, and local action. But the Commission has had no intention of implying that each college, university, or school system should or can operate without relation to other institutions, or that individual staff members do not need contacts with persons from outside their immediate settings. Indeed, the value of school-college relations for the improvement of teacher education throughout its range has been frequently mentioned. And, of course, the very cooperative nature of the national study provided evidence of the Commission's belief in the potential advantages of inter-institutional enterprise. For this chapter, however, has been reserved a systematic examination of the contribution that the Commission's experience showed may come from activities that cut across institutional lines.

Cooperative Enterprise Generally

As an introduction to a more detailed analysis of particular projects that depended on the working together of persons representing different institutions, it will be useful to do two things: first, to consider the possible bases of contact and how the enterprises with which the Commission was associated exemplified these; and second, to discuss what desirable outcomes may reasonably be hoped for as a result of activities of this sort.

Types of relationship

There are four dimensions in terms of which relations that cut across institutional boundaries may be classified. First, there is the geographical basis: participation may usefully be distinguished as national, regional, or statewide in character. Next, consideration must be given to whether the participants are present as individuals or as representatives of schools, colleges, universities, or other agencies. Again, the question of homogeneity versus heterogeneity arises: do those who are working together come from similar specialties or at least similar institutional situations, or is variety in these respects an essential characteristic? And finally, it is important to know the purpose of the enterprise: is it intended merely to provide for mutual education, or is it definitely aimed at some particular kind of action at the points where teacher education must take place?

Various combinations of the above possibilities may be illustrated by the relevant enterprises with which the Commission had contact, and which were referred to in the first chapter of this report. For example, the cooperative study of teacher education itself was national in character; participation was institutional; its members were heterogeneous, representing various types of school system and institution of higher learning; and its central purpose was the encouragement of experimental activity at the places represented. What happened in those places provided the chief basis for what has been said in the two preceding chapters. Later in this chapter further attention will be given to the cooperative aspects of this study.[1]

Even greater space, however, must eventually be devoted to the various statewide studies to which the Commission gave support and which have not yet here received substantial consideration. Participation in these was also mostly institutional in character, at least in theory, although the public school people in question sometimes came in more as individuals. The focus of these studies was on cooperation among colleges and universities, or between these and school systems. All types of institution of higher learning took part—teachers colleges, colleges of liberal arts, vocational schools engaged in teacher education, publicly and privately controlled universities—except that there was one state in which for a period only those places where secondary school teachers were prepared were particularly active. State departments of education also cooperated, frequently providing the leadership, and school systems were brought in though in varying degree. In several states associations of teachers, principals, or supervisors were concerned. In all statewide studies the *purpose* was to bring about changes on the firing line. But, as will be made more evident later on, the exact implications of this purpose and the extent to which it was realized varied somewhat from state to state.[2]

[1] See pp. 187–91.
[2] For details see pp. 208–18.

The national study and the several statewide studies were the cooperative ventures for which the Commission itself had the greatest amount of responsibility. But there were others to which it gave encouragement, financial or moral, that represented contrasting combinations of the dimensions enumerated above. Several of these were regional activities. Among them, the twenty-eight colleges study of the North Central Association of Colleges and Secondary Schools was closest in character to the Commission-sponsored enterprises. Participating institutionally in this were colleges of liberal arts concerned with the education of teachers. This relatively homogeneous, though quite widely scattered, group was specifically interested in stimulating change on the several campuses.

Rather different in character were two cooperative undertakings designed to promote regional uniformity and reciprocity so far as certification requirements for teaching were concerned. One of these was sponsored by the North Central Association, the other by the Southern Association of Colleges and Secondary Schools in conjunction with the Southern University Conference. Officers of state departments of education, faculty members from many colleges and universities, and a considerable variety of school officials took part in these activities, so that various kinds of experience and point of view were represented. Probably only the state departments, however, can be said to have been in these studies institutionally. Certainly the action that it was hoped might result was such as could be taken only by these bodies, though quite as certainly their decisions were bound to be influenced by the judgments of spokesmen for public and higher education and would, in turn, eventually influence practice in the schools, colleges, and universities.

Attention may now again be turned to the national scene for a consideration of two additional projects with which the Commission was associated. The first was the two-week school for executives developed by the American Association of Teachers Colleges. This activity, which was twice carried out and is now scheduled to become a biennial feature of the association's work, represented a novel extension in the program of an organization, membership in which is institutional. The affiliated colleges, invariably represented in association affairs by their administrative heads, constitute a relatively though by no means wholly homogeneous group. The association, in its accrediting and comparable activities, has long undertaken to influence action on the member campuses in definite directions. The school for executives, however, has been viewed as a device for mutual education. It has not been aimed at the formulation of binding agreements; it has rested on the assumption that the participating administrators could be trusted to act, according to their own understanding and the possibilities existing in their own situations, on the ideas formed as a result of their school experience.

There remains to be considered the character of the Council on Cooperation in Teacher Education. This differs from all the other activities mentioned in that its members are neither individuals nor institutions, but voluntary educational associations. All but one of these—there are seventeen—are national in scope, and together they represent a wide range of educational specialties.[3] The basis of membership in several is institutional, as in the case of the associations of teachers colleges, of colleges of liberal arts, of university colleges and departments of education, and of teacher-educating institutions in metropolitan districts. But the majority have individual memberships, being voluntary associations of chief state school officers, of state directors of teacher education and certification, of persons representing various professional specialties at both the school and college levels, or of those with certain other interests. The Council on Cooperation is thus heterogeneous in character. Because of this it has avoided any effort formally to urge action on its member organizations. It has, rather, centered its attention on the promotion of mutual acquaintance and interchange, trusting in the educational value of such experience and in the

[3] For a full list of Council members, see above, p. 47.

probable consequent development of valuable cooperative relationships. [4]

Values of cooperation

The analysis just offered of various group enterprises in teacher education that cut across institutional lines may now be followed by a more explicit consideration of the valuable outcomes to be anticipated from such efforts. Evidently what must be sought after is change of some sort—change that will have the effect of improving the pre-service or in-service education of teachers. The changes to be aimed at may be seen as of three kinds.

First, there is change of individuals. This is always one of the purposes, for even institutional participation in group ventures

[4] Only the national and statewide cooperative studies will be considered in detail in this chapter. Of the other enterprises mentioned, therefore, the following additional remarks may be made.

The North Central Association's study of the preparation of high school teachers in colleges of liberal arts employed techniques very similar to those used in connection with the Commission's studies. It benefited from having a relatively limited geographical base and the sponsorship of an agency with which the participating institutions were long used to working. Upon the completion of an experimental three-year period during which financial contributions by the member colleges had been supplemented by a grant from the General Education Board, the enterprise was not only placed on a wholly self-supporting basis but expanded in size. For a full account of what was accomplished see Russell M. Cooper and others, *Better Colleges—Better Teachers* (The North Central Association Committee on the Preparation of High School Teachers in Liberal Arts Colleges, 1944; distributed by the Macmillan Company).

The two regional studies of uniformity and reciprocity relied chiefly on conference techniques of the sort to be analyzed later in this chapter. A report of the first was published by the North Central Association of Colleges and Secondary Schools in 1941, under the title *A Study of Teacher Certification Conducted and Reported by the Subcommittee on Teacher Certification and Accrediting Agencies*. An account of the other was written and published by the Joint Committee of the Southern University Conference and the Southern Association of Colleges and Secondary Schools. It appeared under the title *A Unified Program of Teacher Education and Certification in the Southern States* (Sewanee, Tenn.: University of the South Press, 1941).

The schools for executives of the American Association of Teachers Colleges were, in effect, extended working conferences. A full report of the first was published by the Commission as *The School for Executives* (Washington: American Council on Education, 1942). The Council on Cooperation in Teacher Education, sponsored by the American Council, has worked through annual meetings of official delegates and ex-officio representatives of the member organizations. In 1943 it held a two-week conference attended by such persons. For a fuller account of the Council on Cooperation see the annual reports of the president of the American Council on Education for 1942–43, 1943–44, and 1944–45.

must be carried out through individuals, and it is only through effects on these persons that any larger consequences may be realized. But only sometimes does the interest of the inter-institutional undertaking come to rest at this point. More frequently, as was noted above, the hope is that the individual participants may be influential representatives of their working situations, and hence that the consequences of the joint activity will be institutional change. Here a distinction must be made. Sometimes the kind of institutional change that may ensue is not a matter of common concern, so long as it represents intelligent experimentation in the particular situation. This was true, for example, in the case of the Commission's national study, which was marked by no drive in the direction of uniformity. Second, a major aim may be institutional agreement, for example, the adoption of common principles of teacher education or even of broadly similar patterns of instruction. Such was one purpose of most of the statewide studies although, as will be made clearer later on, room for individual variation was always preserved.

Finally, the aim occasionally is to bring about changes in the relations existing among institutions, to develop more effective patterns of cooperation among parts of a state's system of higher education, or between colleges and universities on the one hand and school systems on the other. Of course, the several purposes listed are by no means mutually exclusive, but it is helpful to distinguish them. It may be added that it is harder to bring about institutional or interinstitutional changes, and that when these are desired the organization of the joint enterprise and the methods employed by it need to be adapted to such ends.

With these preliminary analyses completed, closer attention may now be given to the cooperative enterprises with which the Commission was most intimately associated. The aim will be to appraise their values, to examine the problems that arise when such efforts are made, to describe certain techniques of operation that were, in practice, found to be fruitful, and to offer suitable recommendations.

THE NATIONAL COOPERATIVE STUDY

The cooperative study of teacher education has been described in such detail in Chapter I, and the experiences of the participating institutions treated so fully in Chapters II and III, that only brief additional consideration is needed here. What is now called for, indeed, is chiefly an appraisal of the whole project as an example of a cooperative educational study.

Organization and control

This particular study was organized by a national commission specially created to encourage improvement in teacher education. The participating colleges, universities, and school systems were selected by that commission, which felt an obligation to ensure that they should be geographically and otherwise representative of the national scene as a whole. The idea of getting together in a joint venture did not originate with the participants. In the nature of the case it could scarcely have done so, for by reason of wide spatial separation they had had few if any prior institutional contacts.

The implications of these facts were well understood from the outset. The Commission on Teacher Education realized that special efforts must be made to develop esprit de corps and to discover what might profitably be attempted jointly. It was aware that the emphasis must be on local institutional change without effort to obtain anything approximating standardization. It had no idea that the participating institutions could be expected to develop continuing patterns of cooperation. When, near the close of the period of Commission support, a spontaneous demand arose that the study be put on a permanent basis, the Commission was gratified at this evidence that the experience had proved valuable to participants. But it was neither surprised nor disappointed when further consideration led to the conclusion that continuance would not be feasible in the absence of extended subsidization.

The central body for the cooperative study was, of course, the Commission itself. But the staff was given the greatest possible freedom in the realms of planning and acting, and it in turn

deliberately undertook to associate representatives of the participating centers in all major decisions. With three exceptions
Commission members were not connected with any of the
centers, and of these one was not in a position to give much
personal time to activities connected with the study. Staff
members, of course, were closer to the situations where action
was hoped for: they spent much time in the field and kept in
continual touch with local coordinators and administrators.
These latter persons, however, were the key figures so far as the
accomplishment of local changes was concerned. Bringing them
together to help with the original planning at Bennington and
annually thereafter for reappraisal and further interchange of
experiences and ideas contributed most importantly to the
success of the venture.

Techniques of value

The Commission's field coordinators advised participating
units as to local organization for work in the study and local
choice of activities in which to engage. In addition, these and
other staff members, as well as temporarily designated persons,
acted as consultants with respect to problems where local needs
were felt. Conferences proved a very important means of accomplishing a number of useful results in the study. They strengthened and kept strong the sense of obligation on the part of key
persons to carry out vigorously and effectively the institutional
obligation that had been undertaken. They maintained the
cooperative spirit and kept the various colleges, universities, and
school systems in touch with each other, resulting in mutual
stimulation and instruction. Better understanding between
representatives of different specialties—for example, education
and various academic subjects—of different types of institutions
of higher learning, and of all these and the schools was
certainly promoted. The Commission feels that it learned a
great deal about conferences in the course of its experience, and
they will be examined more closely further on in this chapter.[5]

The workshops held in connection with the cooperative study

[5] See pp. 218–26.

had many of the values of conferences and influenced many more individuals. Of course, the local workshops, that is, those sponsored by particular school systems, did not provide contacts between workers from several centers, but they had their own virtues as was pointed out in the preceding chapter. Their occurrence was undoubtedly due to the existence of the cooperative study, and they were important elements in its success, but there is obviously no essential reason why they should not have been independently developed. The national and regional workshops, arranged in connection with the Commission's study, brought together persons from various centers and so provided the advantages of opportunity for exchange. No doubt the fact that attendants at these workshops were mainly from colleges, universities, and school systems participating in a common venture had special advantages, and certainly they must be considered as having constituted one of the most valuable of the cooperative techniques. However, it should be said that many of their values can be offered by general workshops on teacher education under the independent auspices of given universities or colleges and without reference to any particular cooperative undertaking.

Favorable local factors

Since the aim of the cooperative study was to bring about local changes, something should be said, even if in partial repetition of statements made in previous chapters, about conditions favorable to the accomplishment of this purpose. Administrative interest and support proved of critical importance, as did interest, intelligence, and skill in group leadership on the part of the local coordinators. The latter point is worth some special emphasis. Most of the local coordinators for the cooperative study were selected at the very beginning and attended the Bennington conference. It was certainly of great value for them to have done so. However, since choices had been made before the character of the study was well understood some selections were made that in time proved less good than would have been possible. And when this fact became evident, making a shift was for obvious reasons difficult.

Had the Commission known in the beginning as much about cooperative studies as it knows now (and as it hopes the readers of this report will know when they have finished it), it would probably have acted differently. It would have suggested at once to administrators the criteria to bear in mind when thinking about the choice of a local coordinator—notably capacity to command general confidence and stimulate widespread activity. It would have recommended that a couple of strong candidates for this position be brought to the planning conference. It would have arranged for a discussion at that conference of the probable duties of a coordinator, the qualities essential for success in the position, and the methods that might wisely be employed in selecting such a person. The result might well have been not only that ultimate decision would have been democratically made at the several centers, but also that the choice would usually have fallen on one of the conference participants. It should be added at this point that the most successful local coordinators found the job to be time and energy consuming, and that they therefore needed some release from other regular duties.

Getting local personnel to share in the cooperative study—a step essential if local action was to take place democratically—required time, patience, and good judgment. The Commission, so far as possible, had selected for inclusion in the study institutions at which some general interest in participation had been expressed. But movement from the expression of interest to vigorous participation is not automatic. Ways and means had to be found for helping more and more staff members to find out what the study was really all about as seen from the center and—which was considerably more important—to enable them to share in determining what should be done in their own situations. As was previously reported some local organization proved essential to the latter end, a more or less representative planning committee being the device usually employed. But this only spread understanding so far and, furthermore, was still an affair of stimulation and coordination rather than of action directly resulting in improvement of the program of teacher education.

There remained, therefore, the problem of extending communication and moving on to the actual action front. How this was most successfully done has been discussed in earlier chapters, especially Chapter III, and need not be repeated here. The methods employed—study groups, responsible subcommittees, support for individual projects, a continuous interrelating of over-all planning and spearhead activities—are not peculiar to cooperative studies. But they are important for any such studies that have as one purpose the promotion of institutional change.

Functions of a national study

It seems fair to conclude that a *national* cooperative study, such as the Commission's, may realize certain unique values but is likely also to suffer from certain characteristic limitations. Its geographical scope makes possible a large degree of representativeness and lends it a dramatic quality. The participating centers receive a special stimulus and the work done attracts widespread attention. Whatever proves to be excellent about the outcomes, therefore, has a good chance of being influential. Conversely, however, the great distances involved add considerably to the expense, and even when this difficulty can be overcome there is not the possibility of as much contact between the member colleges and school systems as in the case of statewide cooperative efforts. A national study is, no doubt, more likely to win substantial financial support. But this advantage can easily be dissipated by lack of firmness in keeping the number of cooperating units down sufficiently: with a whole nation to choose from such firmness is not too easy to summon.

The Commission has not the slightest doubt as to the values of national cooperative studies of an ad hoc character. But it sees them as occasional, ground-breaking projects, necessarily limited as to their period of operation. Statewide studies, however (to which attention will now be turned) have a far greater likelihood of becoming permanent elements in the educational scene. [6]

[6] For further discussion of the cooperative aspects of the Commission's national study, see *The College and Teacher Education* and *Teacher Education in Service*, especially, in both cases, Chapter I.

The Statewide Studies

The state constitutes a political and geographical unit of special significance for teacher education. Its dominant role with respect to education generally was established when the framers of the Constitution failed to list education as one of the responsibilities to be assigned to the new federal government. Its activities with respect to the preparation of teachers are of long standing. Exactly one hundred years before the creation of the Commission, Massachusetts had authorized the establishment of the first publicly supported normal schools in the United States. In the ensuing century every state in the Union had accepted responsibility for helping to see that its children were provided with teachers properly prepared. By the close of the period the vast majority of state normal schools had been advanced to teachers colleges, that is, degree-granting institutions. In the meantime the state universities and land-grant colleges had been founded and these, too, had been given a share in teacher education. The universities had usually developed distinct colleges of education, which offered graduate as well as undergraduate instruction and served as centers of educational research.

Simultaneously state departments of education were being assigned increasing responsibility for the certification of teachers for employment. The resultant regulations established minimum requirements applying to all public schools and to the graduates of privately as well as publicly controlled colleges and universities. The consequence was that relationships having to do with teacher education were developed between the state departments, on the one hand, and the vast majority of institutions of higher learning on the other. These relations at first tended to be highly formal and the colleges frequently resented the power exercised from the capitol, sometimes, no doubt with considerable reason. In recent decades, however, a growing number of state departments have moved away from specialization in a legislative and police function to the exercise of leadership in the cooperative restudy of patterns of teacher preparation. Nor have the state departments been inactive as respects the in-service education of teachers. More and more they have developed programs of stimulation and supervision designed to be of benefit to the public schools, especially those rural in character. Of particular significance have been the statewide programs for curricular revision.

From all this it can readily be understood why the Commission early became interested in the idea of encouraging cooperative efforts for the improvement of teacher education set up on a statewide basis.[7] The relations already existing seemed to offer a readymade basis for such joint ventures. The fact that a major proportion of teachers prepared within a given state were likely to seek professional appointment there meant that the institutions within its boundaries had a largely common service area. And the size of the average state was such as to make frequent getting together a relatively easy matter. Moreover, the Commission believed that if the value of statewide cooperation in the improvement of teacher education could be demonstrated continued financial support would be forthcoming from regular sources.

Participating states

For such reasons the Commission, after its national study was under way, looked around to find a few representative states that appeared ripe for cooperative enterprise. To begin with, it chose three for this sort of experimentation. These states were granted substantial financial aid for from three to three and one-half years: they were, for example, enabled to employ fulltime coordinators and support one or more workshops. Later on the Commission effected affiliation with cooperative undertakings in seven additional states. These ventures received varying subsidies, none very considerable in amount. While one or two of them could not be claimed to have accomplished a great deal the rest achieved genuinely significant results, proving the value of statewide cooperation even when the money available especially for its support is limited. It should be understood that in all ten instances the states in question, and their various

[7] For a fully detailed description and analysis of these studies see *State Programs for the Improvement of Teacher Education.*

colleges and universities, shared in different ways and degrees in meeting the costs of cooperation.

The Commission's all-state program did not exhibit as wide a geographical spread as did the national cooperative study, but the states were otherwise reasonably representative. In population they ranged from 1,000,000 to 7,000,000 inhabitants, in enrollments in the public elementary and secondary schools from 200,000 to 1,200,000, and in numbers of public school teachers from 9,000 to 44,000.[8] The variation in character of economic and social life in these states is indicated by the fact that the proportion of urban population ranged from 20 to 67 percent.

Significant differences with respect to educational situation also existed. Expenditure per pupil for current costs in the public schools was as little as $25 in one state and the average teacher's salary was under $600; at the other end of the scale expenditure approached $96 and the average salary $1,600. One state had only twelve institutions of higher learning; two had more than five times this number. Average enrollment in the colleges and universities of particular states was not so markedly different, the range being from slightly above 400 to a little more than 1,300. Accurate estimates of the total number of undergraduates in each state preparing to teach are not obtainable, but enrollments in institutions specializing in the education of teachers varied from 1,000 to 11,700. Several of the states still maintained two- and three-year courses for the preparation of teachers.

Participation within states

The ten states also differed with respect to distribution of influence on teacher education and to degree of participation in the statewide studies as among distinguishable types of

[8] Figures for the whole of New York State would, of course, exceed the upper limits here given. But since New York City and its environs were not engaged in this state cooperative study the use of such figures would be misleading. All figures in this and the succeeding paragraphs are for 1940.

university and college.[9] In all but one the state university was the only, or at least the dominant, graduate institution. This university invariably participated in its state's cooperative study but in two or three cases the role it played was markedly more influential than in the others. The tenth state had no publicly controlled university of the usual type, but in its study four privately endowed universities played a part, two of them leading parts. The state teachers colleges and other state-supported colleges in which teachers were prepared were invariable participants, in several cases being particularly active.[10] All the states were well equipped with colleges of liberal arts. Four had six municipal universities among them, and four had seven universities under private control. In one study the privately controlled institutions were particularly active and in three or four others they participated unanimously. In two states, however, they did not join at all and in the remainder activity varied considerably from institution to institution.

In the ten states the strength of the departments of education and especially of their divisions of teacher education and certification differed significantly, and was in most cases very definitely reflected in the roles they played in the cooperative study. In seven cases officers of these departments were leading spirits in the cooperative enterprises, in several instances demonstrating outstanding powers of democratic leadership. In one state the appropriate representative of a strong state department gave his full support to the study, but with his entire approval the leadership rested in other hands. In the two remaining ventures, only one of which can be said to have been particularly effective, relatively undeveloped departments played but minor roles.

[9] The statements to follow are made with reference to the situations as determined by participation in the cooperative studies. In most cases all or virtually all colleges and universities were engaged, but in two instances only the state-supported institutions played a fully active part, and in New York participation was limited to institutions located in the upstate area.

[10] Two of the ten states did not operate any institutions classified as teachers colleges but carried out their work in teacher education in one case through five state-supported universities and in the other through the state university and the state college for women.

Pre-existing patterns of cooperation

A concluding word should be said about the extent to which the several states had already moved in the direction of cooperative action that at least had bearings on teacher education before the Commission became associated with them. In two or three cases the Commission's support was given to projects the cooperative foundations for which had already been well laid. In one or two more the practice of having institutional representatives come together to discuss common problems had at least been begun. Two states, on the other hand, launched cooperative studies rather definitely as a result of the Commission's original interest in such possibilities; in another, developments stemmed from participation of a state department officer in a Commission workshop; and there were three in which the presence of an institution that was participating in the Commission's national study was the starting point. The study in one of these last three never got very far, the reasons being institutional jealousies, lack of strong support from the state department, and failure to develop any vital focus. There remains one other venture to be mentioned, one that also failed to develop successfully. As a matter of fact this effort represented little more than a vague idea that cooperation would be a good thing and amounted to little more than one statewide conference. At the conclusion of this conference no clear and compelling ideas as to possible next steps had emerged, and by more or less general agreement matters were carried no farther so far as the Commission was concerned. The eight other studies must all be considered to have been successful.

Leadership in the statewide studies

From the outset the Commission was no more disposed than in the case of its national study to press for uniformity of action on the part of participants in the statewide program. The difference between states, suggested above, would have made any such attempt foolish. So the Commission continued, both as among and within states, to encourage local responsibility and trust to local leadership. Inevitably the several commonwealths focused on varying objectives and organized and operated their studies in different ways. Nevertheless, significant similarities were observable and useful generalizations respecting statewide cooperation in the improvement of teacher education can be drawn.

The success of the all-state studies with which the Commission was associated depended in notable degree upon the nature and quality of leadership supplied on the spot. As repeatedly emphasized, the Commission's policy was to trust and support such leadership. No doubt the Commission exercised an influence, but it avoided building up any structure that lacked local foundations. Chief credit for what was accomplished in these undertakings belongs to local forces. In the majority of cases the role of the state department officials was exceedingly important. In all but a few projects the state directors of teacher education and certification became the key figures. These officers were seeing their jobs in a new light. They were progressively less concerned with making rules and exercising control. They were increasingly interested in encouraging cooperation through the use of group methods, in the statesmanlike use of fundamentally educational techniques. They had discovered the ineffectiveness of unilateral action which subjects staff members in the colleges and universities to resented strain and frequently results in a response which, while it accords with the letter of promulgated regulations, fails to lead to the hoped-for consequences. Experience demonstrated the success of new ways of working, the advantages to teacher education, and the satisfactions to individual leaders. In only one state did such efforts temporarily misfire.

It became evident, in the course of the Commission's period of observation, that a special advantage was enjoyed by those state directors of teacher education who were also in charge of curriculum revision in the schools. Such persons were strategically placed with respect both to the institutions of higher learning and to the school systems; they were in a preferred position to promote school-college relations and to enlist a variety of representatives of both types of situation in attacks on the problems of teacher education, pre-service and in-service alike. They found it relatively easy to keep the focus of attention on the improvement of school programs for the benefit of children—which ultimately is where it should always be.

In two states individual leadership came from one of the universities or colleges. Here some limitations became evident. In one instance the needed degree of statewide unity never was achieved: other colleges and universities were unwilling to follow the lead of the institution whose representative had initiated the enterprise. As a result, little that was substantial was accomplished and the effort was abandoned. In a second situation the dean of the leading state-controlled university thought it best to seek to engage only those other institutions among which cordial relations already existed, along with public school representatives with whom a basis for cooperation had also previously been established. The results of this effort were very considerable: it definitely demonstrated its value. But the enterprise never succeeded in embracing all of the state's teacher-educating forces. It should be noted that in neither of the states just considered was the state department so organized as to make possible provision for the sort of leadership that proved so effective elsewhere.

The last state to be considered presented a rather special picture. The state department was excellently organized and staffed. But the impulse to cooperative action happened to arise, originally, in liberal arts circles, as a consequence of an important impending change in certification requirements. The idea of a joint study, accordingly, was worked out through the state's association of colleges and universities, of which the majority of the state teachers colleges were not at the time members. However, support from the state department was assured in advance and a representative of the teachers colleges was placed on the committee created to guide the projected enterprise. It was decided not to attempt to interest one highly metropolitan corner of the state. The resulting cooperative study was very successful, benefiting greatly from the continued leadership of the originator of the scheme, a man who proved unusually capable of rising above preoccupation with the special interests of his own institution. And the teachers colleges eventually found a place in the program. Since the exhaustion of grants from the Commission, however, this study has not continued on anything like the scale that has marked the situations where state department representatives held the lead.

State councils on teacher education

In the states where leadership was taken by representatives of the departments of education there was a distinct tendency to establish state councils on teacher education. These bodies were customarily made up of an appropriate selection of state officials, designated representatives of each of the colleges and universities where teachers were being prepared, and a selected group of spokesmen for the public schools. The last-named persons were often appointed by the individual state's associations of superintendents, supervisors, principals, and classroom teachers.

These councils provided a means of exchange of views respecting matters relating to teacher education within particular states. They enabled state officials to obtain advice periodically with respect to issues with which they were concerned and to interpret their policies to key workers in the field. Sometimes the councils were assigned a certain policy-making authority; in any case their effect was desirably to influence policy. Their consequence ordinarily was to increase mutual understanding among both state officials and representatives of teacher-preparing institutions, and the latter and spokesmen for the schools. The Commission believes such councils to have demonstrated that they can be very effective contributors to the improvement of teacher education. It recommends that states in which they have not yet been created carefully consider the desirability of instituting such bodies.

Central control in the statewide studies

In some commonwealths central control of the statewide cooperative studies was directly provided by the state councils on teacher education. Ordinarily, however, these bodies were too large for the exercise of continuous planning and supervisory functions. In such cases the executive committees of the councils were sometimes assigned the chief weight of administrative responsibility. Alternatively, creation of special central committees for the cooperative undertakings was authorized, these bodies not necessarily to be made up exclusively or even largely of council members. Experience indicates that central committees, however established, should not have more than ten or twelve members for efficient operation.

Who such members should be is, of course, an important question. In some cases within the Commission's experience chiefly presidents and deans were appointed or selected. The result was that the committee gained prestige. On the other hand such individuals could not be expected to become very active in the field projects which it should be the chief aim of every statewide study to foster; this proved disadvantageous. Indeed, it can be safely said that where central committees were made up of persons in a position to take a leading part in the work done on their own campuses, to act as consultants throughout the state, and to serve on workshop staffs, the situation was ideal. When this was the case the committee's thinking was constantly guided by its members' field experiences, and these members were likewise able to help implement committee decisions once they had been made.

Special mention should be made of the importance of seeing that interested representatives of subject-matter departments should sit on such committees. The closing of the usually existing gap between educationists and subject-matter folk must be one of the leading aims in cooperative efforts for improving teacher education; it is essential that some of the latter should occupy positions at the center. Certainly it is always important that choice of members for central committees should be carefully made with reference to the tasks to be performed and the particular problems likely to be encountered. It was usual, of course, to make sure that public education was provided with a voice on central committees. Not infrequently the state education association was asked to help select at least one member. In one case the commonwealth's associations of principals and supervisors were very effectively brought into the planning and conduct of projects relating to teacher education in service. The more general enlisting of such organizations in statewide cooperative programs would appear to be highly desirable.

Some of the central committees found it helpful to set up standing subcommittees to deal with such matters as evaluation, child growth and development, and the like. More frequent was the appointment of special subcommittees in connection with particular needs as they emerged. For example, in one commonwealth where through the statewide study certain "criteria for teacher education" had been adopted, special committees were established to develop the practical implications of each recommendation and also to lay plans for further study at a forthcoming workshop. Elsewhere the job of working out approved new courses was assigned to bodies of this character. Such subcommittees tended to take on many of the attributes of study groups during the school year, as described in the preceding chapter.[11]

Standing and special subcommittees both offered means of drawing more and more persons into the statewide programs: they were apt to be of fair size and their members were ordinarily chosen in only small proportion from the central committee. Thus, they made possible the full use of people with ideas and of individuals occupying positions of actual or potential leadership and influence on the campuses where change must ultimately occur if the purposes of the cooperative undertakings were to be realized. Here was opportunity, for example, to gain the assistance and good will of more and more representatives of the academic subjects.

Functions of the central committees

The functions of the central committees may now be considered. As in the case of planning committees in colleges, universities, and school systems, their main jobs were to foster

[11] See pp. 146–50.

mutual understanding and joint activity, to see to it that promising focuses for cooperative endeavor were located, and to stimulate action where it counted, that is to say, on the several campuses or in the various school systems. It was not found to be their job to lay down the law. A subsidiary but very important task for a central committee was to develop many contacts throughout the state, to draw into the cooperative undertaking all persons capable of contributing to group deliberation, and of implementing conclusions at their home bases. The exercise of a clearinghouse function was also indicated—the spreading of information about what is being thought and done, not only by committees and conferences and workshop groups, but also by the associated institutions.

The identification of points of attack most likely to arouse wide interest and result in widespread action was a particularly important duty of central committees. Unity among the participants in a statewide study can by no means be assumed at the outset, not even in the limited degree in which it may customarily be found in particular colleges, universities, or school systems. The fostering of such unity becomes, therefore, a matter requiring special attention. Finding goals for joint endeavor that will have the desired effect is not always too easy: some groping may be expected at the outset. But the quest must be vigorously pursued. Central committees should, however, be hesitant about reaching a decision for themselves on this matter without bringing others into the inquiry. An opening conference for a cooperative study along the lines of that held by the Commission at Bennington can be very helpful, as numerous states discovered. Even if the conclusions reached at such a conference coincide with the central committee's own advance judgment, advantages will have been gained. But more than one such conference may be necessary before the best possible decisions can be reached. The achievement of agreements basic to cooperation is essential; but under too much pressure such agreements may prove to be more verbal than real.

On the other hand it would be a grave mistake to press for early agreements too detailed in character or restricting in effect. The aim is to promote both unity and local action—action on as many individual campuses as possible. Anything that looks like an effort toward standardization imposed from without, like an encroachment upon basic institutional freedom, will provoke resistance and delay, hence become self-defeating. What is wanted is merely enough agreement to permit cooperative planning, to make feasible the joint and therefore economical use of consultants, and to promote a sense of common enterprise. The right balance is likely to be found if those who must act on any decisions share in making them. It may well be added that the focus should be on jobs to be done rather than on abstract verbal formulations, to which all may readily agree but the operational significance of which remains obscure.

A central committee will naturally receive proposals from any subsidiary bodies that it may have created, and it has the responsibility of appraising such proposals carefully. It should, however, be hesitant about rejecting suggestions that are the result of earnest endeavor on the part of competent people; and if it has been careful about the membership and guidance of the committees it has set up, it will not be likely to have to do so even though their recommendations turn out to exceed anything the central body itself may have had in mind. Submitting approved proposals to the several institutional faculties is, naturally, another of the committee's functions, as is help in the implementation of recommendations that strike fire. Such implementation may mean, for example, the employment of a consultant, the arrangement of a conference, or the development of a workshop.

The strategic task of increasing the likelihood that action will take place on the local fronts should never be forgotten. Various ways of discharging this task have already been suggested. The Commission observed that success in the statewide studies with which it was associated rested on a mixture of response and of stimulation. In other words the central committees responded to actual and potential developments on the campuses, but they also provided suggestions and encouragement. Thus central activities were geared into local ones.

The importance of the human factor in all this deserves special mention. Successful statewide cooperation proved to be a matter of people quite as much as of ideas. Effective central committees developed esprit de corps. They capitalized on friendships that their members had throughout the state and they built up new ones. They planned carefully to increase participation both in statewide and in related local activities so that more persons might feel a personal stake in the outcomes of the joint venture. It should be noted, however, that the emphasis throughout was on *group* activity. Individuals could not have accomplished a great deal. They had to become parts of study and action groups. Central committees needed to bear constantly in mind that it was such groups that it must reach and foster.

The preceding discussion of central committees and their functions will readily suggest both the extent and importance of their duties. It is apt to raise questions as to whether such duties can possibly be successfully performed by persons who cannot meet with great frequency or for very extended periods. The fact of the matter is that someone is needed who can serve as an executive for a central committee, helping to organize its agenda and making sure that its policies are steadily carried out. In some states with which the Commission worked the committee chairman—usually the state director of teacher education and certification—performed this function. But three were equipped with full-time coordinators for their cooperative studies. This arrangement proved its superiority. Indeed, it may safely be said that statewide programs that really catch hold will suffer seriously in the absence of at least one person who can devote himself pretty exclusively to their affairs.

Getting participation from institutions

Traditionally a good deal of rivalry has often existed between the colleges and universities of a given state. Even when this has not been particularly true assumptions respecting the relative excellence or prestige of the various institutions have colored mutual attitudes. And in any case patterns of coopera-

tion among these institutions have been hardly more than
primitive. Gaining the wholehearted participation of colleges
and universities in statewide studies has not, therefore, been an
entirely simple matter.

It was the observation of the Commission that under these
circumstances some time needed to be devoted, following the
launching of statewide studies, to fostering mutual acquaintance,
appreciation, and trust. It took time for people to become
willing to express themselves with full candor and to learn how
to understand fully what others were saying. It took time for
them to sense differences in institutional situations and to
become willing and able to think in terms of these differences.
It took time to put aside fears that a hidden purpose of the
cooperative effort might be further standardization and the
imposition upon particular institutions of unwelcome requirements. And finally, it took time to discover common ground,
to identify points of attack of general concern. For such reasons
it proved important that an opening conference should not be
hurried, that it should be scheduled to last for from one to
two weeks.

Central committees also found it advantageous to canvass the
institutions that were to be represented in such an opening
conference in order to give them an opportunity in advance to
indicate issues of concern to them. Then it proved helpful for
the committee to select topics of general interest as objects
for conference attention. The identification and highlighting of
some definite social challenge, relating, for example, to the
needs of children or of the communities that they represented,
helped in the development of unity. However, it was not essential, and perhaps not even desirable, to strive to occupy such
high ground at the outset. The challenge was likely to have
more meaning if it grew out of group deliberations where real
situations had been the object of attention. Otherwise, there was
some danger that it might prove a mere matter of verbal
stimulation, being perhaps pitched too high for those who must
plan and act if it were to become influential upon practice.

But when the challenge was realistic, understood, and accepted it lent fire and coherence to the cooperative endeavor.

Since the purpose of the statewide studies was always to stimulate change on the campuses of the cooperating colleges and universities, some general remarks may well be made as to what helped bring this result about. The quality of local leadership was, of course, always important. Where leaders possessed courage and skill in the guidance of group activity effective action could be confidently expected. These qualities were important not only in presidents and deans but also in those selected to serve as local coordinators and group chairmen. Programs of local self-study, leading to a clarification of institutional needs, helped to get things started. The chief thing, of course, was to extend participation in local group activities related to the statewide program as rapidly as could be soundly done. When participation was voluntary and yielded satisfaction, faculty interest grew rapidly and was accompanied by an increasing sense of obligation to help achieve success. Winning the attachment of subject-matter representatives was worth special effort, and particular advantages were yielded by activities that required the cooperation of such persons with members of the department of education. This proved the case, for example, when social scientists and educationists combined to promote better community understanding through direct experiences on the part of prospective teachers. In such instances lines traditionally dividing faculties were advantageously transcended.

Of course, it was always desirable to encourage the expression of new ideas from within the faculties and to cultivate an atmosphere conducive to their being given an open-minded hearing. It may be said that participation in a cooperative study ordinarily served to help in these respects. Local would-be innovators, discovering like-minded persons in other institutions, were emboldened to speak out more freely and hopefully on the home campus; and their colleagues, eager not to be left behind by the faculties of other colleges or universities, tended to listen more sympathetically. The importation of outside consultants, a practice widely followed in the statewide programs, worked in the same direction: not only did local figures often receive support from the visitors but the latter contributed challenging ideas of their own. All these references to ideas, however, should not be allowed to give the impression that decisions were wisely made solely on the basis of speculation. As a matter of fact, the best progress in institutions occurred when decisions rested on an interplay of thought and action. For example, new courses were more successfully developed when major ideas that had won tentative acceptance were tried out experimentally fairly promptly, rather than when action was delayed until a detailed syllabus could be worked out fully in advance.

It proved very helpful, as has already been noted, to arrange that participants in local group activities should, so far as possible, be given an appropriate role in the committee work, conferences, and workshops arranged by the central committee. In this way experience could be shared to the satisfaction and advantage of all concerned. Participants, in consequence, received a strong and supporting sense of the more than local significance of their efforts. And the statewide cooperative endeavor gained meaning and status. In turn, that endeavor proved of value to the various institutions by helping to focus attention on certain key problems. When some such focus was accepted local progress was found to be greater than when an effort was made to work on many problems simultaneously.

Of course, in the studies with which the Commission was associated individual institutions differed considerably in the degree to which they took effective part. Some continued to prefer to pursue their own rather isolated paths. Some never got over their fears that they might be subjected to standardizing pressures. Some were so little concerned with teacher education, or otherwise so different from the main body of participants, that they saw no point in doing more than show their good will. But in most of the states most, if not all, of the institutions whose participation was sought or might reasonably have been expected found a useful and satisfying role.[12]

In concluding this discussion of the interplay between central committees and particular institutions as it developed in the statewide cooperative studies it may be noted that the most successful pattern developed was cyclical in nature. Consideration of common concerns by central bodies, and by larger representative groups formed under their leadership, led to broad general agreements as to problems to be jointly tackled and methods to be employed. This stage was followed by one in which planning and doing on the various campuses took the spotlight. Then came the time for a new conference of local representatives in order that experience might be exchanged, evaluation engaged in, and common plans for next steps developed. Thus continued progress was fostered, central and local activities were integrated, and unity on both levels promoted.

EMPHASES OF THE STATEWIDE STUDIES

A comparison of statewide programs reveals that while most of them selected one, or at most three or four, points of attack near the outset, a few began by trying to move ahead along a very wide front. Efforts of the latter type were to be explained by several reasons. There was a certain assumption that a statewide undertaking should have corresponding breadth of scope. It was recognized that there were many important problems in teacher education and some natural unwillingness was felt to ignore any of them. But there were also factors of another sort at play. For example, where the cooperating colleges and universities varied widely as to purpose and stage of development, finding a focus for activity that could prove generally satisfactory was somewhat difficult. And even where the institutions were similar, fears of the possible emergence of a drive for standardization sometimes made for an approach less likely to result in a rapid getting down to cases.

[12] For further discussion of the internal organization of institutions for purposes of group study and action designed to lead to program improvement, see Chapter II, pp. 62–68.

It may be said, however, that experience demonstrated that this style of operation yielded distinctly limited results. With the program broken up into many elements, it proved difficult to move from the stage of exploration and discussion at the center to that of action at the periphery. Moreover, communication became a serious problem. Even when the central committee published and distributed full accounts of conferences, workshops, and the activities of special committees, the variety of topics treated made for a dispersion of interests so that it was hard for readers to grasp what the study was planning and accomplishing. Not that there were no values in the broad-front way of working. Individuals drawn into the various activities were stimulated, and their practice on the home campus was often influenced. Not infrequently significant changes in given colleges or universities resulted. But these developments were not particularly related and did not strongly support each other. And not a few institutions were left relatively untouched. Most of the states that began by operating along comprehensive lines in time moved to the identification of a few points of common attack.

Indeed, it can be stated confidently that the use of such spearheads contributed a good deal to the success of the more effective statewide programs. Some of the advantages have already been touched on and need not be repeated. Further evidence supporting the generalization will appear as our analysis proceeds. Suffice it here to say that the selection of some particular focus of effort did not prove narrowing when the choice was wisely made. A combined attack on the improvement of student teaching, for example, led eventually to a re-examination and reform of total patterns of professional preparation. If the spearhead selected relates to some integral aspect of a good program of teacher education, consideration of other aspects may be expected to result in due course. In the meantime participants in the cooperative study will have developed a sense of unity; and an intermeshing of activities at the center and on the several campuses will have occurred. This means a greater likelihood of desirable change where change must occur if teacher education is to advance.

The particular problems chosen for treatment in the states with which the Commission worked naturally varied. Choice reflected local circumstances and local interests. Often some development prior to the launching of the cooperative endeavor set the stage. In one commonwealth, for example, the adoption of a requirement that five years of preparation be offered by candidates for certification as secondary school teachers of academic subjects resulted in the statewide effort being first directed to a rethinking of the professional curriculum for such teachers. Elsewhere the slow response to a state-sponsored effort to bring about curriculum revision in the schools had led to the conviction that the teachers were not prepared to employ the new concepts: the natural consequence was that the cooperative study in teacher education should focus on appropriate reforms in the college curricula. A third state's program had its center of interest provided by the passage of a law permitting the development of a single curriculum whereby teachers might be prepared for work at either the elementary or secondary school level, this being an action designed to deal with a situation in which underproduction of elementary and over-production of secondary school teachers had become chronic.

General education

In several states efforts to improve patterns of general education constituted a leading part of the drive for curricular reform.[13] Such efforts had to struggle against the special difficulties described in Chapter II as besetting attacks on general education made in the Commission's national study.[14] An unusually large proportion of any college's faculty has a stake in its program of general education, and these persons represent a large variety of specialties. Moreover, revision of the basic program in general education ordinarily requires changes

[13] For further treatment of this topic see State Programs for the Improvement of Teacher Education, Part Two.
[14] See pp. 78–84.

affecting all or most of these individuals and interests. Finally, while there is widespread contemporary dissatisfaction with the ways in which general education is usually provided for, there is also a great deal of disagreement as to what would constitute a preferable alternative. In all these circumstances, getting agreement and action are both unusually difficult. It may be said, however, that cooperative attacks on the problem on a statewide basis proved to have some definite advantages over independent efforts on particular campuses. Bolder spirits in different colleges and universities were enabled to give each other moral and intellectual support, and the more timid felt happier about innovations when they were related to a program that had statewide prestige.[15]

Professional education

Efforts to improve professional education were also naturally included in the state cooperative studies.[16] Two types were especially prominent. First, there was great interest in the more effective integration of theory and practice. Movement here was usually in the direction of developing a professional block with all or nearly all of the time of some late quarter or semester assigned to it. Such professional units consisted of various theoretical topics blended with each other and especially with student teaching and comparable forms of direct experience. The drive in this direction seemed to reflect, in part, the desire of instructors in theory courses to associate themselves with clinicians in whose help students appeared to find particular satisfaction. The second notable emphasis was on child growth and development. Here the interest was not only in producing new courses, usually scheduled to come fairly early in the preparatory program, but also in instilling the child-development point of view throughout the professional sequence. The interest of the Commission in child growth and development and the

---

[15] The specific changes made in programs of general education in the several states were similar to those discussed in Chapter II and need not be reconsidered here. A similar comment might be made respecting other points of attack dealt with below.

[16] For further treatment see *ibid.*, Part Three.

availability of its services in connection with this subject undoubtedly exercised an influence in several states. Both approaches proved valuable, and on each topic marked progress was in some instances made.

Student teaching

An element in professional education that received definite attention in several states, and that served as the main spearhead in one, was student teaching.[17] Here the most striking movement was usually in the direction of providing a clear block of time during which, near the close of his period of preparation, a student might devote himself fully for from one to three months to off-campus experience in student teaching. Such developments generally had repercussions on the rest of the professional program, supporting the drive to increase the integration of theory and practice. The main difficulties encountered had, of course, to do with scheduling. Subject-matter departments were especially resistant to arrangements which required students to interrupt work in their major fields near the close of the undergraduate program. However, satisfactory adjustments were worked out in time in a large proportion of cases. It may be added that students who had opportunities to engage in good programs of student teaching almost always found the experience particularly rewarding. A further point worth mentioning is that developing substantial programs in off-campus student teaching had the effect of promoting closer relations between schools and colleges, with numerous valuable consequences for the preservice programs.

In-service education

Up to this point not a great deal has been said in this chapter about the role of school systems in statewide cooperative programs. The fact is that by and large that role was not great. Various reasons account for the more vigorous participation of the colleges and universities. It was still usual to think chiefly of these institutions as responsible for teacher education. It was

---

[17] For further treatment see *ibid.*, Chapter VIII.

with them that most state directors of teacher education and certification were accustomed to work. Their numbers were such as to make the problem of developing a pattern of cooperation somewhat formidable, and the inclusion of the very much larger number of school systems would have complicated matters enormously. For these and other reasons the statewide studies usually focused on the improvement of pre-service education. It should be recalled, however, that school people and their interests were by no means ignored. Representatives of the public schools ordinarily sat on the state councils and central committees, and other representatives were usually brought in to conferences, workshops, and the like. But in a very real sense the function of these persons was chiefly advisory with respect to plans relating to teacher preparation.

In two states, however, the statewide effort eventually came to focus on in-service education; in both instances very substantial results were achieved.[18] It is interesting to note that each of these states moved to this emphasis after original experimentation with the broad-front approach. One came to stress the development and improvement of community schools through a series of in-service endeavors cosponsored by volunteering colleges and universities and by one or more school systems in their respective vicinities. The other devoted its attention to the improvement of teaching in rural schools through work with principals and supervisors and the promotion of local clinics, conferences, and workshops.

In each of these two instances the leadership of the state department was a critical factor. In the first department there had developed a deep interest in the improvement of community living through education. Both departments, moreover, were rapidly moving away from the idea that their chief business was certification: they had accepted the function of educational leadership through the encouragement and support of pioneer work wherever it could be developed within the state's schools. The improvement of teacher education, pre- and in-service, was to be geared to these efforts.

[18] For further treatment see *ibid.*, Part Four.

The implication that selective choice was to be made of schools with which to cooperate will be noted. This policy was a wise one. Any attempt to cover the state through an in-service program must surely have broken down because of the large numbers involved and the drag resulting from the inclusion of backward or self-satisfied systems. Moreover, since the intention was to make maximum use of the resources available in the colleges and universities it was desirable to capitalize on the recognized ties existing between these and various systems in their several service areas. The further promotion of such relations proved fairly easy. And the practice of limiting efforts to work with pioneering schools made for progress and satisfaction. It could be expected, of course, that in time the demonstrations occurring at these key points would stimulate emulation in other quarters.

In both states, then, there were developed cooperative relations between particular colleges and universities and particular school systems whereby the former provided continuous field services to the latter. But in one case this sort of thing was overshadowed by arrangements of a more inclusive character. Here, given rural systems frequently drew on several institutions of higher learning for consultant aid in connection with local conferences, workshops, and study groups. Here, moreover, cooperatively staffed summer workshops for rural principals and supervisors were developed, as well as a year-long training program whereby individuals preparing to become county supervisors worked on several campuses as well as in the field. The ability developed by the colleges and universities of this state to rise above traditional rivalries and pool their resources in order to develop a superior program was an outstanding consequence of the cooperative program.

The recognition given in this instance to the key importance of principals and supervisors so far as the improvement of in-service education is concerned deserves special attention. The aim was to strengthen and make more continuous the guidance provided for classroom teachers in their efforts to perform their tasks ever more effectively. It was believed that this implied studying local school needs and ways of meeting them, developing local in-service programs, and planning profitable summer experience for teachers. If these things were to be done principals and supervisors must be sensitive to their importance, have confidence in their personal ability to provide leadership, and be able to work together.

But the principals, by and large, were *not* prepared to assume these responsibilities. Traditionally they had concentrated their efforts on administrative duties and the maintenance of good public relations. They had not been expected to develop skill in the supervision of instruction, and they had not done so. Usually they had not been trained at all in the field of elementary school teaching and hence were particularly unprepared to provide guidance in that area. Moreover, they were not accustomed to working groupwise: for them the accepted pattern of operation was one in which they were invariably dominant. All this was reflected in the usual faculty meeting, at which the principal would announce his decisions, and there might follow some discussion of educational matters that stayed safely at a theoretical level, seldom getting down to real cases. The county supervisors, when they existed, were apt to have a somewhat distant, if not strained, relation with the principals. Moreover, they tended to work with individual teachers in a somewhat censorious fashion, rather than with groups in the role of resource persons. Both the separation of administration from supervision and the individualistic methods of working with teachers were, however, inconsistent with modern curricular goals and with the objectives of democratic group procedure and institutional unity.

The principals' and supervisors' workshops, usually carried on in close relation to one another, proved very effective in correcting this situation. They succeeded in developing new ideas as to ways of working with teachers. Particularly important was the fact that they provided the principals with resources for helping classroom teachers with school problems, thus building the principals' confidence in their ability to give such help successfully. They enabled principals and supervisors to get better acquainted, to develop more mutual respect, and to lay plans that fitted together rather than worked at cross purposes. Finally, they offered an instructive and influential demonstration of ways of working together by group methods that could readily be adapted for use in connection with in-service activities back home. Participants in these workshops emerged with an understanding that teacher growth requires opportunities to tackle real problems arising from the teaching situation and to do so in group fashion. And they felt ready to provide leadership in the development and carrying forward of activities of this character.

The consequences were wholly gratifying. Local clinics, pre-opening conferences, and county workshops for teachers increased rapidly in number and had a distinct success. Consultant services in connection with these enterprises were provided by members of the state's central committee and by faculty members from the various colleges and universities. Thus the central body was kept in intimate touch with the developments it had fostered, and cooperation between the several institutions of higher learning was further advanced. The consequences are suggested by the goals that were set for itself by the central committee at about the time of the conclusion of the Commission's period of association with it. These were to increase the number of community schools, develop understanding of the proper nature and scope of such school programs, determine teachers' needs therein, develop functional criteria for the preparation of such teachers, emphasize local programs of in-service education, and continue and extend the process of integrated and cooperative thinking and doing.

Other points of attack

Among other focuses of endeavor in statewide programs were the working out of more functional master's degree programs for prospective or experienced teachers in the secondary schools, improvement of student personnel work, and increase of student participation in the planning and carrying on of professional preparatory courses. The first, as used in a particular state, led to calling a conference in which deans of graduate schools of arts and sciences and of schools of education, graduate instructors in education and in the several social sciences, and leaders in secondary education in the state spent several days exploring the problems of the high schools and considering their implication for graduate programs for teachers. There emerged a set of unanimous recommendations respecting a divisional master's program in the social studies. These recommendations were promptly accepted and put into effect at the state's leading university. Plans for similar action elsewhere and for moving on in an effort to achieve a similar result with respect to general science were set back by developments growing out of the war.[19] The other points of attack mentioned above worked out satisfactorily but in particular institutions rather than throughout a state.

A number of problems that might have been expected to claim attention in the statewide studies failed, for various reasons, to do so. Of these certification was a notable example. The view is often expressed that certification requirements constitute a leading obstacle to experimentation designed to result in the improvement of teacher education; it may be recalled that the committee of the American Council on Education which prepared the way for the Commission expressed the expectation that this problem would require special attention. Yet at the Bennington conference with which the Commission's national study opened this subject aroused little interest. Moreover, in the course of that study none of the participating colleges and universities found certification requirements to be operating as notable sources of frustration. There would seem to be added significance in the fact that the statewide studies also ignored this topic. The cooperating institutions found, it appears, first, that attention to problems closer to the action front was more rewarding, and second, that state officials were able and willing to interpret certification regulations in ways that kept them from interfering with any soundly thought-out

---

[19] For further treatment of this development see *The College and Teacher Education*, pp. 214–22.

experimental activities. It has already been noted that many of these officers were moving rapidly away from preoccupation with making and enforcing certification requirements toward emphasis on facilitating pioneer activities in the preparation and in-service education of teachers.

Another problem that failed to receive attention in the statewide studies was selective admissions. Here the explanation is doubtless to be found in the circumstances of the times which had a similar effect, it may be recalled, in the national study. During the period of the Commission's field programs a serious teacher shortage was developing throughout the country. For reasons connected with the war, enrollments in teacher-educating institutions were falling rapidly, and experienced teachers were withdrawing from the profession in large numbers. The great problem became one of persuading people to become teachers, not of discouraging their ambitions in that direction. This, of course, had the effect of lowering standards, which seemed to the responsible authorities preferable to leaving children without any instructors at all. With the end of the war this situation can be expected to change. When this occurs it would seem that improvement of selective procedures could become one of the most fruitful subjects for cooperative treatment in statewide programs.[20]

CONFERENCES AS TECHNIQUES OF COOPERATION

The most popular and successful method used for promoting statewide cooperation was the conference.[21] It was a relatively inexpensive device and one whereby it was usually possible to reach all of those whose participation it was important to obtain. Individuals already eager to share in what was going on had little difficulty in arranging to attend, and other persons, whose presence seemed important to the planners but who could not

[20] Attacks on this problem by two states are described in *Evaluation in Teacher Education*, pp. 21–30.

[21] Conferences are given extended treatment in this chapter because they played a particularly notable part in the statewide studies. What will be said concerning them, however, is based on experience in the national study as well, in which they also demonstrated their value.

be counted on to turn up without special invitation, could usually be persuaded to come and see what it was like. Often these latter individuals, for example, subject-matter specialists, caught a vision of the potentialities of the statewide studies and became active workers in the related projects as a result of conference experience. The repeatability of conferences proved valuable, too. They provided recurrent opportunities for old workers to strengthen acquaintance and renew enthusiasm and for newcomers to be inducted into the program under favorable conditions. Recurrence also, of course, conduced to continual revaluation of particular enterprises, to the exchange and appraisal of experience as action proceeded, and to the determination of next steps in the light of fresh deliberation.

It proved very important, in statewide studies, to obtain the participation of several types of person, and in this connection conferences were always helpful. Through them, key administrators could be reached. These individuals could ordinarily not be expected to work very actively in central or in group enterprises, but it was essential that they should have a general understanding of what the cooperative study was engaged in doing and a favorable attitude toward it. Conference attendance helped greatly in bringing this about. Then conferences provided a means in all the relevant states for interesting representatives of the public schools in the planning that was being carried forward. Even where the focus of attention was on pre-service problems continuous check with the field forces was important. Again, conferences made it possible to use efficiently the services of special consultants who, during such gatherings, could present challenging ideas to the entire membership and also work intensively with particular discussion groups. The values of conferences to the main body of working participants have already been mentioned and should in any case be evident.

Administrative features

It should be understood, of course, that the conferences held in the several states (like others with which the Commission was associated through the national study and other cooperative undertakings) had a variety of purposes and accordingly differed in the details of their operation. But there were also similarities. It is possible, therefore, to set down certain generalizations respecting the planning and conduct of effective affairs of this kind.

Careful planning of the conference is the first essential. Purposes, not merely of the planning body but also of the prospective participants, should be carefully considered. Often, especially when a group is being brought together for the first time, it is desirable to conduct a preliminary canvass so as to make sure that the wishes and expectations of those who are to attend can be given due weight. When such a step is impracticable it may be well to plan to spend the first day or two of the conference in drawing the members out and developing a consensus as to the problems to which attention had best be devoted. The latter technique was employed successfully at Bennington. In any case it is well to anticipate that a little time will be needed for orientation at the beginning of any conference at which the participants are relatively unused to working together. It may be added that the problems eventually selected for attention should be not only of general interest but also sufficiently limited in number not to present too great a scattering of effort. Some method of screening proposals is essential. Topics finally selected should not be too broad or vaguely phrased.

It is always well to plan for conference flexibility, so that details may be worked out in response to the judgment of the entire group as the experience together proceeds. This means that advance planning should provide for a variety of anticipated contingencies. "What will we do if this happens?" and "What, if that happens?" are questions that the planners should ask themselves. Since educational meetings traditionally have been devoted largely to listening to speeches and engaging in ideological discussions, those responsible for arranging a conference of the type here discussed are likely to feel some compulsion to make sure that all the time is filled up. They may also feel quite uneasy about allowing leeway for modifying plans and about trusting participants to carry things off successfully without a great deal of guidance. They may worry lest the conference be unproductive and the responsibility be charged to them. It is important then, especially in the case of committee members who have had little experience with working conferences, that they devote enough time to planning so that various possible contingencies can be thought through and a common feeling of confidence in the outcome developed. Moreover, they must expect to meet frequently during the course of the conference, both by themselves and with group chairmen, to appraise developments and make fresh decisions.

The question of the length of a conference is of considerable importance. The Commission's experience indicates that while two or three days is satisfactory for some purposes, a week or even two weeks is much more than proportionately valuable for others. This is particularly the case when cooperative enterprises are being launched. Then it is most important that there should be time enough for acquaintance to ripen and for basic decisions to be reached unhurriedly. Even when a group is meeting a second or third time, about a week can ordinarily be employed profitably up to the last minute. This is especially true when the conference is a large one which must be broken down into sections if it is to operate effectively. Smaller groups such as special committees with limited tasks can often complete an assignment in a briefer period.

Place is also worth careful consideration. Central location and relative inexpensiveness is, of course, desirable, other things remaining the same. But the presence of suitable meeting rooms, good food, good beds, space and opportunity for informal contacts and recreation, and natural beauty should all rank high on a list of criteria for selection. A touch of primitiveness is by no means undesirable: a number of the most successful conferences with which the Commission had to do were held at camps. The atmosphere there seemed to make it easy for people to achieve quickly a friendly footing and a sense of group unity. Big downtown hotels probably provide the least favorable setting. Between sessions members tend to disperse in all directions, and individuals are always slipping off for personal interviews with some old friend in the locality. Full attendance from start to finish is important. It is annoying to have useful participants depart in the midst of things or to have to stop and explain to late-comers what has been happening prior to their arrival. Incidentally the tendency of some educational egoists to think that "looking in for a day" constitutes satisfactory participation should be anticipated and openly discouraged.

The size a conference may wisely be permitted to attain depends on its purpose, its setting and facilities, the skill of its leaders, the familiarity of participants with conference techniques, and other lesser factors. One extremely successful conference in the Commission's experience included well over 200 active members, and several others approximated that figure. Yet there are dangers of permitting such affairs to get too big. A hundred or so people can, in a week or two, develop a real sense of unity: if numbers rise considerably above that figure much of value may still be obtained, but people are likely to go home with less sense of having become part of something single and fully comprehended. This implies, of course, that in some situations it will be unwise to invite to a conference all persons who, in a certain sense, "ought to be there."

Working methods

In the statewide studies a leading task of the first conference or two was to help determine objectives for the cooperative effort. It often proved valuable to develop a list of problems in teacher education in the state and then select some of the items for intensive examination. As has already been pointed out the cooperative process was furthered when it proved possible fairly rapidly to reach common agreement as to a desirable focus and to make progress in the direction of stimulating local action. It was important for succeeding conferences to build upon what had gone before and help move developments along still more. It may be noted, however, that in one state the general conferences were employed chiefly for the exploration of a series of leading problems in teacher education. Here the outcome was stimulation to individual conference participants rather than the promotion of genuinely cooperative action.

In states where a definite focus for joint endeavor was found, special committees charged with responsibilities relating to aspects of the resulting program usually came into being. Such committees frequently found it profitable to hold conferences of their own, at intervals, including not only their own membership but representatives from the central committee, staff members from various campuses where activities representative of the committee's interest were being carried on, and special outside consultants. These ad hoc conferences had many values: they made possible sharpening of purposes, exchange of experiences, development of general course outlines, decisions as to next steps, and—what was very important—enlistment in the cooperative enterprise of additional persons.

The central feature of every conference was the small discussion or working group of from ten to fifteen persons. These customarily met for several hours each day, though in the conferences lasting from one to two weeks a reshuffling or two often took place. Fewer than two or three meetings of the same group seldom proved satisfactory, and many groups found it profitable to stay together for considerably longer periods. According to need groups were organized homogeneously (that is, were made up of persons representing similar institutional situations or specialties) or in cross-sectional fashion. It frequently proved helpful to employ both methods in the same conference: there were advantages in bringing together now like people, now unlike. Both assignment to particular groups and free election by individuals worked out satisfactorily according to circumstances. Sometimes original groups broke up temporarily for certain purposes, and sometimes mergers successfully took place. Group chairmen were usually selected in advance from among the prospective members, being chosen because of their skill in obtaining general participation; the same procedure was sometimes followed in the case of recording secretaries, but it often worked quite well to have these chosen by the group after meeting. Sometimes there were enough consultants to provide for regular attendance with each group, but more often these persons circulated around upon request. As a matter of fact, the risk of providing so much special talent that regular conference members became inhibited had to be guarded against.

Conferences usually opened with a general meeting, of course, but it was found to be desirable to keep this brief and to get to the working-group stage, in which all could participate, promptly. Additional general meetings were fairly infrequent, seldom being called for every day. Sometimes they might be arranged for purposes growing out of the group work, for example, to react to tentative recommendations. It should be said that efforts to keep everyone in touch with everything that was going on were never too successful. Beginning conferees were likely to exhibit concern lest they miss something important, but after things had settled down and they began to enjoy the satisfactions of group experience their concern was ordinarily greatly reduced. The fact of the matter is that it is not possible successfully to learn from others in a few minutes what they have gained from hours of intensive give and take. Occasional general meetings, often in the evenings, were devoted to hearing addresses or panel discussions.

One important conclusion from the Commission's experience with conferences was that it was very profitable to leave considerable time free for spontaneous discussions and recreational activities. Afternoons and some evenings were frequently reserved for such purposes. During these periods mutual understanding and often friendship ripened. There should be no underestimation of the significance of such factors for the success of cooperative enterprise. One of the striking accomplishments of successful statewide programs was the steady growth in the ease with which representatives of institutions, by no means uncompetitive, learned to work together. As acquaintance developed conferences that had been marked by suspicion and caginess were succeeded by others distinguished for trustfulness and candor.

Special and local conferences

It has been noted that statewide programs are likely to result in the emergence of special committees which may well find it profitable to develop conferences of their own. In the experience of the Commission other types of subsidiary conference also developed. For example, in one state where there were a considerable number of teachers colleges, these grouped themselves by twos and threes to hold regional meetings in connection with work on program improvement. Such conferences were very inexpensive and easy to arrange and yielded many values. Exchange of evidence and judgment respecting student needs and their curricular implications took place. Impulses on the several campuses toward more systematic integration of program gained strength by that pooling. And new types of interinstitutional cooperation emerged. There was some advantage to the fact that only a few institutions were concerned.

The example of successful statewide conferences also influenced developments on various campuses and in various school systems. Local conferences increased in number and effectiveness. Some of these were intended chiefly for members of particular teaching staffs: such customarily were held during all or part of the week prior to the opening of college or school. These provided useful opportunities for planning the year's work, especially with respect to activities related to the state's cooperative study and designed to lead to program improvement. It is interesting to note that local conferences sponsored by school systems were usually conducted on school time; in other words, the teachers were paid for the period during which the meetings were held.

Other types of local conference that were found valuable by many colleges and universities were set up either with alumni, on the one hand, or with school leaders on the other. The former served to provide faculty members with information as to how graduates had found their preparation able to stand the test of experience. Alumni made a variety of contributions. Criticism of pre-service programs, for example, was obtained from outstanding workers in the field, along with suggestions as to possible means of improvement. Alternatively the college representatives had the opportunity of bringing their special knowledge and insight to bear on in-service problems with which the school people were struggling. In the state where the co-operative program came to focus on improving community schools, conferences between each of the active colleges and universities and the several school systems with which it was working were held simultaneously. This made it possible to devote part of the time to separate meetings by each group, and part to combined gatherings for the exchange of experience and mutual stimulation.

ADDITIONAL TECHNIQUES OF COOPERATION

In general, very much the same methods and devices that were found useful in the national study likewise proved their value in the statewide programs. These included particularly workshops, the use of outside consultants, intervisitation, and the like. Inasmuch as these have already received detailed treatment in Chapter III, only those aspects call for treatment here that were distinctive in their application to statewide enterprise.

Workshops in the state programs

Reference has already been made several times to the use of statewide and local workshops in connection with the cooperative studies here under consideration.[22] When the former were held before the state's joint program was well under way, had found a focus, and had built itself into local situations they proved to have only limited value. They did help participants to find out what the proposed program was all about, but for this purpose they were not notably more effective than the much less expensive conferences. They also enabled individuals to make progress on their individual problems: this was a good thing, but the same help could have been obtained at a workshop organized independently by some college or university. On the other hand, after interest in the cooperative program had

[22] These were similar in character and accomplishment to those discussed earlier, pp. 155–64.

been widely aroused, and its pattern had become clear and won acceptance, statewide workshops proved to have very special values. Participation increased understanding and acceptance of agreements respecting a given focus for the study. Members of central and special committees were provided with highly favorable circumstances in which to develop and refine their plans. And local action groups were able to benefit by sending representatives to the workshop where they could engage in intensive planning with the help of consultants, central committee members, and persons from other colleges, universities, or school systems engaged in projects similar to their own.

Sometimes state committees established workshops for the definite purpose of promoting some special project to which commitment had been made: the workshops for principals and supervisors already referred to would be examples. Sometimes they promoted the sending of representatives from the state to special-purpose workshops held elsewhere under independent auspices. For example, faculty and school staff members particularly concerned with child growth and development were encouraged to attend the workshop devoted to that subject at the University of Chicago. It may also be noted that the facilities of the Commission's collaboration center were similarly employed.

Mention should finally be made of the local workshops that were developed in one state as a result of its emphasis on the improvement of in-service education. These were held in various counties for the benefit of local teachers. Central committee members and persons who had attended previous statewide workshops took a leading part in organizing them and served as staff members. Thus persons and activities at the center of the cooperative program tied in with activities and persons at a related action front. This was an ideal situation.

Consultants in the statewide studies

The states conducting cooperative studies were in a position to make very effective use of consultants. At statewide conferences and workshops outside experts, including members of the

Commission staff, were brought in, and frequently the same individuals were used in this way on succeeding occasions. This made for continuity of service and proved very effective. Of course, when a consultant did not prove satisfactory he was not invited back.

As programs began to find centers of attention, the central committees sometimes brought consultants into the state to spend a month or more visiting the colleges and universities, sizing up local situations and possibilities, and helping local groups with their activities. Such visits were likely to culminate in a conference where the central committee, representatives of the various institutions, the special consultant, and perhaps others would participate in reaching important agreements. Sometimes the given consultant would make briefer return visits later, working now with one institution and now with another. Or new consultants might be imported for this focalized type of service. It was one of the marked advantages of statewide programs that agreement on some one or more common points of attack made possible an unusually effective and economical use of outside consultants by the cooperating institutions. Individually these institutions would often have felt unable to afford such services, had they, indeed, without participation in a cooperative study been moved to do so. But it proved relatively inexpensive to share in the time of an expert who was making visits to several campuses during the course of a single trip to the state.

Of course, in those states where the central committee was provided with a coordinator on full time this individual travelled about extensively, and incidentally did a good deal of consulting. "Home" consultant service was also very helpfully developed in other ways. Members of central committees, for example, were often able to engage most successfully in this type of activity. Other specialists from the staffs of particular colleges or universities within the state were often called on for help, especially by school systems. And workshop alumni were likely to be found to have developed consulting skills. Indeed it may be said that one of the notable values of statewide studies is their capacity for identifying and producing persons capable of doing a good job as consultants. [23]

Visitation in the state programs

One valuable effect of the statewide programs was that visiting back and forth among the various colleges and universities tended to increase. Some of this took place incidentally in connection with various conferences and workshops held now on this campus and now on that. Some of it was wholly informal, resulting from acquaintance developed at get-togethers of different sorts. In one state, however, intervisitation was definitely promoted by the central committee, providing a very stimulating and satisfying experience for those who took part in it and affecting developments on their several campuses.

In another state a very special form of visiting was arranged for: here the visitors were a panel of outside experts. The cooperative effort in this state had resulted in agreement on a particular set of criteria against which the quality of institutional programs of teacher preparation might be measured. The focus was on five-year programs for prospective secondary school teachers. A fifth-year requirement for certification had gone into effect, and numerous colleges that had never offered more than four years of work were contemplating extending their programs. The state department was in the position of having to decide whether or not such proposals, in particular cases, should be approved. And the state's institutions were as a group in some turmoil over the issues involved. Existence of the cooperative study and of the criteria already referred to led to approval of a suggestion that an evaluation of existing programs and plans in all interested colleges and universities be made by a visiting panel. It was agreed that this panel should make confidential reports to the state department, which would give them considerable weight in reaching decisions with respect to applications for authorization of program extension.

This scheme worked out to the great satisfaction of all concerned. The services of four experts were obtained, all of whom

[23] For more detailed discussion of consultants see pp. 150–55.

had had contact with the Commission's work in some connection or other, and one or two of whom had participated as consultants in various aspects of the particular state's prior cooperative activities. The panel visited the appropriate campuses in succession, remaining on each for one or two days. Each member held a series of individual interviews on those aspects of the program with which he was most concerned. There were also meetings in which the entire panel and a considerable group of local faculty members took part. The visitors prepared both separate and joint reports. Officials of the state department of education found these reports very helpful, and the several faculties testified to the value of the stimulus and guidance that they received from the panel's visits.[24]

Campus and off-campus clinics

In one of the states in which emphasis was placed on in-service education, so-called clinics came to be widely used and proved helpful both in their own right and as parts of the larger program.[25] These were meetings of teachers from some particular school system, lasting a day or two, and held sometimes on a given college campus but more often on the system's home grounds. Consultant service was provided by college and university staff members. These were chiefly drawn from some nearby or from the host campus, but other persons were also brought in, notably members of the central committee. The focus of attention was on developing a consensus among the participating teachers. At the first of a series of such clinics, discussion was usually limited to surface symptoms but, under skillful guidance, was soon directed to underlying causes and eventually to plans for action. Succeeding clinics would be devoted to appraising the success of such action and to rethinking plans in the light of fresh experience.

Clinics produced values other than those immediately evident. Relations between schools and colleges were improved. Not only

[24] For a fuller account of this visiting panel see *State Programs for the Improvement of Teacher Education*, pp. 40–43.

[25] For additional details see *ibid.*, pp. 346–48; compare also pp. 125–32.

did the school teachers receive appreciated help, but the consultants also benefited in their turn from closer contact with school situations and the problems they presented. Pre-service programs did not remain unaffected. Another value was the orientation that classroom teachers, supervisors, and administrators received in group methods. Moreover, out of these experiences there developed an increase in the local use of consultants and in workshop attendance. It may be said, indeed, that as a result of these clinics the effectiveness of workshops and of conferences held by particular school systems just prior to the fall session was probably doubled.

Publications in the state programs

A variety of publications resulted from the operation of the several statewide programs. Few conferences or workshops failed to lead to the production of mimeographed materials of some sort. These ranged from minutes of group meetings, through outlines for proposed courses, to statements of agreement more or less formally arrived at. Significant speeches that had been made were often reproduced. Not infrequently quite complete reports were prepared and made available for general circulation.

It may be said that in general such documents proved of greater value in the statewide studies than did similar publications growing out of the conferences that marked the progress of the Commission's national study. In neither case was it ever possible to convey to persons who had not participated in the occasions reported anything like the full flavor of the experience. But the reports growing out of the statewide activities were likely to have a more definite focus since these studies by and large were more homogeneous and the staffs of the participating institutions were apt to be particularly eager to learn what was going on. These reports, therefore, helped to accomplish a number of valuable things. They were useful in clinching fundamental concepts in the minds first of conference or workshop participants and then of others. They were also widely used as a basis for discussion on the several campuses and in various school systems. Thus they contributed to the spread of understanding, to the clarification of issues, and to the stimulation of thought and action.

In two or three states other types of publication were brought out. The commonwealth that developed a statement of basic criteria for teacher education printed and widely disseminated that document. From the cooperative activity of another state a joint analysis of factors making for teaching competence emerged and was likewise published. This instrument was extensively used throughout the state in connection with orientation programs for prospective teachers, and with the evaluation of the work of student teachers and teachers in service. It has gone through several revisions. A third state developed a particularly broad publication program. Not only were full reports of conferences and workshops prepared, but a periodic newsletter was issued in which progress of the cooperative study was described and accounts offered of new developments at participating institutions of higher learning. At the end of the period during which the Commission was associated with this program —it has been continued under the auspices of the state department of education—a cooperatively produced bound report based on the three and one-half years' experience was published.[26]

CONDITIONS FAVORING STATEWIDE PROGRAMS

It will be useful now to consider what conclusions may be drawn as to the conditions existing in a given state that may be diagnosed as favoring the successful launching and carrying forward of a statewide program of cooperation in teacher education. There can be no doubt that an energetic state department of education, with a strong leader in the position of director of teacher education and certification, is of primary importance. The word "strong" as used here does not, of course, imply a

[26] The three publications referred to in this paragraph are: *Criteria for Teacher Education* (Committee on Teacher Education of the Association of Colleges and Universities of the State of New York, September 1942); *The Ohio Teaching Record*, rev. ed. (Columbus: College of Education, Ohio State University, 1941); and David M. Trout, ed., *The Education of Teachers: Outcomes of the Michigan Cooperative Teacher Education Study* (Lansing: The Michigan Cooperative Teacher Education Study, 1943).

dictatorial habit. On the contrary, it is essential that the leadership should be democratic, eager and able to draw many persons into planning for the enterprise, and to find basic satisfaction not in originating all the good ideas but in eliciting such from any and every source. This implies ability to work groupwise. It does not, of course, imply that it is not a good thing for the leadership to share in the contribution of ideas.

A second favorable condition is the coming of developments that challenge and indeed require rethinking of certain aspects of the program in teacher education. Several examples of such developments may be drawn from the Commission's experience. Particularly useful is an extension of the period of pre-service education required before a certificate can be issued: adoption, for example, of a four-year requirement for all elementary school teachers or of a requirement of five years for teachers in the secondary schools. Such changes may put all colleges and universities under the necessity of recasting their programs; at the very least a considerable block of such institutions will be affected. Moreover, the additional time provided offers leeway for innovations without the necessity of requiring some interests within the faculties to face a certain reduction in their share in the program. This makes internal negotiations considerably easier. With the prospect of a fairly widespread and rapid extension of pre-service education requirements as the impact of war wears off, it is evident that many states will soon have the opportunity to take advantage of this situation in establishing statewide cooperative ventures. Through such cooperation, and perhaps only so, can the tendency merely to extend the old programs uncritically and unimaginatively be avoided.

Other favoring developments in the states with which the Commission was associated were the adoption of regulations providing for an extended period of student teaching or for a single curriculum designed to lead to certification for teaching in both elementary and secondary schools. The fact that both these regulations were instituted only after state officials had discussed matters carefully with representatives of the colleges and universities meant that a specially firm foundation was laid for later cooperative response to the new problems posed. In several states the growth of a statewide program of curricular revision in the schools resulted in pressures on the institutions where teachers were being prepared that inclined them favorably to cooperative action.

Where somewhat dramatic changes of the sort just considered do not provide a special opportunity for organizing statewide cooperative enterprise, other elements in the situation may be found to serve. One of these is the existence of definite common problems, growing out of the situation as it exists and widely enough recognized to encourage positive response to a proposal that a cooperative attack be attempted. Examples would be dissatisfaction with established programs of general education, demands from the field for teachers better prepared to meet the needs of new types of pupil, and concern on the part of superintendents and principals over weaknesses in the school program as currently being conducted. The presence in the state's institutions of individuals and groups marked by innovating drives is also helpful. Such persons, dissatisfied with time-hallowed but doubtfully effective procedures and full of reforming ideas, are likely to welcome an opportunity to join forces and give each other support. It should be noted that when the impulse to bring about improvement is a group rather than a purely individual phenomenon the prognosis for accomplishment is especially favorable. In any case bringing individuals with pioneer ideas together will fail to have concrete consequences on the campuses unless groups there can eventually be brought into the cooperative activity.

The presence in the state of institutions that are taking part in some national study calculated to lead to the improvement of some aspect of teacher education is also an advantage. It will be recalled that in a number of the states with which the Commission worked colleges and universities participating in its national cooperative enterprise were influential in getting a statewide study started. In others such institutions made special contributions to statewide ventures though they were not particularly responsible for launching them. The presence of institutions involved in national studies of general education, education related to regional resources, education for the improvement of community living, and the like, also proved helpful. In all such cases other colleges and universities were interested to share in the advantages enjoyed by certain of their number. Through these latter, moreover, consultant and other services were often obtainable by the statewide studies.

In these ways a powerful and effective social and educational challenge was frequently offered to the cooperating institutions. The existence of such a challenge is, as has already been noted, a distinctly favorable circumstance so far as statewide studies are concerned. But it should be observed that challenge may come from many quarters. It may, for example, emerge from the pervading educational atmosphere: the widespread concern with improving general education in colleges and universities would be an example of this, as would the equally ubiquitous drive toward better integration of theory and practice in the professional portion of programs of teacher preparation. Again the challenge may come from social circumstances and social thought. In our exciting and uncertain times this tends very much to be the case. Such phrases as "the century of the common man," "full employment," "the United Nations," and "the atomic age" suggest some of the contemporary demands on civilization to which American schools, colleges, and universities cannot fail to respond. But how? The existence of that question in so many educators' minds provides an important basis for organizing cooperative efforts to improve teacher education.

A final word may be said regarding the importance of human factors. The need for democratic leadership in the state department of education has already been stressed, and it has also been remarked that an equal quality of leadership is called for in the central committee. The presence on the several campuses and in the several school systems of leaders with similar attitudes, insights, and skills can only increase the likelihood of cooperative success. Nor must the value of good human relations be overlooked. People work together effectively not merely in terms of ideas but also in terms of mutual trust and liking. The existence among the teacher-educating forces within a state of a reasonable degree of friendliness is distinctly favorable to the success of any cooperative venture that may be undertaken. And, as has been emphasized heretofore, it is important that such relations should be deliberately fostered.

IN CONCLUSION

Statewide cooperation among colleges, universities, and school systems was a markedly effective means of improving teacher education. While one or two ventures in the Commission's experience had little success, and an equal number had trouble in moving from discussion to widespread action, the majority chalked up substantial accomplishments. Indeed, the outcome of the state programs exceeded the Commission's hopes despite the special difficulties caused by the war. This was true even when only slight financial support was provided. The value of these undertakings is attested by the fact that most were placed on a permanent footing when the period of association with the Commission was over. This fact further shows that such studies can be fully supported out of state and institutional funds. It should be added, as significant, that during the last few years other states than those with which the Commission worked have set up cooperative ventures.

Joint action on a statewide basis provides encouragement and assistance for progressive forces in the various institutions of higher learning and school systems while at the same time protecting them from yielding to foolish impulses. Few such places are completely lacking in individuals or groups who are eager to experiment with improving teacher education, but these persons are often frustrated by their relative isolation. By coming together in cooperation under the auspices of the state department of education they can gain prestige and new courage. If as a result of skillful planning the central committee and its subsidiary bodies find ways of drawing more and more campus figures into the enterprise, stimulating more action on local fronts, and gearing central and local programs more and more closely together, a considerable renaissance can follow.

But statewide cooperation also decreases the likelihood of bizarre innovations being launched in particular places. A normal outcome is basic general agreement on common points of attack, and while such agreement need not—indeed, should not —have the effect of imposing galling restrictions on particular institutions, it does set broad limits within which developments on the several campuses are likely to occur. Moreover, give and take at committee meetings, conferences, and workshops are calculated to reveal the flaws in poorly thought-through proposals. Since participants in this process of critical examination are likely themselves to be experimental-minded people, the proponents of particular ideas cannot reject their strictures as merely reflecting inbred conservatism.

It should be noted finally that, in a number of states and with respect to a number of problems, cooperation made possible accomplishments that would scarcely have been realized in its absence. Driving efforts by the state department of education working alone could, as past experience has amply demonstrated, have had but little real success. Colleges, universities, and school systems acting separately would have had less motivation, less opportunity, and fewer resources. Cooperative endeavor, geared to common concerns and making possible the pooling of ideas and means of accomplishment, often resulted in more rapid and substantial progress than could otherwise have been hoped for.

The Commission's conclusions, based on its experience with interinstitutional cooperation in the improvement of teacher education, may now be summarized as follows:

1. Cooperative undertakings in which representatives of various agencies participate have proved capable of contributing uniquely to bringing about improvements in the work in teacher education done by particular colleges, universities, and school systems.

2. Effective enterprises of this character have differed considerably as to geographic base, the degree to which individual participants were official representatives of their working situations, the degree to which these situations were similar in nature, and the points at which change was hoped for. Sometimes

the purpose has been limited to change in individuals, sometimes institutional change has also been desired, and sometimes change in interinstitutional relations has been the goal.

3. Cooperative activities of national scope emphasize country-wide similarities among problems of teacher education and may exercise a special influence because of their dramatic scale. On the other hand, the distances involved make frequent contacts impossible even when special financial support is available, and the range of situational difference puts additional difficulties in the way of achieving agreements as to common focus or method of attack.

4. Statewide cooperative studies have proved to possess many advantages. State departments of education are or should be in a position to exercise valuable leadership and to find the funds needed to support such enterprises. The problems facing the participating agencies tend to be relatively similar and some patterns of working relationship are likely to have been developed that will provide a foundation for more formal and inclusive cooperation. Relatively limited distances favor frequency of contact and widespread participation even when study budgets are not very large.

5. Regional studies fall, as to advantages and disadvantages, between the two types just considered. They have proved most successful when their points of attack were limited, when the participating agencies were homogeneous in character, and when sponsorship was provided by established regional associations.

6. Cooperative studies, regardless of geographical base, have been most influential in practice when participants have been institutions rather than individuals and when their purpose has been institutional rather than individual change.

7. There are characteristic advantages and disadvantages to both homogeneity and heterogeneity among participants in cooperative studies. In the former case, finding bases for working together is easier; in the latter, breadth of view and community of understanding are promoted. Some mixture of factors of homogeneity and heterogeneity is most desirable.

8. Successful cooperative studies the purpose of which is the

achievement of institutional change may vary in the degree to which uniformity of such change is an object. There are advantages when a measure of common agreement as to objects to be pursued and methods to be employed can be attained. But such agreements must be genuine and leeway must be allowed for free adjustment to differences in particular institutional circumstances. The possible area of such agreement tends to be positively correlated with the degree of homogeneity existing among the participating institutions. Anything that looks like an external effort to force standardization will reduce the likelihood of successful cooperative effort. There are definite values in cooperative programs even when no attempt to achieve formal agreement is made.

9. A cooperative study can most readily be organized and is most likely to succeed when the lead can be taken by some agency that has the respect and confidence of the various institutions that are to participate, for example, strong national or regional educational associations or well organized and influential state departments of education.

10. A democratic type of leadership is essential. Its aim should be, not to drive for acceptance of its own existing ideas, but to maximize participation, stimulate the expression and friendly but rigorous examination of ideas, promote the use of group methods, and increase experimentation.

11. State departments of education—and especially state directors of teacher education and certification—have special opportunities available to them for the exercise of leadership in cooperative studies in the field of teacher education. Experience shows that work of this character yields more satisfactions and brings more results than specialization in the issuance of regulations, the saying of yea and nay, and in supervising a system of records. Extension of leadership of this character is most desirable. Guidance of a statewide cooperative program is, however, demanding: a competent coordinator on full time will, therefore, ordinarily prove distinctly advantageous.

12. State councils on teacher education consisting of appropriate state-department officials, representatives of each insti-

tution where teachers are prepared, and selected representatives of the public schools are valuable bodies. They provide for interchange of views and improved mutual understanding. They may effectively share in making policy for teacher education in their several states.

13. Every cooperative study needs a central body for planning and guidance. Its membership should be chosen so as to provide competent representation of the major interests concerned, specifically both the public schools and institutions of higher learning. The basic function of such a body is the determination and conduct of strategy, not legislation or enforcement. Ten or twelve members constitute the ideal size; definite advantages accrue when these members exercise leading functions in the activities related to the cooperative venture being carried forward in and by the associated institutions.

14. The early achievement of action on particular campuses and in particular school systems should be definitely aimed for in connection with cooperative studies. There is danger of losing enthusiasm and satisfaction if matters remain too long at the stage of discussion at the center. Moreover, it is important to enlist increasing numbers of persons in the program, in one way or another, as rapidly as possible. This increases understanding and interest as well as the likelihood of substantial achievement.

15. It is important that centralized activities and those on the several action fronts—in other words, in the participating institutions—should be closely related. One helpful way of tying centralized and decentralized efforts together is the development of special committees in connection with particular tasks.

16. There is always danger that a cooperative venture will try to deal with so many problems that effort will be scattered and little will be accomplished in any direction. Selecting a few generally acceptable points for attack should be a first purpose. Such selection will require time enough, however, for the cooperators to become reasonably well acquainted and to achieve reasonable understanding of one another's problems.

17. Institutional responsibility for participation in a cooperative study needs to be located in some person or committee

or both. Local leadership should be assigned to persons possessing status with their colleagues and capacity to work effectively through group methods. Local administrative understanding and support are very important.

18. Special attention should be devoted to bringing an increasing proportion of local personnel into active participation in cooperative studies. Keeping them informed is important, but less so than providing them with an action role. Local projects related to the central program should be encouraged, local personnel should be drawn into related cooperative committee work and conferences, and local conferences may well be developed. Special attention should be given to interesting subject-matter people in the program.

19. Conferences constitute the most valuable single means of carrying on cooperative studies. They are relatively inexpensive, can attract attendance of the needed persons of various types, and are readily repeatable. Such conferences should provide for maximum participation by all in attendance, under conditions conducive to friendliness and candor. They should, consequently, make much use of group techniques, group membership to range ideally from ten to fifteen persons in size.

20. Conferences should be very carefully planned. The purposes of the cooperative study and the interests of the prospective attendants should be thoughtfully considered. Competent leadership should be arranged for, but not of such character nor in such quantity that general participation will be inhibited. Chief reliance should be placed on work in small groups. Time should be reserved for informal activities. The possibility that some arrangements will need to be modified after a conference is under way should be anticipated.

21. A conference should be long enough for its purposes. Less than two or three days' time is unlikely to prove profitable, and conferences of a week's or two weeks' duration have often been outstandingly fruitful. A relatively extended conference is particularly indicated at the beginning of a cooperative study.

22. There is likely to be considerable loss of effectiveness when the number of conference participants exceeds 150, especially if

they are not already fairly well acquainted with one another.

23. The location of a conference is a matter of considerable importance. Consideration should be given to the availability of suitable rooms for group meetings, circumstances conducive to informal contacts, creature comforts, general attractiveness, and—especially in the case of longer conferences—recreational opportunities. Protection from irrelevant distractions is desirable. Camps have often provided unusually satisfactory conference spots.

24. Workshops have demonstrated their great value in cooperative studies. They have been most useful, however, after the study was well established and when the workshop participants represented related activities being carried forward on particular campuses or in particular school systems.

25. Consultants have been widely and effectively employed in cooperative studies. These have often been "outside" experts: their use has proved especially economical in the case of statewide studies that have achieved a definite focus. Central-staff members have customarily served in a consultant capacity, and it has proved of definite value to the studies when members of the central committee could do likewise. Consultant ability on the part of faculty members of participating institutions has often been developed and fruitfully used.

26. Intervisitation among representatives of various institutions participating in cooperative studies has tended to occur and has proved valuable. In one state it was found advantageous to arrange for all the cooperating colleges to be visited by a panel of outside experts charged with the responsibility of appraising programs in the light of criteria set up as a result of the study.

27. Various kinds of publication proved helpful as a means of clearing information respecting the progress of cooperative studies. Periodic reports from central and special committees were customary, as were reports of conferences and workshops. In one state a formal statement regarding the broad purposes of teacher education was jointly produced and widely disseminated. In other instances a newsletter was developed as a means of

spreading information as to progress on various campuses and in various school systems.

28. Cooperative studies have dealt effectively with a wide variety of problems in teacher education. A sense of unity, and movement from the stage of discussion at the center to action in many of the participating institutions, have come most rapidly when it was possible fairly soon to agree on a few common points of attack. It proved important, however, that the spearheads should be employed with careful reference to over-all purposes and to their relation to other aspects of a unified program of teacher education.

29. Cooperative attacks on certain problems—general education, student teaching, and in-service education, for example—seemed to make for distinctly greater progress than separate efforts on particular campuses. Individual staff members who were eager to attempt reforms gained courage when they were brought together, and their colleagues' attitudes became more favorable when their experiments were related to a statewide enterprise.

30. Several statewide studies demonstrated their effectiveness for promoting improvements in the in-service education of teachers. School systems were wisely selected because of their interest and readiness, and while the help of neighboring colleges and universities was particularly employed there was also a pooling of the resources of these institutions. In one state the support of its associations of principals and of supervisors proved very advantageous.

31. Marked changes in requirements relating to the education of teachers within a given state (for example, the extension of specified periods of preparation) provide particularly favorable opportunities for the launching of statewide cooperative studies. Widespread concern with some particular educational problem, such as that of promoting community schools, is also conducive to success. So is general awareness of some important social challenge, such as may come from national circumstances and related thought. In our times all of these favoring circumstances tend to be present.

32. In every cooperative study the human factor has proved to be of marked importance. Democratic attitudes and behavior are essential to success. Good human relations must be deliberately cultivated and taken advantage of. The effectiveness of cooperation in the improvement of teacher education is as much a matter of people working well together as it is of ideas and methods.

V

A Summing Up

WITH THE PUBLICATION of this report the work of the Commission on Teacher Education comes to a close. The event coincides very nearly with the end of the war, which marks the opening of a period in which the further improvement of teacher education is a matter of crucial national importance. The moment finds the schools of the nation faced with many new and difficult problems, reflecting the problems with which society itself is confronted. It finds the schools, furthermore, still staggering under the difficulties that were their portion as a result of war: staffs inadequate both as to quantity and quality; salary levels lagging behind the costs of living; equipment in need of repair, replacement, and supplementation.

The colleges and universities, too, are entering a new era. After years during which enrollments have been sharply depressed they face a period of rapid expansion. The return of veterans to their campuses presents them with a novel challenge. With the ending of selective service—and even if compulsory military training should be adopted as a national policy—the wonted flow of recent graduates of the high schools will be resumed. The upward trend of college enrollments that was so striking a social phenomenon between the wars may be expected to re-establish itself. Moreover, the colleges, like the schools, are under necessity of adapting themselves to the tremendous changes that are affecting the entire fabric of civilization.

Nor can the state departments of education expect to escape the powerful impacts of changing circumstance. The movement already observable before the war toward their achievement of new positions of leadership now becomes a matter of increased importance. The impending expansion of federal aid to education will, it may be expected and must be hoped, add to the responsibilities of these state agencies. Their strengthening must be a major goal in the educational world. Considering the traditional responsibilities of these departments in the field of teacher education it may be anticipated that such strengthening will desirably influence developments in that field.

So pregnant a situation calls insistently for a re-examination of our past in teacher education, a reappraisal of where we stand at the present, and an identification of leading trends and problems that must mark our future. It is appropriate that the Commission on Teacher Education, in the final chapter of its final report, should undertake these tasks briefly. At the same time the Commission may properly offer a concluding summary of its own views and recommendations.

The Significance of Teacher Education

In its first report the Commission stated its views respecting the social significance of teacher education.[1] Its argument may be recapitulated here. Education is the means whereby a democratic society perpetuates its culture and provides for its progressive improvement. While, in a real and important sense, all living experience exercises an educational influence, it is to the schools and institutions of higher learning that our society has assigned a special and chief responsibility for inducting youth into the culture and for developing in them the capacity wisely to modify that culture. Upon these institutions largely depends the nurturing of the nation's human resources. That the schools and colleges should be excellent and influential is, therefore, a matter of prime social concern.

The effectiveness of the schools depends upon many things. What the children that attend them are, by reason of inheritance and the impacts of home and community, sets limits to their accomplishment. So does the quantity and quality of support provided for education by the lay public. Buildings and equipment are important. So are curricula and books. But the children being given, no other elements in educational situations are so

[1] *Teachers for Our Times.* See especially Chapter I.

vitally significant as are the men and women who conduct the schools—the teachers. It is they who must make the most of existing opportunities and conditions. It is they who develop and man the curricula. It is they who select, employ, and interpret the books, maps, movies, recordings, and other aids to instruction. Above all, it is they who day in and day out, year in and year out, influence by their conduct and example the thought and behavior of America's boys and girls. And as these boys and girls steadily extend the average period of their school and college attendance, the power of teachers, for good or for evil, steadily mounts.

The conclusion is inescapable. The quality of teachers is—or should be—a matter of deepest social concern. The nation risks its entire future if it entrusts its children to the charge of men and women who are not intelligent, not informed, not skillful, not democratic, not devoted to young people and to their own calling. The nation needs teachers who are superbly fitted to their important task. It needs teachers who respect personality, who are community minded, who act reasonably, who know how to work cooperatively with others. It needs teachers whose native gifts have been highly developed through sound general and professional education, whose knowledge is accurate, extensive, and increasing. It needs teachers who like and are liked by children, who understand how children grow and develop, who know how to guide learning and mediate knowledge effectively. It needs teachers who live in the world as well as in the school and in the classroom, who function as good democratic citizens in all these situations. And it needs teachers who love their work, who are skillful in evaluating for themselves how effective they are in discharging their duties, and who are continually increasing their stature as persons, citizens, and professional workers. [2]

It is the task of teacher education in the United States to produce teachers of this caliber, teachers fit for our nation and our times. That task is an intricate one and it spreads over many years. Let us consider what it involves. First, there is the

[2] For an expansion of these views see *ibid.*, especially Chapter IV.

need for attracting to the profession young men and women with promise of success, and for guiding into other vocations those would-be teachers who lack such promise. Then there is the necessity of developing the best possible programs of pre-service education. Comes next the responsibility of helping beginning teachers to find berths suited to their interests and competence, and of assisting them to make a good and satisfying adjustment during their novitiate. This responsibility concerns both the institutions in which the teachers have been prepared and also the school systems in which they are beginning their work.

But teacher education is not something that can be considered completed even after a young teacher is off to a good start. The social changes and educational discoveries that mark our times demand that teachers in service should not stand still. The values to any person of continuous development support that demand. It follows that school systems, utilizing the help of institutions of higher learning, state departments of education, and other resources, need to provide teachers with working conditions that will enable them constantly to realize existing powers to the full, and continuously to engage in activities that make for personal and professional development.

The Commission has written elsewhere:

In all civilized communities the task of teaching is chiefly entrusted to a company of experts. In the United States that company numbers approximately 1,000,000; and some 285,000 young men and women are preparing to enter the profession. It makes a difference who and what these teachers are. Social well-being and social advance depend in marked measure on their excellence. But who these teachers are, and what they are, turns directly upon the effectiveness of the arrangements that we make for their education. To improve teacher education is to improve teaching; to improve teaching is to improve the schools; to improve the schools is to strengthen the next generation; to strengthen the next generation is a social duty of the first magnitude.[3]

TEACHER EDUCATION IN THE MID-THIRTIES

When the Commission was created in 1938 a hundred years of public teacher education in the United States was drawing to

---

[3] *Ibid.*, p. 24. The second figure quoted, a prewar estimate, would of course be too high for the war years; but it is likely to be reached again in the near future.

a close. The colleges of liberal arts, of course, had produced teachers from the earliest days of the American colonies, and they along with the universities (institutions much more recently developed) continued to constitute the chief source of teachers for the secondary schools. But the vast proportion of elementary school teachers had long come from the state, county, and municipal normal schools. Of these the last two types had by the mid-thirties all but disappeared, while the former had almost universally undergone a metamorphosis into degree-granting state teachers colleges. These colleges, moreover, were increasingly entering the field of preparing high school teachers.

The pre-service situation

The situation, so far as teacher preparation was concerned, was far from stabilized and far from satisfactory. The teachers colleges were on the march, but had not yet fully found themselves. Their facilities and faculties, while steadily improving, were still frequently inferior. The opportunity, provided by lengthening their courses, for the radical rethinking of their curricula according to functional criteria had not been widely or fully employed: the response in many institutions had been mainly to do more of what had been done in the normal school stage; elsewhere there had been a tendency to adopt liberal arts practices without too much consideration of their suitability for teacher education. The colleges of liberal arts themselves were in a state of great uncertainty with respect to their role in teacher preparation. The role was one they had long performed, and for perhaps most of them the loss of the opportunity would prove disastrous. Yet they liked to pride themselves on being nonvocational in character, and their faculties, outside the departments of education, were not likely to feel much devotion to the job of preparing teachers.

Between these two types of institution, indeed, an ill-concealed conflict frequently raged. The teachers colleges resented what they saw as airs put on by the older institutions, and doubted the efficacy of teacher education where concern with the task seemed often to be centralized in a single department and where such facilities as campus schools seldom were to be found. The colleges of liberal arts, for their part, were likely to take a lofty view of their own superiority in scholarship and in tradition and to criticize the new arrivals in the degree-granting field as largely concerned with "methods, psychology, and administration—with anything, in short, except the subject to be taught." They were also disturbed by what they felt was a propensity of the state-controlled institutions to use their close relations with legislatures and state departments of education to get laws passed and rules adopted whereby their position was consolidated and unwelcome pressures brought to bear upon their rivals. Feeling ran particularly high when, as had begun to be the case, the teachers colleges offered curricula designed for students who were not intending to teach. The fact was that some of these institutions were tending to become general colleges.

The universities occupied a somewhat special position and had their own particular problems. With few exceptions they had developed schools or colleges of education which offered both undergraduate and graduate instruction. These were able to attract the services of the most prominent professional experts, and to this degree had an advantage over the teachers colleges. But on the other hand they seldom were in a position to exercise any control over the various subject-matter departments, which were customarily parts of the universities' colleges and graduate schools of arts and sciences. And these latter divisions, with which it was necessary to work, ordinarily shared quite fully the attitudes toward teacher education and faculties specializing therein, already described as characteristic of the independent colleges. Things were further complicated by the fact that university undergraduates destined for teaching usually registered during their freshman and sophomore years with the colleges of arts, and were often later provided with the option of either continuing in that division or shifting their allegiance to the school of education.

The situation described was obviously unfortunate. The schism between educationists and professors of the various

academic subjects—observable, it should be said, on the teachers
college campuses as well as elsewhere—constituted a formidable
obstacle in the way of achieving anything like integrated programs of teacher preparation. Such achievement was equally
militated against by the prevalently atomistic pattern of curriculum construction. For more than half a century the elective
system had been encouraging and increasing proliferation of
courses, out of which curricula were constructed much as a
child builds houses out of blocks. The individual course, half
course, or even quarter course, given independently by an
individual professor, had become the educational atom, and by
a process of aggregation these atoms were employed to create
the various educational universes. The only generally recognized
test that such a universe *had* been created was that it should
include enough courses to add up to at least 120 semester hours
of credit.

There was emerging, however, a distinct demand for educational programs more integrated, and hence more meaningful,
in character. This demand was being expressed with respect to
college education generally, not merely to that designed for the
preparation of teachers. Moreover, it was being felt by subject-
matter professors as well as by professors of education. This
common interest was favorable to the ultimate achievement of
a greater degree of rapprochement. The trend was favored by
another development. The rapid increase of college enrollments had meant the appearance, on all sorts of campuses, of
undergraduates whose abilities, interests, and purposes varied
markedly from those of the students with whom the colleges had
been accustomed to deal. These newcomers did not respond too
satisfactorily or with too much satisfaction to the standard
curricula and standard methods of instruction. An uneasiness,
accordingly, had begun to spread widely throughout the
faculties. A demand for substantial curricular reform, especially
with respect to general education, was increasingly being heard.
And the word "functional" was now on many lips. This word,
long familiar to the educationists, implied that education should
be planned in conscious relation to the needs of students and

of the culture in which they were to live. More common ground was being built up.

Another factor making for reform in the higher educational sphere was, of course, the mounting social crisis. The first world war had been followed by a period of unprecedented prosperity, and then by one of equally unprecedented depression. Social and economic changes were cracking the established patterns of national life. And the tragedy of another world conflagration, certain to be more devastating than the last, was inexorably drawing near. The period was one in which all educators save the most obtuse found themselves driven to face fundamental questions about their work.

The in-service situation

The word from the schools was also calculated to encourage reform so far as teacher education was concerned. These institutions were being subjected to influences similar to those operating upon the colleges. The skyrocketing of enrollments in the secondary schools, far more phenomenal even than the increase in college attendance, had brought with it a quantity of critical problems. The unsuitability of traditional high school curricula for the large proportion of "new" students had become undeniably clear. Experience with the CCC and NYA programs during the depression had cast further light on the unsatisfactory situation existing in these schools. The public school authorities were disturbed by the prospect of a rival educational system being developed under federal auspices. They knew the threat could be warded off only if they themselves succeeded in meeting the needs of all American youth. But this required teachers who knew how to do the job, and teachers of the requisite character were not customarily being developed by the colleges and universities. Upon these institutions, accordingly, there descended a mounting volume of criticism from the field.

The schools, however, could not afford to wait for replacements from the colleges even if these institutions should have suddenly begun to turn out teachers according to ideal specifications. Action had to be taken more closely to home. School curricula had to be re-examined and refashioned. And this had to be done by teachers already on the job, teachers who on the *average* had been in service for a dozen years or more. These experienced teachers had to learn how to work in new ways. In a word, the situation called for a blend of program improvement and of in-service education.

In this connection, too, criticism was voiced respecting the customary contributions of colleges and universities. Their patterns of in-service education had been developed in a more primitive day when the teachers who came to them were mainly satisfied to complete the courses requisite to the award of the bachelor's or master's degree. Considerable magic was presumed to reside in these degrees. School boards and superintendents had encouraged teachers to attain them by making promotions and increases in salary dependent upon them. Since few teachers could afford to take a year or two off for further study they did the work required mainly at summer sessions or through extension courses. To such piecemeal effort the course-and-credit system was admirably suited. Eventually the teacher might hope to accumulate whatever "met the requirements" and be awarded the coveted degree. But this system not only provided for little in the way of integration; it fostered the offering of professor-planned, theoretical courses —often identical with those prepared for undergraduates— which frequently made but limited connection with the problems the teachers were actually facing in their schools. As such problems became severe, both the classroom teachers and the administrative leaders in the schools became more and more critical of the in-service work of the colleges and universities.

Special influences

In the meantime a number of other occurrences had begun to point toward innovations in the education of teachers. A rapid cumulation of significant research respecting the growth and development of human beings, and especially of children and adolescents, had yielded numerous conclusions that had important implications for teaching. The bearing of emotional, physical, and social factors on intellectual growth and the development of personality was discovered to be profound; and the new insights respecting human wholeness and human dynamics cast serious doubts on the suitability of many school arrangements and teaching practices. From another quarter, in response to mounting sensitivity to social problems, came the criticism that too little of education was related to the problems and needs of contemporary communities and their populations. The idea of the community school as an instrument for the improvement of ordinary living began to be vigorously propounded. What shall it profit a child, it was asked, if he gain a knowledge of Caesar and trigonometry and lose an opportunity to learn how to raise standards of health, housing, and citizenship?

A third influence was the result of the mounting attention to educational evaluation. Broadening the objectives and bases of traditional testing and measurement, the proponents of evaluation raised searching questions respecting educational goals, asked what behavior on the part of students might be presumed to indicate the attainment of such goals, and developed qualitative as well as quantitative means for gathering evidence in regard to such behavior. Moreover, they emphasized the pooling of all such evidence, the importance of viewing the child as a whole and not from some limited angle. The effect was to stimulate teachers in both the schools and the colleges to ask themselves more sharply just what it was they hoped they were achieving and just what reason they had to think that they were being successful. The emphasis upon behavior carried the teachers' eyes beyond the final examination, and the stress upon the whole student increased sensitivity to the importance of interests, attitudes, and skills along with that of the attainment of knowledge.

One additional element in the emerging situation should be mentioned: this was the increased concern with democracy, its preservation and its better realization. For a century and more the American people had taken it for granted that democracy was destined ultimately to sweep the globe, and events closely following the end of the first world war seemed to promise the early realization of that expectation. But suddenly the tide had set in the opposite direction. To be sure, the rise of totalitarian governments had at first seemed anachronistic. But by the mid-thirties it was becoming evident that democracy was faced with a formidable adversary. Men who loved freedom and who sensed the crisis became deeply disturbed. Their concern was not lessened when they observed developments in our own country—in the citadel of freedom—which showed that the new yet reactionary doctrines were capable of finding a sympathetic hearing even here. Such men, not few of them representatives of the schools, colleges, and universities, began to urge that American education must increase its effectiveness as a developer of democratic ideas and actions.

Thus it will be seen that, at the time when the Commission was appointed, forces at work within institutions of higher learning, in the public schools, and in American society and the world at large all combined to set the stage for serious thought and action in educational circles. More specifically, the world of teacher education was ripe for change.

What the Commission Stood For

This then was the situation that faced the Commission on Teacher Education when it came into being. It had been told that "the new task confronting teacher education is, in part, the breaking down of the control of tradition and outworn practices and, in part, the building up of new concepts of education and a creative approach to the problems of teaching." It had been advised to encourage "more experimentation, demonstration, and evaluation, on the bases of hypotheses in which there is reason to have confidence because of previous careful study," to press for "adjustment within existing institutions" and to rely upon "the leadership of those directing teacher education and the public schools."[4]

The Commission's first duties were to formulate a point of view by which it might be guided in its action, and then to

[4] *Major Issues in Teacher Education*, pp. 7–8 and 43.

develop a program. What that program was, how it developed, and what it accomplished have been described in the earlier chapters of this report and also, more fully, in other reports, prepared for it and previously issued. The point of view that the Commission adopted was developed in detail in its own first report, *Teachers for Our Times*.[5] It seems to be desirable here to rehearse the main tenets of that philosophy and to suggest how it operated to control the Commission's course of action.

Ideas about democracy

The Commission began by formulating a democratic philosophy of life and undertaking to see what it would mean if it were fully applied in the schools, in the colleges and universities where teacher education is carried forward, and in control of its own actions. It saw as basic elements in the American faith to which it was prepared to give allegiance, belief in the unique worth of personality, belief in the interdependence of the individual and society, and belief in reason and reasonableness as the sovereign means of determining goals and solving problems. It accepted the idea that freedom is the proper state for man to live in, and that popular government offers the best guarantee that that state will be approximated. It embraced the view that the boundless potentialities of men, if permitted to express themselves in a free and reasonable social order, may result in progressive improvement both of personality and of society. The Commission suffered no illusions as to the degree to which the American faith had thus far succeeded in controlling American behavior. But if it saw the blemishes upon our national life it neither exaggerated them nor accepted them as evidence that the faith was false. The Commission believed in America; it also believed that America could and should move nearer to what its deepest convictions implied.

Ideas about social trends

In an epoch when the age-old issue of man versus the state was again rampant the Commission felt it necessary to examine

[5] Especially in Chapter II. For the titles of the other reports see the appendix.

this conflict. It emerged with the conclusion that the issue was mainly illusory. It saw "the individual" as every member of society, born and destined to live and die dependent upon social relationships. It saw freedom as something that must be realized in a social context, as indeed an ineluctably social phenomenon. It rejected the idea of the slave state, a mystical entity superior to all men and by right the master of all men. But it also rejected the notion that government, however popular, must always be an enemy to freedom, a natural despoiler of the rights of individual man.

As a matter of fact the Commission reached the conclusion, from the evidence of history, that there is an irreversible trend toward the wider use of collective powers in the affairs of modern society. An examination of economic and social movements, whether confined to the national scene or spread to embrace the whole world, revealed that with the rise of modern technology and the development of a steadily greater degree of human interdependence men were faced with a basic dilemma. Either they must learn to cooperate more effectively, to employ their political powers and institutions more affirmatively, or they must expect some tyrant to undertake to manage the complex machinery of contemporary civilization for them. The third alternative was chaos.

Yet the doubts with which many citizens see government becoming more powerful and more extended were recognized as being by no means wholly lacking in foundation. The possibility of big government becoming a heavier-handed master than big business or big finance is a wholly real one. The problem, then, is to keep government the servant of the people while employing it more widely. The necessity is to plan; the need is so to plan as to magnify, not restrict, freedom.

In examining this issue the Commission became impressed by the idea of a balance of centralization and decentralization. It saw in the example of the Tennessee Valley Authority a demonstration of how government may be employed in such fashion that great enterprises may be planned and realized in conjunction with one another to the advantage of the people—

whose will is constantly consulted, whose participation is continually made possible, whose understanding is progressively increased, and whose welfare is steadily enlarged. The secret seemed to lie in a clear concept of the roles of leader, expert, and worker, in the maintenance of open and sensitive channels of two-way communication, and in a decentralization of administration to balance a centralization of control. There were things worth doing that could be accomplished only by group action on a very large scale. But the action at the center must be kept responsive to the wishes and capacities at the periphery; and the actions at the periphery must be determined not merely by decisions reached at the center but also by the judgment of those most directly concerned, with free reference to locally ruling circumstances. The key to the problem was responsible participation.

Ideas about personality and human relations

All these views the Commission found supported when it turned to consider personality and human relations. Personality it saw as a social phenomenon; and in the efforts of modern man to escape the obligations of his social nature it found the explanation for many social ills. This line of inquiry led to a re-examination of the concept of freedom. It now appeared that this concept has been largely interpreted, during recent centuries, in a predominantly negative way. Man has sought freedom from those very relations that distinguish him from the rest of creation. He has resisted what is most human about him: his capacity to plan and work with other men. Seeking freedom from his obligations to others, he has found only loneliness and fear. And then sometimes he has fled such freedom, preferring to recover a sense of belonging by sacrificing his individuality in slave service to the totalitarian state or to the anonymous authority of a mechanized, standardized culture.

The remedy for this situation appeared to the Commission to be a recovery of positive freedom, of man's freedom to think, feel, and act for himself, not as a refugee from society but as a willing accepter of the implications of group membership.

Isolationism has been tried and has failed in more spheres than the international. Men need to realize anew that we are all members one of another.

Only by freely joining his lot with others, only by accepting full responsibility for cooperative planning and action, can the individual—whether child or man—attain that sense of belonging which is his desperate need. Involved is the necessity for understanding oneself and others, for being sensitive to the rights and needs of all, for guiding personal action according to such sensitivity and understanding. Above all, personality must respect personality: only by freeing others may oneself be free.[6]

The study and improvement of human relations thus seemed to the Commission to constitute major needs in our times. It saw modern man led astray by the example of the machine, a thing of standardized interchangeable parts, made of non-sentient materials. A machine could be fully planned in advance, built imaginatively as a blueprint, and once constructed counted upon to run according to specifications. Its operation was in response to power supplied from a single source. Its efficiency was subject to a certain amount of mechanical friction, but this could be accurately estimated and allowed for in advance as well as kept at a minimum through regular lubrication. Once the switch was pulled the machine would run as expected, cog turning repetitively on cog, and a standardized product emerging at a standardized rate. Man had been trying to develop human enterprises according to this pattern and to operate them according to these concepts. He had not succeeded, and he could not expect to succeed. Modern personnel research had revealed what might have been comprehended in the first place, namely that human beings are persons and cannot successfully be treated as cogs.

The Commission believed, then, that undertakings for which men and women, boys and girls, are of the essence must be thought of, planned, and conducted with reference to human nature and human relations. It must be understood that the "parts" of such enterprises are persons with all that that implies.

[6] *Teachers for Our Times*, pp. 81–82.

Each is a potential source of power and all that power should be released, pooled, and magnified. Each has ideas and feelings of his own, and those ideas and feelings cannot wisely be ignored. Each is a changing being whose changes cause whatever he participates in to have an inescapably dynamic character. And each of these persons reacts variously to other persons with whom he is associated. It follows that the successful operation of human enterprise calls for methods and concepts quite different from those suited to a machine's work. Greater and better understanding of these matters seemed to the Commission to be a prime necessity for our times.

Ideas about thought and action

A related idea that came to prominence in the Commission's thinking remains to be presented. This was that in the modern world thought was too frequently divorced from action. The Commission declared:

By specializing in thinking some men have made great advances in understanding but they have always run the occupational risk of losing contact with reality. Moreover, the results of their speculations when systematized and taught to other persons lacking in related practical experience have not infrequently had dangerous consequences. The mistaken idea that theory and practice are unrelated has been encouraged; so has the notion that the universe, including its human aspects, is a mechanical entity any part of which may be abstracted and treated as if it were without organic relationship to the whole.[7]

It appeared that this condition had been fomented by a high degree of intellectual specialization. Noting a trend toward greater cooperation in this sphere and a more organic type of thinking, the Commission developed the view that specialists should be encouraged to pool their powers in joint efforts to deal constructively with real situations, complex and changing. It concluded:

. . . the test of reason in modern man must be the skill with which he applies thought in the guidance of action in an interdependent world. Since the world—our world—is predominantly social, and since skill is the fruit of practice, extended experience with group methods

[7] *Ibid.*, p. 82.

is indicated. Such methods may be applied to the simplest as well as to the most complex of situational problems. They require a combination of thought and action, each leading to the other, turn after turn.[8]

Effects on the Commission's program

The reader who has followed the earlier chapters of this report should be able to see for himself how the program of the Commission reflected the views summarized above. That program sought to exemplify the principles of democracy and of democratic planning. It was marked by respect for personality; it emphasized the organic character of group enterprises such as colleges, universities, and school systems; and it placed its trust in the efficacy of reasonable procedures in which all might play a part. It sought to attain a balance of centralization and decentralization whereby individuals and groups and institutions might work freely, yet in organic relation to one another. It promoted participation in the formulation of inclusive agreements, and trust in the individual to bear his share in the implementation thereof. It encouraged cooperation yet strove to enlarge positive freedom. The program paid much attention to factors of personality and to improving human relations. It was not mechanical. Finally, the program sought constantly to increase thinking in relation to doing, and the reverse: to demonstrate the values of pooled intelligence when applied to problem situations.

It should be noted that the Commission's basic ideas not only determined the procedures employed by its staff—members of which fully shared these ideas and had, indeed, participated in their formulation—but were reflected in the activities engaged in within particular school systems, colleges, universities, and states. Democratic participation increased on all these fronts. The quest for institutional unity was stimulated there. A balance of order and possibility was more fully achieved. Cooperation was extended, human relations improved.

The Commission would not wish to make any undue claims as to the success of its procedures. Its members and the members

[8] *Ibid.*, p. 85.

of its staff, as well as the thousands of persons throughout the country with whom it was associated, were all fallible humans. Moreover, the point of view that it held and the methods it employed were not wholly developed at the beginning, requiring steady refinement as matters progressed. It took time for the ideas to be worked out and communicated, and for the procedures to be developed and put to the test. Mistakes were naturally made along the way. But the Commission believes that, as a whole, its effort *was* a success. It emerges from its experience with its basic convictions corrected in detail and further clarified, yet fundamentally confirmed. It has evidence that those convictions have achieved better understanding and wider acceptance among the many persons who shared in its work.

The question now naturally arises, what were the results, so far as changes in teacher education are concerned, of action according to such ideas and with reliance upon such procedures as those that have just been set forth and suggested? The Commission did not anticipate as spectacular immediate consequences in the colleges, universities, school systems, and states with which it was associated as might have been attained by the use of forcing procedures predicated upon autocratic assumptions. It believes, however, that its several reports reveal the occurrence of changes that were substantial in quality, represented distinct improvements, and were solidly grounded. It believes that the ways of working together that were developed will continue to be fruitfully employed. The Commission has no hesitation in recommending these ways to others. It has no doubt that their extended use will result in steady improvement in teacher education. And it is convinced that they constitute examples of the ways in which all men must learn to work together if democracy is to remain triumphant in our times.

Leading Issues and Promising Trends

The leading issues in teacher education have been repeatedly dealt with in this and other reports of and to the Commission. In those same volumes there have been repeatedly set forth the conclusions of the Commission and of its staff respecting directions of movement likely to lead to improvement. It seems proper, however, in drawing this final statement to a close to sum up briefly with respect to these matters. The purpose will be to suggest points at which continuing attacks should be aimed, and reforms that in the Commission's opinion deserve particular emphasis.

The conditions of teaching

It must be observed at the outset that the improvement of teacher education depends fundamentally upon an increase in the attractiveness of the teaching profession. The ablest young people cannot be recruited to teaching—or if they are persuaded to prepare for the profession, will not enter and remain in it—unless the conditions surrounding their work are satisfying. Moreover, unless this is the case teachers on the job will not be able or encouraged to make the most of their powers, or likely to behave in such fashion as steadily to increase their competence.

Salaries are, of course, of basic importance. The worth apparently placed on teaching by the American people (the *average* salary they provided for classroom teachers, supervisors, and principals in 1944–45 was less than $1,800) does small credit to their presumable regard for the welfare of their children and of their society. Salaries must be increased. And since many states are financially unable to raise teachers' salaries to respectable levels through their own efforts alone, federal aid to education is indispensable.

Occupational security is another matter to which much more attention must be given. Too many promising prospects have been kept from entering upon teaching, and too many promising teachers have been prevented from realizing their full potentialities, by the insecurities that frequently beset the profession. Competent teachers must be assured of tenure. Arrangements with respect to sickness and the like must be at least as enlightened as those provided for industrial workers. And pension systems, or comparable guarantees of income after retirement, must be further instituted.

The right to live a normal life must be granted to teachers. Too many communities make unreasonable demands on members of the profession so far as their out-of-school hours and private lives are concerned. It is justifiable to expect that teachers should be good specimens of the culture, and it is desirable that they should play the part of good citizens in the general life of the community. But to insist upon a hypocritical simulation of a standard that the lay community itself does not live up to is a destructive procedure. Such a practice can only breed rebellion and reduce teaching effectiveness. It is equally indefensible to forbid teaching by married women including mothers. This not only represents a discrimination that has lost any sanction in other feminine occupations, but it excludes from the schools women with a type of experience that is likely to enhance their competence.

Democratic administrative leadership greatly increases the satisfactions felt by teachers, enables them to work up to the limits of their existing abilities, and encourages them to engage in activities that result in professional growth. The best preparation in the world will not produce a teacher who can do a good job in an atmosphere of suspicion, disdain, or tyranny. The Commission's experience has demonstrated how favorable administrative attitudes and practices make for the improvement of teaching in service.

An in-service program of teacher education, centered in the school system, can further enhance the satisfactions of teachers and consequently the attractions of the profession. Teachers like other human beings enjoy learning to do a better job. When they are helped to do so by methods such as those described in this and other Commission-sponsored reports they appreciate the values of the experience.

Recruitment and selection of teachers

There can be no doubt that many young men and women capable of becoming superior teachers never even consider entering the profession. This is partly because its rewards are never sufficiently called to their attention, partly because they cannot afford the preparation required. It is also regrettably true that no small number of individuals are permitted to complete preparation for teaching, and subsequently to become teachers, who are not adequately suited to the work. It is important that steps be taken to correct these situations.

Recruitment is a responsibility that should be shared by the faculties of both high schools and colleges, and that may receive helpful support from state departments of education. The basic approach should be through developing firstrate programs of general vocational guidance. The task of helping young people to select a life work wisely is one that educational institutions should take very seriously. The ultimate responsibility of choice should be reserved to the individual, and he should be encouraged and helped to weigh alternatives. But if the advantages of the teaching profession—its social worth and personal satisfactions—are adequately set forth there can be little doubt that more able persons will be attracted to it.

Colleges that prepare teachers have an opportunity not only to help high school students understand what becoming and being a teacher means, but they are also ordinarily in a position to engage in effective recruitment on their own campuses. Incidentally it should be recognized that individual faculty members often exercise a negative influence, so far as recruitment for teaching is concerned, by reason of their prejudice against work in the schools and sometimes against colleagues who specialize in teacher preparation. Finding ways to bring such persons into closer contact with school situations and school people, and to gain their participation in local planning for the improvement of teacher education, has been found helpful in desirably modifying their attitudes.

More financial aid for firstrate students who are eager to become teachers is undoubtedly needed. The fully attested fact that as many able young Americans never go to college as do so is disturbing evidence that our educational system falls far short of serving the public weal to the degree it ought. Measures designed to provide equal educational opportunity regardless of occupational intention are demanded by American ideals. The introduction of such measures is no doubt likely to come piece-meal in relation to particular social needs. The shortage of young scientists and the prestige of science resulting from the war have given rise to a strong demand that special provision be made to facilitate college training in this field. But in the world that science has been shaping, better education for all citizens through the public schools has certainly become a primary need. The provision of such education requires better teachers, better prepared. Society cannot afford not to provide the means whereby these teachers may be produced.

Selection must, of course, be made from among those who propose to become teachers: all such cannot be presumed to possess adequate ability and promise. During the war the critical shortage of teachers inevitably resulted in a relaxation of selective procedures. But conditions now developing promise to become favorable to a resumption of efforts along these lines. Institutions where teachers are prepared ought, consequently, to renew their efforts to develop effective techniques of selection and to apply them with increasing vigor. Selection should normally be a continuous process, cumulating evidence being used as a basis for periodical reconsideration of earlier decisions. Furthermore, the students themselves should be given some responsibility in the selective process; they should be helped to interpret the evidence bearing upon the question of their suitability for the teaching profession; and joint rather than unilateral decisions should be sought.

Preparatory programs

Reform of programs for the pre-service education of teachers requires continuous attention. The Commission knows of no program now existing that could be considered wholly satisfactory. It assumes that none ever will exist. In other words, it believes that as certain problems in teacher education are for the time being satisfactorily solved, others take their place. For teacher education is a dynamic business. The needs of children and society, the needs of the schools, change. Hence the demands on teacher preparation change. Meantime the institutions where preparation takes place, the persons responsible for guiding that preparation, and the knowledge and beliefs by which they themselves are guided, change as well.

The Commission has chosen, then, to emphasize continuous improvement rather than to imagine and set forth some ideal program. It has stressed the process whereby teacher education may hope to become steadily better. It has also, however, reached a variety of conclusions respecting key problems in the preparation of teachers, and trends in the treatment of these problems that deserve support. Its views with respect to these matters having been set forth in detail and also summarized in Chapter II, only a brief additional statement is called for here.

Greater institutional unity is a prime need in programs of higher education. This implies a more effective integration within and between the various parts of each college and university, and also greater ability among faculty members to work together groupwise. Integration suggests moving away from reliance on a patchwork of brief courses in the direction of programs made up of related units, each commanding a relatively large block of time. Such a movement is discernible as respects both general and professional education and deserves support. In both of these areas, moreover, there may be observed commendable efforts to combine theory and practice, classroom study and direct experience, more effectively. So far as staffs are concerned, the increase in group study and action is wholly desirable. A focus of attention on such shared elements of concern as students and their needs, communities and their problems, and schools and the challenges they face has proved exceedingly useful in increasing the ability of staff specialists to work effectively together.

General education promises to become one of the leading objects of educational reform during the coming years. Here, too, a quest for unity is fundamentally at work. The improvement of general education for prospective teachers, the great majority of whom will themselves function in the field of general education, is clearly a matter to which much time and intelligence should be devoted. Aims need to be clarified and educational experiences developed that are calculated to serve these aims. More provision needs to be made for art in general education.

As respects professional education, two trends—aside from that toward better integration—are particularly to be observed. One is in the direction of making better provision for bringing about an understanding of child growth and development, not only through creating directly related instructional units but also through saturating the professional program with the child-development point of view. The other trend involves more attention to communities and their problems, leading on to promoting broad social understanding. Each of these trends deserves encouragement.

Student teaching is being widely re-examined as an element in the preparation of teachers. Several promising movements may be noted: toward providing more experience with children, schools, and communities prior to student teaching proper; toward relating earlier professional study more intimately to student teaching; toward arranging for an extended, full-time student teaching experience off campus.

Student personnel is a subject commanding increasing attention in institutions that prepare teachers. The movement is in the direction of enabling larger and larger proportions of faculty members to participate in the work of guidance. In this connection central staffs of specialists are giving increasing time to helping their colleagues share the responsibility for guidance. Such arrangements assist in providing a basis for more effective group attacks on common educational problems.

Advanced subject-matter offerings are being influenced by the situations that have developed in the secondary schools. Subject-matter specialists who have learned at first hand what the contemporary problems and needs of these schools are, have come to favor the development of divisional majors and of courses more functionally designed for the preparation of teachers.

More student participation in the planning of their own educational experiences is increasingly being provided. This trend is supported both by democratic theory and also by the belief that if prospective teachers are to learn how to guide the learning of others, they should better understand the process as it operates in their own cases. Further experimentation in this direction is recommended.

Evaluation is coming to play an increasingly useful role in the field of teacher education. Its effort is to devise the widest variety of means of checking progress in relation to an integrated pattern of educational goals, and to employ all the evidence consequently obtained respecting students and their behavior as a basis both for guidance and curricular revision. Judgments respecting individual development and program effectiveness are thus simultaneously arrived at and employed as a basis for modifying action. There is a commendable tendency toward providing those on whom light is to be thrown by the evaluative process—instructors and students alike—with opportunities to participate responsibly therein.

In-service programs

One of the most striking developments in teacher education in the years lying immediately ahead is likely to be a rapid increase in attention to its in-service aspect. Developing conditions call for early and substantial changes in the school curriculum. Leaders in curricular revision have come to believe firmly that the planning of modifications must be shared in by the teachers whose task it will be to carry them out. The function of supervision has also come to be regarded in a new light. The supervisor who was supposed to know the one right way of teaching, and to see to it that the classroom teachers followed it, is being succeeded by a person who respects individual teaching differences, who thinks of himself as a resource to teachers, and who sees the use of group methods as the best technique to be employed in his work. Superintendents and principals are becoming sensitive to the role personnel relations play in making a good school system, and are rising to the challenge of an opportunity to become educational leaders in a new sense. All of these trends point to the expansion of system-centered programs designed to improve educational services to boys and girls and at the same time to help teachers to grow in competence.

The Commission believes this movement offers extraordinary promise. It considers that its experience has clearly demonstrated the positive values of such a development. It sees in this direction one of the great opportunities presented to teacher education.

Tasks growing out of teaching situations provide the starting point for such in-service programs. The teacher's personal and professional concerns become the focus for attention, as they should be. Helping the teacher to do better what he sees as his job, and to see better what his job might be, becomes the goal. Democratic group methods provide the procedure to be employed. Through policies councils, planning committees, study groups, conferences, and workshops teachers can be given a share in educational planning and doing. Thus the teacher gains respect—his own and that of others. Thus the power inherent in the ideas possessed by all teachers has an opportunity to express itself fully for the advantage of the schools. Teachers who are able to help form policies and encouraged to act responsibly and freely in implementing them find new satisfaction in their profession. They learn by doing. And the educational program improves.

Colleges and universities are also faced with new opportunities in the in-service field. Through developing closer relations with school systems they may find ways of field service that are more effective as well as more rewarding than those to which they have been accustomed. They can help by developing consultant services, conferences, and workshops. Incidentally, such ventures will assist the institutions of higher learning to discover how they may increase the functional effectiveness of their programs of teacher preparation. Problems of adjustment to new in-service roles will offer some difficulties. But much experimentation can be expected along these newer lines, and it is desirable that this should be the case.

Interinstitutional cooperation

Another exceedingly promising development is that of interinstitutional cooperation for the improvement of teacher education. Statewide programs of this character have proved particularly easy to organize and effective as to results. Such programs are creating a new and more positive type of leadership in state departments of education, leadership in the management of cooperative enterprise. The Commission believes that its experience has demonstrated the unusual value of such undertakings. They offer encouragement and support to all who are eager to promote improvements in teacher education, they facilitate the drawing into experimental activities of more and more persons, they are as adaptable to the betterment of in-service as of pre-service education. The Commission hopes that programs of statewide cooperation will rapidly spread.

School-college cooperation, which deserves strengthening under any and all circumstances, may be notably promoted by statewide cooperative programs. The schools need access to the resources represented by the colleges and universities, and the latter need close contact with the situations in which teaching is actually being done. From such contact wiser planning of pre-service curricula will come, and better service to teachers on the job. The gap between thought and action will be narrowed, and improvement will ensue. The Commission commends all efforts at bringing schools and colleges closer together.

The unity of teacher education

The Commission would call attention, in conclusion, to the similarity of problems of teacher education whether the college, university, school system, or state is being viewed and to the applicability in all these situations of the same methods for dealing with these problems. The qualities that make for good teaching are not something that can be fully attained once and for all. The same needs of teachers are relevant to the determination of both pre-service and in-service programs. And both students preparing to teach and experienced practitioners of the profession respond favorably to educational methods that show respect for their personalities, that combine thinking and doing, and that employ group methods.

ENVOI

The work of the Commission on Teacher Education was part of a development that had a past and that has a future. The Commission built on what had been accomplished by its predecessors. It sought consciously, during its own existence, to take full advantage of the skill, understanding, and good will of its contemporaries. It now passes the torch to its successors, to whom it addresses its final words.

The world, and our country with it, is on the verge of a new and revolutionary era. The changes that have already occurred are only a beginning. Whether man can meet and master them remains a question. If that question is to be answered as we pray it may be, education must meet the challenge. The schools provided for our future citizens must prepare them to make a better world. The schools must change. And if the schools are to change, teachers must change as well. This calls for change in teacher education.

But change merely for its own sake is not what is to be desired. It must be change consistent with fundamental values and guided by responsible purpose. It must be change intended to provide conditions conducive to the fulfillment of personality and the achievement of community. It must be change intelligently and imaginatively planned, brought about by men and women of good will working together to good ends. Such change will mean improvement.

The Commission has tried to promote improvement in teacher education. It has sought to further ways of working together that are most likely to have such a result. It has felt the social challenge of these tasks.

But the challenge has been shared by others, and with these others the Commission now confidently leaves it. The challenge is to the colleges and universities where new teachers are prepared and where there are great resources for helping teachers in service. It is to the school systems which have the opportunity and obligation to make full use of all their teachers' powers, and to help these men and women to grow steadily in skill and understanding. It is to the states which by promoting cooperation can increase the capacities for advance possessed by individual colleges, universities, and school systems. It is to the educational associations which can inspire their members to continued study, steady improvement in practice, and promotion of unity through earnest participation in joint endeavors in their several working situations.

To all these the Commission commends the great task with which it has been concerned: the improvement of teacher education that we may have teachers—classroom teachers, supervisors, principals, administrators—who can meet the challenge of our times and help to make them great.

Appendix A

Personnel

A GREAT MANY persons participated in the program of the Commission on Teacher Education. There were the members of the Commission itself and of its regular central staff. There were a considerable number of persons who served in various connections as special consultants or who carried out certain special studies. There were those who acted as members of planning and directing committees or as local coordinators in the participating colleges, universities, school systems, and states. Beyond all these were the numerous administrative officers, professors, and classroom teachers in the units cooperating in the national and statewide studies who shared in local activities and—in many cases—attended conferences, workshops, or the collaboration center in child growth and development. Finally, mention should be made of the not inconsiderable number of persons belonging to none of the above categories who helped in various ways.

It would be gratifying to be able to recognize all of these contributors to the Commission's work by name, but a full and accurate compilation is not practicable. Completeness, then, being out of the question it has seemed best to list below only those individuals who devoted at least half—usually all—of their time to the Commission's field program for a year or more. The membership of the Commission itself is given on a front page of this volume.

CENTRAL STAFF WITH HEADQUARTERS IN WASHINGTON, D. C.

Karl W. Bigelow, director; professor of education, Teachers College, Columbia University.

W. Earl Armstrong, field coordinator; formerly head, School of Education, Mills College, and later dean, School of Education, University of Delaware.

C. Leslie Cushman, field coordinator; formerly director of curriculum and research, Denver Public Schools, and later associate superintendent, Philadelphia Public Schools.

Helen E. Davis, associate in charge of the clearinghouse and editor; specialist in social research.

Ernest V. Hollis, field coordinator and associate in college teacher education; formerly instructor in education, College of the City of New York, and later principal specialist in higher education, United States Office of Education.

C. Robert Pace, research assistant in evaluation; formerly on the research staff of the General College, University of Minnesota, and later director of the field research division, Bureau of Naval Personnel, United States Navy Department.

Charles E. Prall, field coordinator; formerly dean, College of Education, University of Pittsburgh, and later director, Joint Commission on Education, American College of Hospital Administrators and American Hospital Association.

Harold E. Snyder, assistant to the director and research associate; formerly instructor in education, University of Rochester, and later director of the training division, United Nations Relief and Rehabilitation Administration.

Maurice E. Troyer, associate in evaluation; formerly professor of educational psychology, Syracuse University, and later director of the evaluation service center, Syracuse University.

STAFF IN CHILD DEVELOPMENT AND TEACHER PERSONNEL WITH HEADQUARTERS AT THE UNIVERSITY OF CHICAGO

Daniel A. Prescott, head of the division; formerly professor of education, Rutgers University, now professor of education, University of Chicago.

Lawrence L. Jarvie, associate in teacher personnel; formerly chairman of the educational research committee, Rochester Athenaeum and Mechanics Institute, and later lieutenant colonel, Army of the United States.

Fritz Redl, field consultant in child development; formerly instructor, School of Education, University of Michigan, and later associate professor of social work, Wayne University.

Caroline M. Tryon, field consultant in child development; formerly research associate, University of California, and later assistant professor of education, University of Chicago.

STAFF OF THE WORKSHOP ADVISORY SERVICE WITH HEADQUARTERS AT NORTHWESTERN UNIVERSITY

Kenneth L. Heaton, associate in charge of workshop advisory service; formerly director, Cooperative Bureau for Educational Research, and later chief of the research section, Civilian Personnel and Training Division, Office of the Secretary of War.

Francis C. Rosecrance, field consultant; professor of education, School of Education, Northwestern University.

COORDINATORS OF STATEWIDE STUDIES

Georgia: M. E. Thompson, formerly state director of teacher education, certification, and curriculum, Georgia, and later state commissioner of revenue, Georgia; and John H. Cook, coordinator of teacher education, state department of education, Georgia.

Michigan: Harvey L. Turner, formerly director of rural education and teacher training, Michigan State Normal College, and later president, Hillsdale College; and David M. Trout, formerly head of the department of psychology and dean of students, and later dean of administration, Central Michigan College of Education.

New York: Harold E. B. Speight; formerly dean, Swarthmore College, and later dean of students, Cornell University.

Appendix B
Publications

THE EXISTENCE of the Commission on Teacher Education led to the publication of a considerable amount of material. It produced a variety of books, pamphlets, and mimeographed reports as well as a monthly *Newsletter*. Similar materials were brought out by many of the universities, colleges, school systems, and states associated with the Commission. In addition, numerous articles relating to the Commission's work appeared and are still appearing in the periodical literature. A complete bibliography of these items would be of limited interest. It has accordingly seemed best to list below only the printed publications of the Commission, a selection of mimeographed material produced at the collaboration center in child growth and development, and bound volumes issued by cooperating units. Unless otherwise indicated the publisher in each case is the American Council on Education; the starred items are out of print.

MAJOR PUBLICATIONS

1938

Major Issues in Teacher Education, American Council on Education Studies, Series I, No. 4.

> An analysis of needs leading to the recommendation that a commission on teacher education be established.

1939

*Cooperation in the Improvement of Teacher Education.

> A brief statement on the plans of the Commission.

*Bennington Planning Conference for the Cooperative Study on Teacher Education: Reports and Addresses.

> An extensive account of the conference at which the national cooperative study was launched.

1940

EPLER, STEPHEN E. *The Teacher, the School, and the Community.*

> An annotated directory of organizations and agencies concerned with community problems, and a bibliography of items relating to school-community relations.

277

Cultural and Social Elements in the Education of Teachers. Washington: American Council on Education and the Educational Policies Commission.

Contains addresses delivered by Karl W. Bigelow and Lewis Mumford at the Bennington planning conference.

**The Commission on Teacher Education: A Brief Statement of Its Origin and Scope.*

A description of the various aspects of the Commission's program, listing the cooperating units and the names of a considerable number of persons connected in various ways with the work.

The Newsletter of the Commission on Teacher Education of the American Council on Education.

Published monthly, except August and September, from October 1940 through July 1943. A running account of Commission activities and of other developments in the field of teacher education.

1941

*Engleman, F. E., and Matthews, J. C. *Progress Report on Seven Teachers Colleges Participating in the Cooperative Study of Teacher Education.* Preprinted from the twentieth *Yearbook* of the American Association of Teachers Colleges.

A description and evaluation of what the authors discovered when they visited the institutions in question at the joint request of the American Association of Teachers Colleges and the Commission.

Curriculum Committee of the School of Education, Syracuse University. *A Functional Program of Teacher Education.*

The developments at Syracuse described in this report occurred quite independently of the Commission, which, however, recommended and helped finance publication of the volume.

Klein, A. J. (ed.). *Adventures in the Reconstruction of Education.* Columbus: College of Education, Ohio State University.

The developments at this College of Education described in the report largely antedated that institution's participation in the Commission's national cooperative study; the Commission, however, helped finance publication of the volume.

Linton, Ralph; Fisher, Mary S.; and Ryan, W. Carson. *Culture and Personality.*

Contains three lectures delivered at the Commission's summer workshop of 1940.

1942

This War and the Teacher.

A folder devoted to emphasizing the importance of good teaching in wartime and to urging experienced teachers to stick to their posts.

EVENDEN, E. S. *Teacher Education in a Democracy at War.*

A survey of the adverse effects of war on teacher education in England and the United States from 1914 to 1918 and after, and in England from 1939 to 1942, leading to warnings against the risk of similar developments during the war just entered by this country, and concluding with recommendations for teacher education during the war and postwar periods.

The Training of Secondary School Teachers: Especially with Reference to English. Cambridge: Harvard University Press.

This report by a joint committee of the faculty of Harvard College and the Graduate School of Education was drafted quite independently of the Commission, which, however, helped finance the volume.

The School for Executives.

An extensive account of a two-week conference of teachers college presidents held in June 1942 by the American Association of Teachers Colleges.

EVENDEN, E. S. and BUTTS, R. FREEMAN (eds.). *The Columbia University Cooperative Program for the Pre-Service Education of Teachers.* New York: Bureau of Publications, Teachers College, Columbia University.

A staff report of the three-year demonstration conducted by Barnard College, Columbia College, and Teachers College as their contribution to the Commission's national cooperative study.

1943

BLACKWELL, GORDON W. *Toward Community Understanding.*

A report specially prepared for the Commission on college efforts to aid students, particularly prospective teachers, to develop capacity for a better understanding of communities; based on visits to fourteen campuses.

FAULKNER, RAY N. and DAVIS, HELEN E. *Teachers Enjoy the Arts.*

A report specially prepared for the Commission on the character and value of informal art activities as engaged in by experienced teachers at five summer workshops; based on questionnaires and extensive interviewing of classroom teachers and administrators in three school systems participating in the Commission's national study.

TROUT, DAVID M. (ed.). *The Education of Teachers.* Lansing: Michigan Cooperative Teacher Education Study.

Contains the findings respecting various aspects of teacher education of participants in the Michigan statewide cooperative study carried on for three and a half years in relation to the Commission's program.

1944

Teachers for Our Times.

A statement of purposes by the Commission on Teacher Education, this volume constitutes the first in the Commission's series of final reports and an introduction to the others.

TROYER, MAURICE E. and PACE, C. ROBERT. *Evaluation in Teacher Education.*

Prepared by two staff members on the basis of experience in the Commission's program with evaluative problems, techniques, and procedures connected with all stages in the education of teachers; one of the series of final reports.

PRALL, CHARLES E. and CUSHMAN, C. LESLIE. *Teacher Education in Service.*

Prepared by two staff members on the basis of experience in the Commission's program with school-system efforts to facilitate the growth of teachers on the job; one of the series of final reports.

ARMSTRONG, W. EARL; HOLLIS, ERNEST V.; and DAVIS, HELEN E. *The College and Teacher Education.*

Prepared by three staff members on the basis of experience in the Commission's program with the activities of universities, teachers colleges, and colleges of liberal arts designed to improve the preparation of teachers and to assist in their in-service growth; one of the series of final reports.

1945

Helping Teachers Understand Children.

Prepared by the staff of the Commission's division on child development and teacher personnel on the basis of Commission experience with an extended child-study program in a particular school system; one of the series of final reports.

HOLLIS, ERNEST V. *Toward Improving Ph.D. Programs.*

Prepared by a staff member on the basis of an exhaustive study of the positions and duties of persons who received the Ph.D. and Ed.D. degrees in the United States during the 1930's, together with other inquiries into the satisfactoriness of graduate school practice, especially as relating to the preparation of college teachers; one of the series of final reports.

1946

PRALL, CHARLES E. *State Programs for the Improvement of Teacher Education.*

Prepared by a staff member on the basis of experience, in the Commission's program, with statewide cooperative efforts to improve the preparation of teachers and to assist in their in-service growth; one of the series of final reports.

The Improvement of Teacher Education.

A concluding report by the Commission, summarizing its experience and containing its recommendations with regard to various aspects of teacher education and the processes found effective in obtaining improvement therein; the present volume and the last in the series of final reports.

MIMEOGRAPHED MATERIAL ON CHILD STUDY

All of the materials listed in this section were produced at the Commission's collaboration center in child growth and development. They are grouped as study guides for teachers, bibliographies, and miscellaneous study materials. While the supplies of these items are virtually exhausted, requests for further information may be addressed to the Collaboration Center in Child Development, Department of Education, University of Chicago, Chicago 37, Illinois.

Study Guides for Teachers

COMMITTEE ON LEARNING. "Child Development and the Psychology of Learning." 1941.

A series of generalized statements with illustrative implications for education, a bibliography of secondary sources, and an appendix of expanded statements on experimental research with samples of the application of principles to specific problems.

COMMITTEE ON THE PHYSIOLOGICAL ASPECTS OF GROWTH. "Physiological Aspects of Child Growth and Development." 1941.

An attempt to draw from available data on human growth concepts of importance to teachers, and to arrange them in orderly fashion for the convenience of persons directing further studies in this area; practical implications are indicated and a bibliography is furnished.

COMMITTEE ON THE PSYCHOLOGICAL ASPECTS OF GROWTH. "Aspects of Child Growth and Development." 1941.

Part One contains selected generalizations on human development with sample implications for education; Part Two consists of detailed analyses of the personal-social, motivational, emotional, and intellectual aspects, with examples to assist the teacher of teachers; a general bibliography is included along with an expanded topical bibliography.

COMMITTEE ON SOCIALIZATION. "The Socialization of the Individual." 1941.

Contains generalizations on aspects of social and economic change, American class and caste structures, and the social development of the individual; there is a separate section on the educational implications as well as a bibliography of secondary sources.

Bibliographies

KNOX, W. T. "Adolescent Behavior in Interpersonal Relationships." 1941.

A selected and annotated bibliography classified according to the process of socialization, cultural determinants of social growth, socialization in other societies, the family as an agency of the culture, social techniques for college students, the development of social attitudes, the school as an agency of society, education for personality development, and education for family and social relationships.

LEVIN, BERNICE. "Selected Bibliography on Human Growth and Development." 1940.

Annotated references exclusive of general textbooks on the following topics: the biological background of human development, the role of culture in personality formation, significant research in child development, general source books in child development, and child development and education.

Miscellaneous study materials

BALLER, WARREN R. "The Case of Mickey Murphy." 1941.

An instrument based on the development of an actual child constructed so as to test the user's own growth in judgment and understanding of the case, and to reveal abilities and other characteristics of teachers; usable as a device in teaching, discussions, and self-evaluation.

————. "The Relation of Evaluation to the Improvement of Teachers' Understanding of Child Growth and Development." 1941.

A brief summary and discussion of current practice in evaluating a teacher's understanding of child growth; contains also a short bibliography.

BARKER, ROGER G. "Science and Education." 1940.

A discussion of the uncertain role of science in modern society, the nature of science, and the place of science in education; includes a bibliography.

OLSON, WILLARD C. in cooperation with SARITA M. DAVIS. "The Case Method Applied to Recurring Educational Problems: Case B." 1940.

An instructional document based on a classroom experience in reading, with illustrations from actual case evidence.

———. "Graphic Summary of Observations for a Child." 1940.

A trait-action scale for recording a teacher's observation of a child.

REDL, FRITZ. "Exercises in Applied Thinking." 1941.

Brief case situations to emphasize the importance of applied thinking in child study and guidance, with an analysis of reactions to the instrument and illustrative examples of its use.

———. "Helping Teachers Study Their Children." 1940.

A discussion of some of the most frequent difficulties teachers run into when first attempting to study children intensively.

———. "A Method for Determining Training Needs of Teachers." 1940.

In the following six parts: the teaching function, the situational approach to teacher education, teaching equipment, discovering training needs, a tentative instrument for analysing the training level, and suggestions for practical application.

———. "Suggestions for a Case-Discussion Method for the Purpose of Child Study and Educational Training." 1941.

Contains plans for handling the fresh-air camp-clinic of the University of Michigan, discussions based on experience, and an analysis of the logical steps involved in child study and educational planning.

———. "What Should We Know about a Child?" 1940.

Suggestions to aid teachers in studying children in their classrooms.

STOKE, STUART M. "Keeping Behavior Journals." 1940.

A critical discussion of methods for keeping incidental and cumulative records of child behavior in the classroom, and a short bibliography.

———. "The Social Analysis of the Classroom." 1940.

A discussion of the "Guess Who" technique with illustrative cases.

THE AMERICAN COUNCIL ON EDUCATION

GEORGE F. ZOOK, *President*

The American Council on Education is a *council* of national educational associations; organizations having related interests; approved universities, colleges, and technological schools; state departments of education; city school systems; selected private secondary schools; and selected educational departments of business and industrial companies. It is a center of cooperation and coordination whose influence has been apparent in the shaping of American educational policies as well as in the formulation of American educational practices during the past twenty-eight years. Many leaders in American education and public life serve on the commissions and committees through which the Council operates.

Established by the Council in 1938, the Commission on Teacher Education consists of the persons whose names appear on a front page of this publication. It operated through a staff under the supervision and control of a director responsible to the Commission.

Date Due
